Religion and Social Change in Modern Turkey

SUNY Series in Near Eastern Studies
Said Amir Arjomand, Editor

Religion and Social Change in Modern Turkey

The Case of Bediüzzaman Said Nursi

Şerif Mardin

State University of New York Press

To F. C.

Published by
State University of New York Press, Albany

Printed in the United States of America

For information, address State University of New York Press, State University Plaza, Albany, N.Y., 12246

Library of Congress Cataloging-in-Publication Data

Mardin, Şerif.
Religion and social change in modern Turkey.

(SUNY series in Near Eastern studies)
Bibliography: p.
Includes index.
1. Nursî, Said, 1873–1960—Philosophy.
2. Nurculuk. 3. Islam—Turkey—History. 4. Sociology, Islamic. I. Title. II. Series.
BP80.N89M36 1989 306'.6'09561 89–4280
ISBN 0–88706–996–7
ISBN 0–88706–997–5 (pbk.)

10 9 8 7 6 5 4 3 2 1

Contents

Preface

This book is a preliminary exercise in attempting to gain an understanding of the ways in which religion and society interlock in modern Turkey. The specific appeal of Bediüzzaman Said Nursi for his own followers provides a useful focus for a description of this type of articulation and for an analysis of the social processes which project the dynamic counterpart of the intermeshing of religion and social relations. I have tried to follow parallel developments in a number of fields such as those of the world communication (and communications) revolution, Turkish political and social reform, Turkish intellectual development and aspects of religious history that are relevant to a study of Said Nursi's biography. I have not attempted to set out any strong causal linkages between these parallel streams. Nevertheless, I believe that they produce pictures which complement one another. I hope the interconnections I have plotted will serve as a springboard for further studies of the role of religion in modern Turkish society.

I have to thank many persons for important assistance on my way: Professor Albert Hourani and the Middle East Center of St. Antony's College, Oxford University, for their invitation to join the college as a visiting fellow in 1980–82; Professor Hourani for continued encouragement, and for reading preliminary versions of the manuscript; Dr. Roger Owen for his remarks on some early chapters. My debt to Professor Ernest Gellner of Cambridge University is especially that of keeping in mind the questions he would have asked should he have taken up the same subject for study. Professor Dale Eickelman encouraged me to believe in the worth of my analysis by asking to quote material from one of my chapters. Professors Michael Meeker and Allen Duben have read the completed versions of the manuscript. Professor Hamid Algar led me to believe that the analyses of Islamic material I was proposing was not too far off the mark. From all these contributors I have gained, although the blemishes which may remain in my exposé are my own responsibility.

I owe a special debt of gratitude to my friends in the editorial offices of the *Yeni Nesil,* the newspaper published by the followers of Said Nursi. I would like in particular to thank Mr. Necmettin Şahiner whose biography of Said Nursi provides information essential to anyone attempting to study the Nur movement. Finally, I would not have taken up the figure of Bediüzzaman for study had I not been alerted by the late Cemil Meriç to the former's substantive contribution as a religious thinker. I shall always be grateful for the insights he let me share with him.

I have not mentioned by name the many friends who read chapters of the book, but they, of course are not forgotten. I would like to thank Marilyn Semerad of SUNY Press for her excellent care throughout all the stages of publishing.

Transliteration

ANY BOOK WHICH covers Ottoman and modern Turkish history runs into insuperable problems of transliteration. Turkish is a language which has a structure that differs fundamentally from that of Arabic. Yet—and this is where the problem arises—speakers of Turkish and Arabic share the Arabic culture of the Qur'ān, and the terminology devised by the early Muslim theologians. Ottoman culture has also shared many aspects of Muslim Persian culture and of its vocabulary. Modern Turks have adopted the Latin alphabet. Neither Arabs nor Persians have.

In the face of such difficulties the method followed here was to use the modern Turkish spelling of words which have an Arabic or Persian origin. This was followed—in the first instance of the use of such words—by a transliteration based on the system of the International Journal of Middle East Studies.

Examples:

Cemaleddin or (a moot point) Cemalettin Efgani (Jamāl ad-Dīn al-Afghānī)

Icaz–'Ijāz.

The main exception to the rule is the spelling of Qur'ān and 'ulema.

Introduction

ISLAMIC STUDIES DID not flourish in Turkey in the early years of the Turkish Republic (est. 1923). The foundation myth of the republican regime, based as it was on the idea of a secular state, precluded such a flowering. The history of the first twenty years of the new Turkey, with its dramatic secularizing reforms, underlined these aspects of the myth. Between 1925 and 1950 the main source of information about the religious debates which had engrossed Ottoman intellectuals in the first decades of the century was dusty brochures dating from pre-Republican times.

With the deceleration of secularization since 1950, publications on religion have grown significantly. Part of the latest religious literature consists of transcriptions of Islamic classics into the Latin alphabet or into Turkish. Recent scholarly books on religion, on the other hand, are overwhelmingly studies of institutional Islam: catalogues of leading *şeyhülislams*, surveys of educational centers, descriptions of the so-called "learned institutions" (*ilmiyye* in Turkish), i.e., the class of learned Ottoman Muslims who up to the nineteenth century filled the positions of theologian, judge and professor.

All of this is of interest to the student of religion, but these studies do not give us a clue to the deep commitment and virulence which appears in the everyday discussion and debates on religion in contemporary Turkey as reflected in the local press and a number of polemical books. They do not indicate that Turkish conservatism rotates around a religious axis and that a "progressive" attitude is that of Kemalist Jacobinism. In fact the current debate on religion in Turkey is lively, and all Turks realize that it implicates some of the ideological foundations of republican Turkey with secularism in the forefront. For some time, Turkish intellectuals have carried a vehement campaign against the resurgence of sect (*tarikat*) activities, the spread of religious education and the subversion of young minds by charismatic preachers. Muslim fundamentalists—nowadays better prepared to find chinks in their opponents' stand—have replied with their own ammunition. Deep-seated world views, values and attitudes clash here, and these are part and parcel of the arrival of Turkey into the modern world.

Among the religious figures that have attracted the bitterest criticism on the part of Turkish secularists is Bediüzzaman Said Nursi (1876–1960), a person who, to them, is the very incarnation of backwardness. For many years his followers had to cover up their religious identity lest charges of illegal religious propaganda be proferred against them. Their legal status is sufficiently vague to attract periodically the ire of state prosecutors.

True, since the 1950s a more quizzical concern on the part of the secular intelligentsia has replaced invective, but the real threat to a secular mode of life unleashed by the recent regurgence of Islam in Turkey has again resulted in a hardening of attitudes. One would have expected that the success of a religious leader like Said Nursi would have aroused the curiosity of his very detractors and that they would have made an attempt to unravel the intricacies of his influence. Such adjectives as reactionary, tricky, and exploitative do not fill this need.

Some ground has been covered in the last ten years by respectable scholarship in elucidating the religious affiliation of the "*nurcu*"* and in addressing other issues raised by Republican secularization. Political scientists have led the field. Marxist theoreticians have also begun to explain the influence of Islam as a means of protection for and an assertion of the disinherited. But, in fact, the problem has many more aspects to it. The present work is an attempt to clarify the foundations and origins of the influence of a man like Said Nursi. It consists of a description of the many strands of influences which converged on him during his life. It does not give a *systematic* explanation of the interrelation of elements which contributed to his life as a religious leader. It does, however, take a stand in the very selection of the elements which it considers important and the concepts which it considers shed most light on the life of Bediüzzaman and his influence on disciples. These concepts are those of culture and, within culture, those of idioms of social relations, discourse and social practices. By "idiom" I refer to a special language used in a specific sphere of social

*Followers of Said Nursi, "*Nurculuk*"—membership in the movement.

relations; by "discourse" the way in which this idiom is structured by a more specific set of practices.

Every author who has written about Islam has indicated that Islam is more than simply a religious belief, that it structures the social life of Islamic societies, that it provides the foundations for political obligation and that, in short, it penetrates the smallest interstices of daily life and of social and political organization. What these authors have not elucidated is the process by which such a society is reproduced. What I suggest is that the reproduction of Islamic societies is linked to a common use of an Islamic idiom by the members of such societies.

A Note on the Use of "Idiom" and "Discourse"

A clarification of what I mean by idiom and discourse may be necessary at this point. I can illustrate the meaning of idiom by referring to its constituent parts, which I shall characterize as root paradigms.

"Root paradigm" is a term used by Victor Turner to characterize clusters of meaning which serve as cultural "maps" for individuals; they enable persons to find a path in their own culture. In Turner's own words:

> Where processes are unconditioned, undetermined or unchanneled by explicit custom and rules, my hypothesis would be that the main actors are nevertheless guided by *subjective paradigms* which may derive from beyond the main stream of sociocultural process with its ensocializing devices such as education and imitation of action models in stereotyped situations. Such paradigms affect the form, timing and style of behavior of those who bear them. (Turner, 1974, 67)

In our study we shall see that Said Nursi appeals to a large number of persons for whom "customs and rules" are either deficient or have been improverished or have been proclaimed to be illegitimate. In these circumstances residual root paradigms provided the foundations for Said Nursi's influence. An example of a root paradigm would be the variety of meanings carried by the term *gazi* (*Ar. ghāzī*) (*E.I.*[2], II, 1043–45) in Turkish culture and the multiplicity of situations in which it operates as an effective frame for the behavior of Turks.

Ghāzī is a general term used in Islam for someone who has scored an impressive success on the battlefield. The connotation of the concept is seen against a vast background in which some of its effectiveness in social relations emerges with greater clarity. A *ghāzī* is not only a courageous and able fighter but, even more important, a fighter for the faith. His deserts are not only of this world, they shall be counted in the afterlife. The behavior of thousands of Iranian *Shi'ites* who take the *ghāzī* as a role-model for suicidal attacks in war suffices as an illustration of its contemporary substance for Muslims.

However, there exists more than one battlefield in which one can become a *ghāzī*. One's soul is also the field of a battle waged to control one's baser appetites. There is, then, an internal as well as an external dimension of *ghazw*, the action imputed to the *ghāzī*. *Cihad* (Ar. *jihād*), the struggle for internal as well as external mastery is the term more often used for this control over the self. As to its special place in Turkish culture, *gazi* is used to describe the fighters for the faith who are considered to have laid the foundations of the Ottoman Empire. But the term has never lost its force.

A *gazi* is an extremely prestigious person in modern Turkish as well as in ancient Ottoman society. Throughout the history of the Ottoman Empire one encounters *gazi*s, the last one of which is *Gazi* Mustafa Kemal Paşa as Atatürk was first known, in view of his victory over the Greeks and the fact that he had saved the Muslims of Anatolia from conquest by the infidel. The town of Antep is known today as *Gazi*antep; this name was given to it in the same years because of its resistance against the French.

The *gazi-gaza* cluster makes up a cultural constellation which is still active in contemporary Turkey and which shapes social behavior in important issues. At the time of the Cyprus conflict it was around the concept of *gaza* that large masses were mobilized for action and this seems, by and large, to have been a spontaneous movement.

The internal dimension to the *gaza-cihad* cluster is also relevant in contemporary Turkey. In the periodical *Girişim*, a radical and intellectually extremely interesting Islamist periodical, jihād is used as the equivalent of the South American radical *conscientizacion*, as the name for an active posture which is meant to raise consciousness among the masses. It is also used to characterize one's attitude of militancy to force the recognition of Islam as a force in international relations.

An adumbration of this use may be found in its use by Said Nursi in the 1940s. At one stage in his life, pointing to a pile of periodicals published by his followers and having spread his message he states: "Gazidirler . . . they are *gazi*s," i.e., they have waged a battle against unbelief. (See below p. 205.) This is a rather unusual use of *gazi*, but one with which Said Nursi legitimizes the use of mass communication media and the transition from orality to scripturalism.

The *gaza-gazi* cluster is a root-metaphor providing lines of force which shape social relations and at the same time enable these to be transformed.

I have selected only one root-paradigm, but I could go on to do the same exercise with the concept of "*haram-harem*" (Ar. *ḥarām-ḥaram*) as the core of one constellation of social behavior, the concepts "*namus*" (Ar. *nāmūs*) (honor), "*hürmet*" (Ar. *ḥurma*) (respect) for family life, "*kanaat*" (Ar. *qanā'a*) (frugality) and "*rizk*" (Ar. *rizq*) (just deserts) for the sphere of economics, "*hak*" (Ar. *ḥaqq*) (right) and "*adalet*" (Ar. *'adāla*) (justice) for questions regarding equality or "*insan*" (Ar. *insān*) (man), "*hayvan*" (Ar. *ḥaywān*) (animal) for issues concerning man. All of these are concepts which are drawn out of a fund of Islamic culture.

A question still remains unanswered. How is it that the untutored audience of Said Nursi could bring these concepts into their daily life strategies? After all, they could not read Arabic. Therefore, the production and reproduction of Ottoman Islamic culture and of its root-paradigms could not be based on a knowledge of the text of the *Qur'ān*. An immediate answer would be "by knowledge transmitted in the family." But this knowledge itself was nourished by what Nazif Shahrani has called "popular knowledge of Islam." Shahrani shows (Shahrani, 1985) that in Afghanistan the sources of this knowledge were popular "catechisms," narratives of the lives and pious deeds of the Prophet Muhammad, biographies of Muslim holy men, poetry and love stories placed in an Islamic setting. Exactly the same holds true for Turkey. Here epic poems and other products of Ottoman Islamic culture were brought to villages by bards who recited stories based on the same frame for centuries. A selection of Turkish equivalents of Shahrani's inventory of religious folk literature would include the *Kara Davut*, *Necat ül-Müminin*, *Envar ül-Aşikin* and the *Muhammediye* of the Yazıcızâde brothers at the village level, and in more Sufi-inclined circles, the *Müzekki ün-Nufus* of Eşrefoğlu Rumi, the *Mebahis-i iman* and the *Mebahis-i Salat* of Muslihiddin.* All of these are "catechisms," but their influence can hardly be compared to that of *Mevlud* of Süleyman Çelebi, a story of the prophet's life; a similar work is the *Siyer ün-Nebi*. Religious epic poems which had wide circulation were the *Muhammed Destanı*, the *Gavazat-i Ali der Memleket-i Sind*, and the *Gavazat-i Bahr-i Umman ve Sanduk*. *Yusuf ve*

---

*The 17th century author of these two works may be considered a predecessor of Said Nursi insofar as he speaks of his own mission as an attempt to boil down compendious works on religion into something easily understood by the people.

Züleyha provided a basic model for innumerable variants of the love story. In the province of İsparta, where Said Nursi's message was propagated for the first time to a rural audience, such knowledge was taken for granted. Said Nursi's influence was founded on such priming. One should also keep in mind the peculiar way which the message was legitimated. In many cases Said Nursi's homiletics were *read* to an audience by persons who already had acquired religious prestige. Only after the 1950s, after his books were taken off the list of banned publications, can we speak of a wider circle of *readers* for his works. It is the *aura* carried by this *performance* which in the early days legitimated his ideas, rather than the *words* which he used, which in many cases could not be understood by villagers or even townsmen.

One may detect at least two levels at which the folk-Islamic texts exerted an influence on social behavior. First, as exemplars which sometimes subtly and sometimes quite explicitly provided models for conduct. But at a second level one finds a less visible network of influences where the motive forces consisted of *intimations* about values and conduct. In a somewhat different conceptualization which is, nevertheless, meant to convey the same dichotomy, Anthony Giddens (1979, 5) has distinguished between "practical consciousness, as tacit stocks of knowledge which actors draw upon in the constitution of social activity and . . . 'discursive consciousness' involving knowledge which actors are able to express on the level of discourse."

This double level of signification makes for flexibility in the actor's interpretation of the exemplary content of the text.

While Shahrani's clues are important for a study such as mine, I would wager that the functioning of the "root paradigms" I have mentioned assume a special color in the Islamic setting which may be loosely described as "linguistic," and at this point we go deeper into the process of sharing the texts of a culture. What I see is that the Islamic "idiom" is pervasive in the sense that it covers all aspects of life in society and that it is shared more equally by upper and lower classes than its equivalents are in the West. Daily life-strategies are framed by the use of the religious idiom, and the fund of *Qur'ānic* symbols on which it is based has a widespread popular usage. This sharing of an idiom to structure life strategies may be the foundation of what observers of Islam see as its "democratic" or "populistic" aspects. We can then understand why some fundamentalist Muslims correctly state this "democracy" not to rest anything resembling the parliamentary bodies of the West.

It is because this idiom is shared that there appears something which we could name "social legitimation" in Islamic societies, a legitimation that derives from the widespread use of this idiom. As long as the common idiom is used by individuals to procure their needs, the social process functions smoothly, and it is legitimated by use. Anything that upsets this use of the idiom for everyday purposes becomes illegitimate. Thus, when the Ottoman reformers of the 19th century began to change the day-to-day space configuration of women's activities, allowing them to show themselves where they had not appeared before this was (in the meaning frame of the fundamental idiom) an anti-democratic move, a means of escaping from popular control by changing the idiom used. I believe that Said Nursi's success was in part due to the "re-democratization" promised by his revival of the traditional idiom.

In short then, the concepts which I have described as "root-paradigms" functioned at two levels: as "maps" which provided personal guidance in and projected a picture of an ideal society but also as items in a cultural knapsack which integrated the individual's perception of social rules and positions with signifiers for images, sounds and colors. In this second sense what Said Nursi was doing was promoting key concepts in the language of the periphery, of the underprivileged (Mardin, 1972), a language which expressed the special character of peripheral status. Latife Tekin, a contemporary Turkish novelist who has tried to describe the culture of the Turkish periphery, underlines the same idea when she says to a Turkish intellectual during an interview: "You shall never understand the type of knowledge that underlies the signs with which I communicate with the poor, with the people of my quarter of town" (Tekin and Savaşır, 1985, 146).

Of course, the most important effect of such a fund was in its *use*, i.e., in the way in which it not only functioned as a directive but constituted the materials for personal strategies aiming to promote one's welfare, deflect dangers and engineer coalitions. This is what Michel de Certeau has named knowledge for a "doing" (*un faire*) (de Certeau, 1984).

So much for "Idiom." *Discourse* is a word which I use to bring in the plasticity of the root paradigm. The way in which the idiom is used depends on the social position of the user (in this case a cleric trained in Nakşibendi seminaries) the selection made from a large inventory of possible themes, the particular slant of the message and the way in which the meanings carried by the themes selected are transformed to suit current purposes.

My own use of "discourse" has relatively little overlap with the same term as used by Foucault (Foucault, 1977). Foucault's discourse is held together by relations of power; my own use of the term refers to cognitive problems. Foucault underlines that the users of discourse are an exclusive set privileged by this very use. I, on the contrary, try to delineate an aspect of increasingly wide access to the use of an idiom which exists in the background of discourse. Foucault's stress is on the discursive in its classical sense as well as on discursive as a derivative of discourse. My use covers this area and, even more, that of metaphorical practices. The overlap between my use and his consists of seeing discourse as practice and thus constantly mobile and transformational.

Community and Society in Ottoman Modernization

In the most general sense, structured templates which guide our conduct in society are part of our cultural inheritance. The manner in which we arrange our daily life is no random exercise. We eat, drink, love, kill and think from within a set of cultural frames which shape our lives. These frames already exist when we are born, and our maturation consists of adapting to their imperatives. (For a study of the imperatives for followers of Bediüzzaman analyzed from the perspective of symbolic exchange see Schiffauer, 1984.) It is true that these frames have an entropic quality: the reproduction of a cultural pattern as it existed at the time of our birth is not automatic. Errors, changes in the environment, idiosyncratic perception, interpretations and manipulatory strategies are sources of this instability. But another element which changes the cultural setting within which we operate is the intrusion into our lives of alien cultures. When these external forces impinge upon and force us to change our set ways, we have to decide how we shall deal with them.

The life and teachings of Bediüzzaman Said Nursi, the Muslim thinker whose tribulations I try to unfold in the following pages, may be seen as shaped by a reaction to such an intrusion. Since Said Nursi was a so-called "gate-keeper" of Islamic culture, a cleric, he had a special role to play in these spheres. Said Nursi's writings claim to serve one main purpose: to stop the inroads into the Muslim culture of what he saw as the materialism of the West. To combat materialism he is engaged in missionary work to revitalize the Muslim heritage of Ottoman and, later, Turkish Muslims. What we also gather from his life history is that many of his disciples saw the same intrusion in the simpler terms of the advent of an alien thing.

The point at which Said's thought met with the silent musings of his clientele was that, while he combatted materialism because it negated Islam, he also realized that the influences of Western ways (ideas, institutions, practices) were destroying the cultural frame that Muslims used to establish a rapport with the everyday world.

An informed reading of Bediüzzaman's arguments enables us to draw a somewhat fuller picture of the points at which Ottoman reform from 1839 onwards created cultural constraints for a large number of its subjects and established a foundation for his influence. These areas of friction were underlined even more heavily after the inception of the Turkish Republic and its secularizing reforms. In the perspective of this second reading, Bediüzzaman's struggle against materialism emerges as a stand taken against a new image of social relations and a protest against the practices linked to this image. The novel concept of social relations which came with reform was one which ignored a code of conduct drawn from Islam and the personal relations which formed around this code, and superseded them with an understanding of society as an impersonal machine. A short excursus into Ottoman history and Western European social thought will explain what I mean.

The venue into modernism of late-comer nations is one which starts with a cultural confrontation and a cultural transformation. Often no other option exists: the process of European nation-building was too far advanced when Ottoman Turkey clashed head-on with it for the Ottomans to be able to replicate the European trajectory to modernity. The latter had included a long gestation of economic forces which was missing in Turkey's experience. A few earnest Ottoman attempts at industrialization in the 1840s and 1850s having failed, Ottoman reformers of the so-called *Tanzimat* era decided to streamline military training, transform education, reform administration, secularize courts of justice and modernize communications, hoping that these changes could eventually win them a place among the powerful.

This process of cultural transformation occurred relatively quickly, but its leadership, limited at its inception to a group of top-rank bureaucrats, was small. For a long time Ottoman culture had been two-tiered, with a high and a low, or folk, component. High culture was in turn divided into the more secular culture of bureaucrats and the Islamic culture of the *'ulema,* the doctors of Islamic law. The tacit understanding that Islam was the premier element in Ottoman culture kept all three of these segments interpenetrating under an Islamic umbrella.

Through their secularizing reforms, the bureaucrats of the *Tanzimat* were alienated from both the doctors of Islamic law and the folk, whereas in the past a commom idiom and code of conduct linked these elements. But in the 1890s something occurred which resulted in a distancing of the new generation from its Islamic roots. This distancing may have derived from unstated premises in the thinking of the new intelligentsia shaped by the bureaucrats' reforms. Ernest Gellner has described its earlier equivalent in the West as a "universal conceptual currency," i.e. "one single language" to describe the world (Gellner, 1923, 21).

Scientific objectivism replaced a "faire", theoretical knowledge overwhelmed practical knowledge and judgement. The significance of this change was that practical knowledge had also been the foundation of the Ottoman elite's view of the world. In this sense, in the earlier setting the elite had been closer to popular "know how" composed as it was of "multiple but untamed operativities" (de Certeau, 1984, 65) drawn out of Islamic culture than was the scientism of the new generation (for which see Devereux, 1979 c.f. Bernstein, 1985, 38–39 for further connotations).

A consequence was that the newest generation of reformers of the 1890s was drawn into a conception of social relations that relegated man to be an epiphenomenon of more general laws of nature and society. In this perspective, society and nation were seen as real entities to which real persons were and should be subordinated. For them, one worked for the good of society through laws of nature and not for one's family as dictated by traditional norms, i.e., an explanation of how one should act on the basis that it had happened before. Yet, and this is the crucial point, in the nation-state—which the new intelligentsia increasingly saw as a necessary stage of political evolution—all citizens are required to believe that one works for society. "Society" is the cement of the social order, and this ideal becomes food for thought in all strata. One single legitimate discourse prevails. Neither Turkish clerics nor the folk took easily to this conception. In fact, they combatted it tenaciously, and this for the following reason.

Modern theories of society from Hobbes onward start with individuals and their disposition but then immediately proceed to examine the social function not of individuals but of aggregates constituted by individuals. Leviathan, general will, *geist*, state, society, are some of the nuances of these aggregates. The social and political institutions created during modernity replicated this understanding of a society of blocks.

Islam does provide equivalents of such abstractions, but these do not paint a picture of a machine-like, self-moving society. (At most, the Ottomans used Ibn Khaldun's sociological *'umrān*—civilization—a concept which was abstract but extremely diffuse.) Inevitably, there existed more or less anthropomorphic views of God in the ideal of an Islamic society. For a majority of rural Ottoman subjects, the anthropomorphic picture prevailed. The sacred was personalized and the cult of Muhammad's person was one of the ways in which traditionalism was modified in the nineteenth century in what may be named the peripheral areas of society. But in a more fundamental sense, Islamic culture made considerable use of concepts which related individuals to other *persons* in society such as the father, the mother, the master and the sultan. Both in theory and in practice, Islam banked on human networks and not on "blocks." Its educational institutions were based on the relation between a mentor and his pupil, its courts on the personal intercession of the judge (a shorthand notation for Weber's "*kadi* justice" – Ar. *qādī*), and this was still a feature of Ottoman culture before nineteenth century reform. This characteristic of social relations in Islamic societies still evokes many contemporary echoes, and numerous examples may be cited of a modern Muslim nostalgia for an ideal *gemeinschaft* in which intimate, face-to-face relations would set the tone. Modern Islamic radical thinkers and, among them, Sayyid Qutb, the ideologue of the Muslim Brothers in Egypt, look back wistfully to such a golden age. For Qutb, a fundamental flaw of Western parliamentary institutions is the climate of anonymity which they promote, whereas to him the Muslim consultative institution used in the *urzeit* of Islam, the *Shura*, was "personalized and fraternal" (Carré, 1984, 96–97). Said Nursi has a more positive attitude towards an Islamized parliamentary system but "fraternal" relations are as important for him as for Qutb.

The idea that to understand any Islamic society one has to give a structural value to persons was one which I found indispensable for analysis. What gives body to Ottoman civil society, to the areas circumscribed by the Şeriat is the bedrock of personal relations which occupy such an important place on Bediüzzaman's preachings. These relations have only recently become a legitimate subject of study among social scientists. In Eickelman's words, "In many parts of the Islamic Middle East and elsewhere it is increasingly apparent that social structure can also be conceived with persons as the fundamental units of social structure" (Eickelman, 1976, 89).

If this "personalistic" component of traditional Ottoman culture did, in fact, constitute part of the mental "repertoire" of the Sultan's "ordinary" subjects, then a number of consequences follow. One has to do with the impact on Ottoman culture—of the European culture of the Enlightenment. This culture was built on a view of stellar bodies in movement (Galileo-Newton) which together operated as a system. The projection onto the understanding of the state of this particular conception of a system is that the state is also a system of interrelated parts which operate mechanically: the state is a machine.

An outcome of the permeation of the Ottoman Empire by Western ideas concerning the state was that the reformers of the *Tanzimat* attempted—with variable success—to build such a machine. What they inherited from the Ottoman state system made this relatively easy for them. Not so for the common citizen to the extent that their religious culture concentrated on persons, their worth and the rules applying to control of their bodies. My thesis is that adopting the mechanistic view of society was more difficult for the clientele of Said Nursi than taking over the Newtonian *physical* system.

Note that the contrast between society seen as a machine and society conceptualized as a set of personal networks does not stem from the value which Muslim theorizing attributes to individualism as we know it in the West. Neither Said Nursi nor the idiom he is trying to revive have anything good to say for individualism. Rather, they bank on the *gemeinschaftlich* aspect of interpersonal relations. Said Nursi's ideas have their own holistic dimension. They are not those of a society viewed as a machine but those of a community interlinked with ties of personal obligation. And at still another level, rules for the control of bodily expression (cf. Colonna, 1979).

The changes which occurred in the Ottoman Empire during the *Tanzimat*, and continued during the Republic attacked the traditional Ottoman system by the extent to which it "de-personalized" it. The role of the patriarch, the father, the patrimonial ruler was gradually eroded and bonds of personal allegiance were replaced by Western-type contractual ties or by the type of affiliation that prevailed in a society of blocks. I intend to take up this point in detail in Chapter III. Eventually, it was to be this gap which Said Nursi filled by setting out to repersonalize Turkish society through the personalized stamp of the *Risale-i Nur*—yet giving to depersonalization to the extent that he denied the legitimacy of personal guidance after his own demise.

The mode of life encompassed in the traditional, Muslim, personalistic system was changed relatively quickly during the reforms of the *Tanzimat*. This occurred in two stages. First, there was a reassertion of the state and its bureaucratic apparatus in the early years of reform. Then came the Young Turks of the 1890s among whom a subservience to a universalistic conceptual universe brought in its train a view of society once again underlining elements working beyond the person. Individuals were still accepted in this new outlook; they were still seen as units of society, but their interrelation was conceptualized as that of lifeless atoms driven by laws of nature. I do not need to go into greater detail in this modern denial of organic connections between individuals since it has been studied in many other contexts. One remark, however, may bring greater depth to a well known proposition. I refer to the recent discovery that "the ratiocination by which we understand the world actually occurs more through non-propositional that propositional means." In other words, "performative language," the use of primary imagination and "displacement through metaphors, are actually better confirmatory means of what the world as reality consists that the true/not true questions of standard, formal logic" (Parkin, 1982, XXVII). What the Young Turks, and later the Republic, had done was to eliminate the discourse based on non-propositional means which gave life to inter-personal relations for the average Ottoman. Said Nursi's contribution was a reaffirmation of the norms set by the Qur'ān in such a way as to re-introduce the traditional Muslim idiom of conduct and of personal relations into an emerging society of industry and mass communications. I consider that a large part of his appeal was due to this philosophical-sociological approach. In the pages that follow, I analyze a number of other forces that marked his life. However, the centrality of his contribution in reviving the traditional Ottoman idiom of social conduct and relations and his own discourse as a variation of the latter constitutes a good synoptic explanation of his influence in modern Turkey.

A number of important uses of this idiom by the non-govermental, i.e., middle and lower classes of Turkey, highlight the great value that Bediüzzaman's followers attached to it: it offered them a means for spiritual development; it provided for their maturation as persons and the building of their personality; it gave them the means of constructing a social sphere which may be described as delimited by private law, and also the means for building a new base of ultimate legitimacy; it generated arguments, if not instruments, to keep the state at bay when it wanted to invade their sphere; and, finally, it was a map for community action. Depending as it did on a flexible discourse rather than on block-like institutions (such as the Church in Christianity) it showed a remarkable reliance on and adaptability to modern conditions while maintaining the integrity of its message.

The perdurance of the Islamic idiom through thick and thin during the various stages of Ottoman modernization was due to the richness and flexibility of its conceptual apparatus. In our story this apparatus enables persons steeped in the rural world, but alerted to the transformations that were taking place around them, to take their first steps into an increasingly Western-oriented urban cultural sphere. Said Nursi saw himself as the guide who would lead them into this stage while at the same time shoring up their religiosity.

From what I have stated it follows that, in my story, the two camps which are locked in combat do not take their force from the realm of theories or theologies but are opposites that spring from the bedrock of everyday life. Even though they can be seen as the expression of an abstract historical dialectic, and even though Said Nursi states that he is combatting European philosophers, "especially atheist philosophy," the combat he is waging assumes greater clarity when it is seen as unfolding on a field which is that of the "common-sense world."

Let me underline, however, that what we are dealing with here is the appeal for his followers of *what is absent*. It is as much a yearning for something which one feels is missing from the social fabric as it is an interest in the substance of this element. Bediüzzaman's disciples were drawn to him by the feeling that a key element had been driven out of the social structure in which they were immersed, a sense similar to that of a man who is sitting at a table with one of the legs somewhat shorter than the others. We may go even further: this element had been driven out at a time when they dimly perceived that it held out new possibilities for an expansion of their universe. In our case then a *lacuna* becomes a sociologically significant element. This consciousness of a potential, the charismatic appeal of an esoteric style as items in the power that builds up a faith movement such as the one I study, still remain somewhat mysterious, and I have not attempted to decipher them but take them as irreducible elements of the religious experience. The clue to these paradoxes may be that "poetry" and "mystic marks" are more integral parts of the "common-sense world" than many would admit.

I think it is clear by now that I see religion—Islam—as social practice. This approach seems to have suffered undeserved neglect. But then, that does not clear up the issue of the structural frame within which the idiom I am pinpointing operates. What I mean is that the idiom has to be linked to the dynamics of statuses and positions, and that power has also to figure somewhere in one's explanation. These interlinkages may be studied in a Foucauldian or Weberian frame. I have chosen Weber. The relation between idiom and "status-positions" is, in any case, one between two different levels of abstraction. Even if one were to delimit these two contexts as field or spheres one could probably not find a way of fitting them together.

A similar problem is that of the consistency of all the pieces of one's image of society. A number of social scientists have speculated that inconsistencies within a given system of representation are necessary for the functioning of society (Leach-Gellner). Reminding oneself of this approach also seems salutary at this point. What I would venture to suggest is that there exists a social dialectic which attempts to overcome these inconsistencies—a major theme in the pages that follow—but that these are in the end never resolved.

Internal States

Delineating the type of influence which Said Nursi exercised over his clientele reveals three fundamental axes around which one may build an explanatory frame. One of these is the "idiom" he was reviving, and I have already covered this aspect of his biography. The other two dimensions of his effectiveness as a leader are linked first to a world-wide development which I call the "communications revolution" and second, to his followers "internal states." I take up the international relations component of his life-world in Chapter I. In the following pages I develop the idea of the psychic demands to which he was responding, placing these in the Ottoman-Muslim cultural setting.

An analysis of the motivation of individuals proceed at two different levels. One of these is to take the subject's understanding of his own cultural system as providing a means for his as well as our understanding of the way society functions (Gidden's "tacit stocks of knowledge"). I have attempted to cover this aspect of the behavior of Said Nursi's followers with the concept of "idiom." Let me rephrase once more what my use of the concept implies for me by citing yet another remark by Giddens:

> . . . in a basic way, a social investigator draws upon the same sort of resources as laymen do in making sense of the conduct which it is his aim to analyse or explain; and vice versa . . . the practical theorizing of laymen cannot merely be dismissed by the observer as an obstacle to the "scientific" understanding of human conduct, but is a vital element whereby that conduct is *constituted* or "made to happen" by social actors. . . . . the stocks of knowledge routinely drawn upon by members of society to make a meaningful social world depend upon knowledge, largely taken for granted or implicit, of a pragmatically oriented kind: that is to say, "knowledge" that the agent is rarely able to express in propositional form, and to which the ideals of science-precision of formulation, logical exhaustiveness, clear-cut lexical definitions etc.—are not relevant . . . the concepts employed by

> the social scientists are linked to or depend upon a prior understanding of, those used by laymen in sustaining a meaningful social world. (Giddens, 1976, 52–53)

A second level of analysis which would attempt to shed light on the behavior of the individuals who were attracted to Said Nursi would involve inquiring into the psychological processes which operate with even less of a conscious choice than is the case in rule-governed behavior. Because the *nurcu* often use items of the Islamic idiom for unconscious processes of identity-building and accomodation with the ambient world, I believe that a more psychological tack is necessary to shed light on the inner drives of the *nurcu* clientele.

It is clear that the pains that Bediüzzaman took to promote the revitalization of Islam were a consequence of changes in his own "internal states" as well as those of his clients. His psychological disarray caused by the penetration of Western European influences into the Ottoman Empire was paralleled by a similar malaise among his followers. For them too, affiliation with the *Nur* movement appears to have been triggered off by certain motivations or psychological dispositions. An interpretation of the dynamic of the movement requires an understanding of these dispositions.

A peculiarity of the times I cover in this study is that a number of social institutions such as craft guilds, religious orders, religious communities and powerful families of provincial notables—all of which made up the mosaic-like peripheral structure of the Ottoman Empire—were undergoing a process of breakdown and deterioration (Berkes, ed., 1959, *passim*). However, a national identity had not yet emerged to take the place of these segmental affiliations. This was particularly true of the Ottoman provinces. In many of these outlying areas—one of them being Said Nursi's first base, İsparta—sufficient change in the segmented structure had taken place to create a general feeling of anxiety in the rural and provincial population. In this perspective it is reasonable to assume that the resources for identity building which at one time flowed from the controlling force of the peripheral institutions were dissipated and that the revitalization of the Muslim idiom offered by Said Nursi was a bounty that could be made use of in the elaboration of the self.

Indices which became stronger as I studied the reception of Said Nursi's ideas seemed to indicate the persistence of a venue into *Nurculuk* linked to psychological quandaries. I therefore have attempted to give aglimpse of this process at various times in my study.

The Person's Involvement in Religion

Said Nursi was a deeply religious man. In contrast with the Islamic proto-nationalist thinker Cemaleddin Afgani (Ar. Jamāl ad-Dīn al-Afghānī), he eventually abandoned the more clearly instrumental stance he had assumed at the beginning of his practices of Muslims. The materials that were available to me in the case of *Nurculuk* brought to the fore an aspect of what may be termed the mytho-poetic dimensions of religion. This aspect concerns the maintenance of the integrity of the self worked through a symbolic mytho-poetic repertoire. Not all *nurcus* fall into his category; for a number, the revitalization of Islam in order to regain the power it once held has first priority. For others, whose distinguishing characteristic seems to have been lower age brackets, the dynamics of the venue into the *Nur* sect appear to be linked to the solution of quandaries concerned with the maintenance of the integrity of traditional sets of "positions" (Giddens, 1986, 83), and this they work out by embracing religious symbolism. There are indications that Said's success in the vicinity of Isparta around 1925–27 may be related to the reaffirmation of the legitimacy of these symbols at the time they were coming under fire in the Republic. The important contingent of small town dwellers with some education but an inconsistent status—part modern, part traditional—which one finds among the first propagators of Bediüzzaman's message in one of these indices.

Theological Foundations

To see the revitalization movement of Said Nursi as one which sustains the use of an idiom in a time of troubles is a first step in getting an understanding of his influence. A second step requires that one brings to bear into one's analysis the specific characters that one has attributed to "Islamicate" cultures (Hodgson, I, 1974, 57) and the way in which they shape social behavior. Although a repetition of a theme I have already broached, I have to underline once more at this point that the basic perspective which I assume is that the believer's conceptualization of what religion-means to him in relation to his everyday life cannot be dismissed as an epiphenomenon which "masks" a more basic dynamic of religion.

What has focused the attention of students of Islam in the past has been an aspect of Islam which is best rendered by the term "revelation" (Makeen, 1980). It is the "revelational" aspect of the *Qur'ān,* the fact that the *Qur'ān* is the revealed word of God, which sets boundaries to options available to man. These boundaries provide one clue to the study of modern

Islamic society in the sense that the correct attitude a Muslim should adopt towards modernization can only be drawn out of the religious sciences. Here, Said may be seen as an expert in Islamic sciences who has drawn from the *Qur'ān* principles of Muslim behavior appropriate to our times. Nevertheless, two other pieces of the problem are needed before we can understand Said Nursi's influence and his transformation of the Islamic revelational idiom. One of these is the quality which the Islamic idiom assumes in an Ottoman context, another the conditions regulating access to God in Islam.

In the *Qur'ānic* discourse it is difficult to separate the private and the personal from the public field. There is no equivalent of the Western separation of public and private law. The Ottomans were able to circumvent this feature of Islam only because they brought their own store of clearly political symbols of legitimation with them (İnalcık, 1958). Ottoman institutional specialization produced an extensive vocabulary of politics and a new mental world related to political action. This special Ottoman demarcation of the state from religion was one of the reasons for which Ottoman statesmen of the *Tanzimat* could consider the translation of the French civil code into Turkish without flinching. Said Nursi was constantly faced in his life by this mode of thought which accorded the highest priority to the salvation of the state. Said himself conceptualized the central problem confronting Ottomans as one of the revitalization of the Islamic *community*.

This duality of the visions regarding the place of religion vis-a-vis the state placed many stumbling blocks in Said's way. The problem gains from being studied as an aspect of the role of the community in Islamic societies.

Islam first coalesced into a religious *community*. Leaders of the Islamic forces were leaders of this religious community, and their prestige arose from the fact that they were repositories of religious charisma. Somewhat later, the mechanism of a patrimonial state was imposed upon these arrangements. The *Qur'ān* defined with some detail how the religious community was to operate, although it was not so precise concerning the structure of the state. Thus, Islamic societies and their theoreticians had a tendency to see the state as an extension of the religious community, existing for the protection of the community. The emphasis was on the life of the community, not on the life of the state. An independent body of political formulae, which attained its highest form in Turko-Mongol-Ottoman practice, did develop, but this view was somewhat alien to the Islamic theory of the community insofar as it saw the state as the primary mode of society. Both before and after the Ottomans, the *de facto* heavier weight of the state (than had been planned for an ideal Islamic society) was reluctantly accepted by the *'ulema* but the theoretical hiatus could not be made the subject of profound disquisitions because the very concept of a state was alien to pristine Islam.

In the Ottoman Empire, the majority of the *'ulema* who did not have much contact with state practice, did not confront the secular formulae of statecraft head on. They brought out what they had learned about political obligation in Islamic sources whenever the opportunity arose. Even though daily Ottoman practice differed from what would have been a strict application of Islamic principles, their acceptance of the existing institutions did not mean that the *'ulema* had rallied to the bureaucrats' view of the state, but rather that doctors of Islamic law had better means of testing the legitimacy of an individual caliph than assailing his machinery of rule. Neither did they have the practical means of reasserting the power of the community, except by backing community outbursts against the central power or palace intrigues to topple an administration. In times of discontent the *'ulema* could invoke Islamic principles to rally the people around them, but routine administrative practice with its unorthodox features was accepted by all subjects, including the *'ulema*.

In short, in a study involving the Ottoman Empire one always has to remember that political legitimacy was bicephalous. Some of the sultans can be shown to have had a fine understanding of this balance between religion and the state. Sultan Abdülhamid II (1876–1909) was—contrary to all that has been written—a person who deeply sensitive to the concept of the survival of the state. He used appeals to the Muslim community to band together, but he could also shape a policy for the Ottoman state which had as a goal the preservation of the state itself. In search for new sources of income, he could go through the existing religious foundations with a fine tooth comb. It is probable that what appears to be the sultan's rebuff to Bediüzzaman's own reform proposals in 1896, during an extended stay in Istanbul (Kutay, 1966–67), was due to his suspiciousness of the special place that Said gave to the Kurds in his proposals. He may well have believed that this was a divisive factor which would undermine the unity of the state. His successors, the founding fathers of the Turkish Republic, were to level the same accusation against Said in the 1920s. Said Nursi figures as the representative of the culture of the *'ulema*, more precisely as a member of that sub-set of this culture that had strong links with popular culture.

Man's Access to God

That Islam, in its most orthodox aspect, posits a God that is perceived as pure potency and creativeness, and is devoid of anthropocentric characteristics, has often been underlined. One of the best summaries of this feature has been given by Robert Bellah:

> Without intending any disrespect, one can speak of a certain poverty of symbolic reference to God in the *Qur'an*. Ancient Israel, according to George Mendenhall and other contemporary scholars, first built up its conception of a transcendent God on the model of the ancient Near Eastern great king. God was above all King, Lord, Ruler. Christianity continued this line of analogical thought, but added to it a stress on God as Father which was much less central in Israelite thought. In the *Qur'an* God is understood, first of all, neither as king nor as father but simply as God. The only analogy for God is God. (Bellah, 1970,155)

As a proposition about Muslim theology, this may be somewhat one-sided. But it does highlight one aspect of Islam which one of the most prominent of Muslim theologians, al-Ghazālī, underlined when he stated: "As to God's love (for man) there are few who believe in it. Some sages (*'ālim*) have even denied its possibility" (Ghazālī Trs., 1925, IV, 533).

This condition is compounded by certain ecological conditions prevailing in the Middle East. Ernest Gellner has shown how, for the tribal illiterate, these difficulties of access result in the necessary intercession of holy men between man and God (Keddie ed., 1972, 311) even though many of the theologians of Islam decry such an intercession.

The urban Islam of the orthodox *'ulema* which is "legalistic, restrained, arid" (Keddie ed., 1972, 309) has opened a door to another understanding of God, and that is Sufi mysticism. Classification should not stop here, however, as the votaries of city Sufism also consist of two groups: the sophisticates, who are learned in the ways of Sufism, and the masses. Kâtip Çelebi, the Ottoman encyclopaedist of the 17th Century, provides a description of the mode of affiliation to the latter which was still a received idea among educated Ottomans in the early 20th century:

> "Most of the Khalwati orders have based their rites and observances on the community of aspirants. They have founded lodges and have made the *Hay*! and *Hu*! which are the essentials of their society . . . This is the reason why the brutish common people flock to them and votive offerings and pious gifts pour into their lodges . . . ." (Kâtip Çelebi, 1957, 43–44)

Sufi *şeyh*s were not above providing for such needs or dealing in magic cures. In modern times the mobilization of the masses has given a new twist to their mode of participation—not anymore a gross "Hay" or "Hu"; I try to describe this development and the emphasis on a softer understanding of man's relation to God in Chapter V.

For both the learned and the masses, mediation between man and God was provided by a guide, a *pir* or *mürşid*. It is possibly this overwhelming need to establish a chain linking man and God that explains why so many of the orthodox *'ulema* were affiliated with a mystic order. For the traditional Anatolian masses the mediator was the image of the Prophet, which stressed his kindness, his physical make up, his well-groomed person and his sense of justice and fairness. The *pir*, the spiritual guide, is one person who, as a link in this chain, also emerges as father figure, a father that smooths access to the ultimate father. What theology denies is provided by day-to-day practice.

Father images were also in tune with the principles of organization of Islamic societies which underlined the homologous roles of the *pater familias* and the teacher. But if we look at Ottoman Islamic society as a social structure, we notice that the *pir* (hypostasis of the personalistic system) figures as a metaphor of the entire social system: the father image fits into this structural slot.

In conclusion, two characteristics may be underlined which I believe are relevant to an understanding of what is "truly" religious in *Nurculuk*: one is the centrality of the symbolic store in a person's involvement in religion. A second is the malleability of the set of religious symbols at an individual level. Ernest Gellner, in a seminal article, showed some years ago that the necessary ambivalence of our symbolic apparatus opens a door to social change (Gellner, 1970). We may extend this insight to religious symbolism in the sense that there are avenues of freedom in the very process of using one's culturally determined apparatus to reach God (as I shall try to argue in Chapter IV). Gellner was referring to conscious processes, but there is no reason why his suggestions could not be even truer of unconscious processes. Depriving a person of his ability to use the set of symbols which shape his individual approach to God may be a more distressing blow to him than depriving him of other values. It may be easier to take defeat on the battlefield than to be deprived of the means of personal access to the sacred, especially if this access is one of the processes that make for mental equilibrium, personal satisfaction and integration with the rest of society. If millenarian movements are the product of some form of deprivation, I would speculate that their driving force is not only a matter of recapturing means of controlling power and influence (Burridge, 1967) but, in addition, an attempt to reconstitute a shattered "numinous grammar" which, when re-established, can bring back a mode of reflecting about the sacred, but also the ambient, world.

I shall try to show that the impoverishment of religious symbolism was felt with great force among a certain strata of Turkish Muslims at a time when this symbolic fund was being devalued. I am unable to offer any "proof" of this proposition, but that Said Nursi's success was due to his revitalization of the religious idiom at the individual as well as at the social level may become more evident as I proceed. Social change, as manifested by the birth and development of the *Nur* movement, is unraveled in this perspective.

Last, but not least, we have taken up problems of power, and here we have to back-track to the macro aspects of the study. The neglect of micro studies of social dynamics in Muslim societies has led me to over-emphasize these aspects in my treatment here. Nevertheless, the ubiquity of power in an Islamic setting and the extent to which social relations tend to be conceptualized as power relations is a theme which spills over into the sphere of religious practices. That the life of Said Nursi was framed by power as a *leitmotif* and by issues related to the legitimation of power and leadership emerges even in the most sketchy of descriptions of the sage's career. It is precisely because of the segmented structure of Middle East societies that the role of a charismatic leader such as Said Nursi is highlighted. In this particular case, the charismatic leader in his role as an innovator imposes new obligations on his followers, although he works through a traditional setting.

Said Nursi's task seems to have been promoted by the new life which certain traditional Muslim institutions acquired during the process of modernization in the Ottoman Empire. What we have here may be described as over-determination. The expansion of *medreses* in İsparta at the end of the nineteenth century is only one example of these developments. Others are the promotion of *tarikat* activities both in the diffuse sense in which such bodies as the Sanusi acquired a new function and in the more instrumental sense in which Sultan Abdülhamid used Islam as a tool for mobilization among his Muslim subjects. But at the other end of this over-determination we have the disenchantment of the modern world and the opportunities created by this blow to the integrating mechanism of Muslims in Turkey.

CHAPTER I

Preliminary Approaches to the Biography of a Turkish Muslim Fundamentalist Thinker

THE TOWN OF El Cerrito, California has not made a special mark by its contribution to the development of contemporary intellectual history. It is, however, a center from which, in recent years, a series of pamphlets with special importance for Turkish religious history has been issued. The *Qur'ānic* commentaries and homiletics which make up the Turkish originals of these brochures are a segment of the published doctrines of the protagonist of this study, Bediüzzaman ("Nonpareil of Our Times") Said Nursi (1876–1960). Together, these pieces constitute what is known as the *Risale-i Nur* (*The Epistle of Light*).

Even if one takes for granted the well-known eclecticism of California culture, the speed and the extent of diffusion of Bediüzzaman's message is remarkable. To the limited extent that it has thus joined a group of movements of spiritual revitalization—which have recently transcended their local origins and have stepped on to the world stage—Said Nursi's message may be considered to have entered one stream of modernization. The internal organization of the "faith movement" of the *nurcu* is a diffuse one which—it has been advanced—consists of the hierarchically arranged categories of *talebe* (student), *kardeş* (brother), *dost* (friend) and *sevgili* (beloved) (Spuler, 1981, 428). *Talebe* and *kardeş* are said to have to retain their bachelor status for the first five to ten years of their "apprenticeship" and to concentrate exclusively on study and on tests assigned to them. The step from *talebe* to *kardeş* depends upon the internalization of the message of the *Risale-i Nur* as well as on establishing an activist record. Organizational responsibilities appear at the level of the *dost*. The highest rank consists of persons who have inherited the tradition of Said Nursi from the man himself. The number of these is decreasing all the time. Actually, these categories, derived from the writings of a Turkish journalist have no basis in fact and are distorted reflections of the way Said addresses himself to his audience. (See *Barla Lâhikası* and *Emirdağ Lâhikası*). My own observations are that Spuler's categories are a reification of more transactional processes where one accedes to the top through a constant, informal evaluation of the organizational-Islamist utility of a person and its relation to the goals of the *nurcu*, the ladder of leadership being lowered from the top down.

There also exists an "assembly" of the *nurcu* which is convened informally and meets every few years. An important aspect of *Nurculuk* (membership in the faith movement) is that just as men gather every week to discuss passages from the *Risale-i Nur*, a number of women's gatherings are also convened for similar discussions. This parallel structure is not reflected in the leadership, which is all male. Schiffauer (1984) has, nonetheless, shown how the availability of such women's circles allows some of the Turkish women guest-workers in Germany to achieve an autonomous identity for which there was no place in their village of origin. In fact, the relation of the movement to modernization is quite intricate and also begins earlier than one would suspect (see below, Chapter III).

Modern Muslim revitalization movements have been linked with an early stage of global modernization processes and one can follow this link through the effect on revitalization of modern communications. During the 18th century, Mecca was already drawn into the new density of Mediterranean communications, and from Mecca issued the ferment which propelled Islamic revival movements in Asia and Africa. In the 19th century, the world communications revolution, though originating outside the Islamic world, gave a fresh impetus to the enhanced interaction of Muslims. The rise in the number of Meccan pilgrims has been mentioned by a number of authors (Geertz, 1968) as a development due to the improvement of communications but, in turn, generating communications effects. The same enhanced effectiveness applies to the *Nakşibendi* "sect" with which Said Nursi had such close links. During the 19th century new opportunities for the expansion of the *Nakşibendi*s' proselytizing activities seem to have opened up in the Ottoman Empire and Said's life was marked by these antecedents. It is only the latest expansion of this network which brings into focus the Risale-i Nur Institute of America.

In Turkey, the *Nur* movement acquired its most striking universalistic characteristics between 1950 and 1975. Paradoxically, these followed upon, and were organically linked with, the modernizing policies of the Turkish Republic. The *Nur* movement may thus be seen as having been carried to its internationalization on the crest of Turkish Republican modernization. As we know, during the Republican era (1923 to date), Turkey increased its interaction with the world at large: it opened up unequivocally to the Western world by adopting Westernization (*garplılaşma*), as one of the ideological tenets of the new republic (Lewis, 1968, 176f.) This external stance was duplicated by internal policies of reform that stressed education, science and secularization. Between 1923 and 1938 the entire cast of Turkish society was penetrated by some of these reforms carried out under the aegis of Mustafa Kemal Atatürk. The *Nur* movement had, therefore, to accept as a datum of social life those reforms—such as universal education—which, gradually, had become part of the birthright of modern Turks. Spuler (1973, 105), earlier, had already perceived the connection between the Nur movement and modernization. Her emphasis, however, has to be reversed. It was not because of the modernization of pan-Islamic propaganda that the movement acquired new impetus after 1950, but because it could by then work with modern materials and ideas which had been integrated into the new culture of Republican Turkey and become part of the patrimony of the Turks. A striking—although not typical—example of this transmutation may be seen in the question posed by a *nurcu* (1983): "Have you ever read the following quatrain of Rilke? He shows so well what Said Nursi meant."

The *Nur* movement also found some of its strength in Republican failures. Outstanding among these was the inability of secular Republican ideology to replace Islam as a world view. This failure paralleled what Western civilization was beginning to perceive as a drawback, namely the absence of strong bonds of belief and the "anomie" prevalent in industrial society. The *Nur* movement's ability to direct its operations through a cultural framework partly imposed by the Turkish Republic, together with its rhetoric, which incorporated a strain of Islamic mysticism, answered the operational mode and the spiritual demands of a Turkish clientele. "*Nur*" also answered the longing of a new world clientele to which it could now begin to address itself. This, then, is the process by which El Cerrito came into the orbit of Bitlis, Said Nursi's birthplace.

The *Nur* movement first took shape in western Turkey in the 1920s at a time when Said Nursi was exiled to a provincial hamlet by the government of Republican Turkey. The social characteristics of its earliest following, just as those of its present votaries, are difficult to pinpoint. Since it does not operate on the model of a traditional Islamic sect, but claims it is a medium for the dissemination of the truth of the *Qur'ān,* its boundaries are diffuse: every person who joins in the task of dissemination is *ipso facto* a disciple. There are no initiation rites and there is no formal organizational structure; a precise count of the membership is, thus, impossible. It is, nevertheless, incontrovertible that the fundamentalist views of Bediüzzaman have acquired a large following in Turkey since they were first propagated in the 1920s.

The specifically Turkish circumstances in which the movement was born remind us that its most significant aspect is not its improbable encounter with the affinity of Californians for esoteric lore. Neither is the *Nur* movement best characterized by its recent importation by Turkish guest workers, into Western Europe thereby adding to its clientele a small contingent of Western Europeans. The *Nur* movement makes greater "sense" when it is investigated in the context of a number of similar Islamic movements in the Islamic world. It is this approach that provides us with clues to an understanding of the complicated social processes which it tapped in Turkey. I shall, therefore, attempt to bring out its features as an aspect of the "revitalization" of Islam, a term which seems to me to be a fair equivalent of *tajdīd*, the word used by Muslims for the process of renewal in religion (Ayoubi, 1981; Dekmejian, 1980; Dessouki, 1982; Esposito, 1980; Gellner and Vatin, 1981; Gilsenan, 1982; Humphreys, 1979; Ibrahim, 1980; Mitchell, 1969).

Bediüzzaman was a Muslim thinker who encountered problems similar to those faced by other Muslim thinkers in other parts of the Islamic world in the nineteenth century. The religious idiom that he inherited, and the ways in which he stated problems in this idiom, show a strong Muslim medieval imprint. The external forces impinging upon him which impelled him to modify this idiom, however, are thoroughly contemporary: they were part of the process by which new communications media were penetrating the globe and reducing its dimension.

The study of the ideas of Said Nursi and the analysis of the social movement he created, then, fall under at least two headings: one related to the state of Islam in Turkey in the last century, the second to a world-encompassing process associated with modernization and—possibly—to a Turkish version of the spiritual crisis which accompanied modernization (Berger, Berger and Kellner, 1973; Wallis, 1978). In short, Said Nursi's attempt to "revitalize" Islam was the product of a change in the scope of Ottoman social relations which was, in turn, part of a more universal process known as the "social communication" mutation. What may be seen as the more clearly indigenous Ottoman development with a dynamic emerging from *internal* sources generated a separate set of variables which were just as important for Bediüzzaman as the exogenous forces. (An example would be the growth of the *medrese* network in the province of İsparta, where Said Nursi was to find his first disciples). Today the perspective one needs to adopt in studying the *Nur* movement has changed once more: a largely rural movement which gained strength in small provincial towns has become enmeshed with problems created by rural–urban migration and by the rapid growth of large cities in Turkey.

There are other aspects of Said Nursi's career and contributions which cut across my basic two-dimensional categorization, one Muslim, the other universal. The first of these possible alternative classifications is biographical: Said's life may be divided into two periods. The first covers his activities up to the early 1920s; the later one has as its focus the creation of the *Nur* movement in Western Anatolia and ends with Said's death in 1960.

The Setting

Said Nursi's first involvement with Islamic revitalization goes back to the early part of his life (1876–1896): this is the historical context in which the variables which turned him into a fundamentalist activist came into play. For Said, as well as for his contemporaries living in Bitlis, an outstanding characteristic of the troubled era they were traversing was that it placed them at the terminus of a chain reaction of social change. This movement had been set in motion in the West, where it had been proceeding for some time before it finally reached Eastern Anatolia. But what reached these provinces belonged more to the superstructure of change; it consisted of items that could be broadly described under the heading of "communication" such as linkage with the center, government services, education, conscription. On the other hand, the original communication revolution which the West had experienced had arisen together with a concomitant groundswell of infrastructural transformation; communications were the multiplier of a material transformation. In Europe, the expansion of the road network, the propagation of mass media and the growth of modern educational institutions had been linked to antecedents such as the expansion of commercial capitalism, the growth of the cities and the birth of industrial civilization.

Neither the area under study here, nor other parts of the Ottoman Empire were ever directly involved in all of these features of the infrastructural modernization of Europe.

Although the Ottoman Empire itself was only drawn into what may be termed sub-processes of modernization—the most conspicuous aspects of Ottoman modernization being governmental reform and educational expansion—the involvement of the Kurdish-speaking regions in these changes was even more limited. Some new educational institutions and the outlines of a new administration appeared. Yet, while this region experienced almost no infrastructural development and saw little local change in the technology of communications, it was, nevertheless, brought into contact with the relatively developed social communications network which grew out of 19th century Ottoman reform.

This reform movement was the end-product of an extended confrontation of the Ottoman Empire with the West. The sequence of change in the streamlining of Ottoman institutions was that reform was applied first in the more developed western parts of the Ottoman Empire. Changes of political structure were planned in Istanbul, carried out with some loss of content in Western Anatolia and then—with varying lags—affected the eastern regions. Changes in economic structure changed life in Beirut and Aleppo and then trickled to Eastern Anatolia. Economic changes affecting the Middle East also worked towards eastern Turkey through Persia and Iraq. In all these cases Bitlis was the end point of the process of change.

While Bitlis did not suffer from the direct intervention of the West—and thus seems in the short run to have been relatively insulated from the adverse repercussions of Western industrialization on its manufactures—neither was it directly affected by economic imperialism. In short, the impact on Bitlis of the momentous changes which were reshaping the world in the nineteenth century were mediated, indirect and partial.

The situation was different in the more developed areas of the Ottoman Empire, where the impact of the West was felt earlier and more directly. The Anglo-Ottoman Treaty of Commerce of 1838, which set a model for many others to follow, *did* impose onerous conditions on Turkish manufacturers, just as Ottoman administrative and economic reform was directly inspired by European enlightened despotism. Liberal trade policies and the copying of legal, administrative and educational institutions of the West were to become the hallmark of the Ottoman era of reforms.

It will have become clear that I use "communication" in a special sense. The meaning it carries in my exposé derives from Karl Deutsch's "social communication" (Deutsch, 1966). Deutsch takes up the social changes which took place in Europe up to and during the nineteenth century—and nationalism as one product of these changes—as a function of their widening of the scope of social relations. In Deutsch's own words: "Clusters of settlement, modes of transport, centers of culture, areas and centers of language, divisions of caste and class, barriers between markets, sharp regional differences in wealth and interdependence, and the uneven impact of critical historical events and social institutions all act together to produce a highly differentiated and clustered world of regions, peoples and nations" (Deutsch, 1966, 187).

The "clustering" which Deutsch mentions is an important datum of the history of Eastern Anatolia in the nineteenth century: as the forces of differentiation set to work in the Kurdish-speaking region, the setting emerged which shaped Said's behavior and ideas. The Ottoman government and administration upset an existing system of authority relations which had provided tolerable conditions for the rural population. Christian missionary work expanded the horizons of converts, while the sultan's support of Muslim-Ottoman activism encouraged the sects to work with Islam as a flag under which Muslims would re-group and be energized. But the theory that changes in communication patterns can influence social behavior can only be substantiated if we add to it a corollary which often goes unstated. In a setting like that of Bitlis the acceleration of social change was promoted by certain uniquely influential—in our case, psychologically shattering—events. (Lyman, 1978, 81) For Turkey, a series of clear defeats on the battlefields had constituted such events and had brought Westernizing reforms in its wake. For the heavily *tarikat*-influenced culture of the area in which Said Nursi was raised, the threat to Islam of an upsurge of activity of Christian communities had constituted such a salient event. This saliency was the product of a tradition which incorporated conventional perspectives for highlighting distinctive aspects of historical developments. We know that the type of resentment caused by such an event, and by what was perceived as a slight to Islamic civilization, affected not only Said Nursi, but a number of persons from contiguous regions. Thus, while Said was—as we shall see—setting out to elaborate a form of Ottomanism (an integration of all ethnic groups in the same national unit), three young students of the military medical preparatory school in the capital, Ishak Sukûti, Abdullah Cevdet and Ziya Gökalp—all from the Eastern Ottoman provinces—were led by a similar sensitivity towards the decline of their ambient culture to join libertarian movements with a liberal-constitutionalist ideology. The first two of these were among the four founders of the earliest form of the Young Turk organization, the Committee of Union and Progress.

The Tanzimat

The beginning of a policy of institutional reform in the Ottoman Empire may be traced to the reign of Sultan Mahmud II (1808–1839) and his successor Abdülmecid (1839–1861). It was officially inaugurated in November 1839, by the reading of the *Hatt-ı Humayûn* of Gülhane, the charter which described the aim of reform. It continued to be implemented up to and beyond the reign of Sultan Abdülhamid II (1876–1909). The latter, although systematically maligned as an opponent of the *Tanzimat*, is seen in some important recent works as a willing heir to reform policies. The Young Turks (1908–1918) disassociated themselves from the 19th Century reform movement with a claim that they had introduced a radical element into reform; however, their policies were in the mainstream of the *Tanzimat*. In reality, the *Tanzimat* continued into the first decade of the twentieth century, and its latter part thus overlaps with Bediüzzaman's youth and early manhood.

The general trend of current research on the nineteenth century has been to belittle the achievements of the *Tanzimat*. One accent of this criticism is the extent to which peripheral areas of the Ottoman Empire remained untouched by modernization. This was true for the remoter regions, such as Bitlis, but part of the problems of the Eastern provinces of the Ottoman Empire was related not to the failure, but, on the contrary, to the *success* of the *Tanzimat*.

Even though these provinces did not profit from industrialization or commercial capitalism, they were drawn into a vortex created by Ottoman governmental reform, and had to face at least two developments which were the outcome of an Ottoman modernist policy. First, the Ottomans undertook to tighten their own system of provincial administration. This resulted in the elimination of local rulers who had possessed considerable adminstrative and political autonomy before the 19th century (van Bruinessen, 1978, 220f.). In addition, the new administrative structure of the Ottoman state began to penetrate into the area.

Still underdeveloped during the *Tanzimat*, Bitlis and its environs was, neverthless, drawn into some of the political and social outcomes generated by the Western communications revolution and its trickling into all of Eastern Anatolia. For instance, while this region did not benefit from many new schools, railroads or even highways, it became the field of activity for Protestant missionaries who now had easier access to the region (van Bruinessen, 1978; Darkot, 1944, 660). This is a good example of the mediated effects of the communications revolution proper. It is a development which is known to have had tragic consequences for the Nestorians, whom the missionaries were proselytizing (circa 1850).

The restructuring of the central apparatus of Ottoman government during the *Tanzimat* had important consequences for social communication. This recasting introduced new relations of subordination into the bureaucratic hierarchy: it brought the central administration of the Ottoman Empire closer to a true Weberian model of rationalized bureaucracy. "Ministries" emerged, the bureaucratic network itself was much expanded, within ministries bureaucratic linkages emerged which had not existed before, and new regulations appeared, accompanied by a novel "administrative law." All of these changes created networks of communications which resulted in the intensification of social interaction at the administrative level, but such developments also meant that an older system of administration which was well-worn but understandable was replaced by a new set of subject-official relations which had yet to be deciphered. Bitlis is a case in point.

A positive aspect of the Eastern Anatolian area's encounter with the *Tanzimat* was the increasing competence of provincial governors. The upper bureaucrats who went into the provinces as governors were expected to be inspired by a new ideology of reform. Good governors did, indeed, concentrate on building road systems, on establishing local governmental gazettes, and on founding systems of agricultural credit; they also tried to wrest the control of publicly auctioned state projects out of the hands of corrupt notables. The Ottoman government had established the first Anatolian newspaper in Erzurum in 1867 with the purpose of influencing local public opinion in this leading Eastern province (Yaşar, 1971, 30). This, again, was a novel channel for influencing populations to side with the government.

A consequence of the expansion of the world communication network was that, starting with the fourth decade of the nineteenth century, Ottoman mass media also grew. In the early 1840s, the Ottoman state divested itself of the monopoly of printing. Some years later, the growth of journalism created a new audience of readers in Istanbul and in some of the larger provincial towns. It was through his access to newspapers that Said Nursi learned of the intellectual currents in the Ottoman capital, just as it was there that he acquired some basic information concerning world affairs.

A further aspect of the changing pattern of social communication was the transformation of modes of thought. The infiltration of Western literary genres into the intellectual life of Istanbul between 1840 and 1900 occupies a central place in this process. Western rationalism and positivism had a harder time getting established, but were clearly gaining strength in Istanbul by the end of the nineteenth century (Ülken, 1966, I, 200f.). Traditional Ottoman literati had been eclectic. They had seen no harm in taking over ideas, such as those of modern Western education which had tangible, practical uses (Berkes, 1978). But the new secular philosophy derived from the West had an uncompromisingly materialistic problem-setting mode which presented novel dangers for religion. This new intellectual outlook brought its own problems with which Said had to grapple in his mature years; it must have caused him considerable inner turmoil even during the years he was in Bitlis (1876–1907).

Another area of change in the Ottoman capital was that the group characteristics of "carriers" of ideas changed: circles of literati gave way to a more homegeneous group of an intelligentsia which took up the new Western "culture of critical discourse" (Gouldner, 1979, 8–44). Esotericism lost its appeal: explanation became a much more frequent *leitmotif* in literary products. The newspapers and magazines replaced expostulation by arguments which were addressed to the presumed shared rationality of the readers, while the readership of printed books made up a public unknown to the traditional culture of Bitlis. All of these changes found an eventual echo in the provincial setting. In Van in the 1890s, Said was part of a circle of bureaucrats surrounding the Governor, who spent many a pleasant afternoon discussing current developments in world politics and other items of the Turkish press.

An excerpt of the 1880s from the Bitlis *Gazette* shows that the Ottomans considered they had a "civilizing mission" to carry out in these areas (Appendix 1). Some of the consequences of the policies of the *Tanzimat* were unanticipated even by the reformers themselves. The Ottomans were content to defeat local princelings and did not attempt to break up the social structure of the area directly, yet this was the unanticipated consequence of 19th century Ottoman reforms. Simply by imposing centralization and a new pattern of territorial sub-divisions, the Ottomans broke up the earlier social structure and caused what has been described as a "retribalization" of the area (van Bruinessen, 1978, 228f.). A movement partially reversing this trend emerged at the very end of the century. The sultan relinquished a degree of authority when he placed some tribal leaders at the head of local militias created for policing the area. But once again, it was an object of—not a source of—change. The build-up of the strength of Kurdish notables was an unanticipated outcome of the sultan's policy, but it was not consciously pursued by him. Instruments of rule, yes; autonomous groups, no.

Important educational reforms were carried out in the Ottoman Empire between 1840 and 1900 which changed the entire cast of Ottoman education. Among these was the establishment of a basic, three year post-primary school, the *rüşdiye* (Unat, 1964, 42). In the absence of a developed set of institutions of secondary education, the *rüşdiyes* served a portion of the population which up to that time had only received primary education followed immediately by professional training. Another new educational stream was that of military education. The system was first tried in Istanbul; its expansion into the Ottoman provinces began after 1876. Eastern Turkey profited somewhat late from the educational benefits of the *Tanzimat*. In the 1890's only two military lycées functioned in all of eastern Turkey to the Persian Gulf (Felgenhauer, 1887, 61). In Bitlis, however, a military *rüşdiye* was established in 1890 (Griffiths, 1966, 94, note 2). The point to be made here is not one of scarcity: one military *rüşdiye* in town and two lycées in surrounding areas were no mean achievement, but the existing military schools did not operate with the purpose of alerting students to the plight of the eastern region. On the contrary, they were established to draw their attention to the problems of the center and to socialize them into becoming loyal members of the Ottoman central bureaucracy.

The contrast between the paucity of educational institutions in the Bitlis-Van area and western Turkey was marked, but more by "relative" than by "absolute" deprivation. The best way to describe this is to point out that Bitlis had (in 1889) four civilian *rüşdiyes*. This meant one per 63,500 inhabitants, as compared to Izmir, which had one *rüşdiye* per 25,000 inhabitants (Cuinet, 1891). But in Bitlis, this ratio changes to one institution of secondary education per 1,100 inhabitants if one includes in the reckoning the 18 *medreses* which still operated as institutions of secondary education.

The problem for Bitlis, then, was to retain its prestige as an educational center, a prestige which it had acquired long before the end of the nineteenth century.

One final item in the pattern of change which affected the Ottoman Empire during the nineteenth century, and which also had repercussions in the Eastern region, was immigration into Turkey. As the Empire was diminished in size by a Western diplomacy underpinned by a new war-making machine, large groups of Muslims left the areas that had to be ceded to non-Muslim states. Especially after the war of 1877–78 with Russia, and the Balkan Wars of the first decade of the twentieth century, many refugees were settled in Anatolia by the Ottoman state. The exodus had started much earlier at the time of the Crimean War. One area affected by this type of migration was Eastern Anatolia (Pinson, 1970; Bishop, 1891) and the Van area contiguous to Bitlis.

The enumeration of the "modernist" aspects of the policy of the *Tanzimat* should not be taken to signify that these processes worked only in one direction. The stream of Westernization also sometimes introduced an unanticipated bonus for the defense of established religious ideas. The history of printing in the Ottoman Empire provides us with some examples to this effect. Printing had been introduced into the Ottoman Empire in 1727–1729 (*E.I.*[2], III, 997). After a brilliant first series of publications by the founder of the trade, it stagnated for a long time, reviving again in the first half of the nineteenth century. This new expansion brought with it the opportunity to print and reprint Islamic classics which had been favorites of the literate public. These went through numerous editions and became more widely available, selling at a much lower price than their manuscript version. An example would be the guide to the lore of Muslim mystics by Yazıcızâde A. Bican, which appeared in nine catalogued editions up to 1893 (Karatay, 1956, 60). On the other hand, the number of books on what may be broadly described as enlightenment philosophy was much smaller. Consequently, while Said Nursi was propelled by the conviction that a return to the *Qur'ān* was essential for the moral soundness of the Empire, he was aware that the modern technology of mass media could be used to service conservative ends.

Leadership, Power and Ideology

In Bitlis, in both town and country, *tarikat* leaders, some of whom had also assumed the role of teachers of religion, played an important role in community affairs. After the middle of the nineteenth century, new opportunites appeared for these men. Before the *Tanzimat*, the influence of the Ottoman center had filtered through a local structure of Kurdish princelings and of tribal leaders. The *Tanzimat* crushed the leaders and gave an end to their rule. Local tribes thereafter became locked into petty feuds which in the past had been pre-empted by the princes. This gave the religious leaders—the so-called *şeyhs*—the means of assuming the role of arbitrators in areas where they had already established their spiritual prestige (van Bruinessen, 1978, 291 ff.). Political influence also followed. Said's reaction to this state of affairs is interesting: after an initial try, he gave up the attempt to fill the position of an arbitrator for tribal disputes, the latter being one way of establishing one's reputation as a political leader. Neither did he work for very long on another project, that of taking on the role of a community leader protecting the interest of local communities against the state. He tried his hand at a local variant of city politics which involved the gathering of a clientele of religious votaries, and failed. His own final solution to the problem of acquiring personal prestige and entering a world of action was to propose the establishment of a university (according to some commentators, a *medrese* for higher studies similar to the early reformed al-Azhar) in eastern Turkey (Şahiner, 1979, 75–76). The proposal was bold and somewhat unorthodox and carried an unusually modern flavor.

This project of Said Nursi's, which echoes an idea of the British Military Consul in Van in these years (Col. Chermside), goes a long way to show that the accusation that Bediüzzaman was a Kurdish nationalist in the 1890s should be taken with a grain of salt. Somewhat later, as a consequence of his contact with a type of pan-Islamic thinking which the sultan supported, a clearly discernible pan-Islamic element did emerge in Bediüzzaman's outlook. This strand of thought became clearer after the Young Turk revolution. What we may say with certainty is that, just as it was the case for the Maronite Church in the Lebanon in the 18th century, the possibility of transcending networks based on kinship and the operation of channels activated by the new principle of participation and public interest were also opening new political horizons for Bediüzzaman (Hurik, 1968, 125). This is the structural origin of his unusual concern for the population of the area.* This attempt to exploit new possibilities was hesitant, tentative at best, resembling the similar ideas of his contemporary in Syria, Butrus al-Bustānī, who was trying to promote "Ottomanism" and "Arabism" at the same time (Abu Manneh, 1980, 189). Bediüzzaman's concerns were focused on a distinct Kurdish identity, but he simultaneously expressed the conviction that all ethnic groups in the Empire could collaborate as Ottomans.

In the early stage of his activities, in the 1890s, Said Nursi was led to action by his feelings both that his community was losing ground within the Ottoman Empire, and by his increasing conviction that the Islamic world was losing ground to Christianity; it is in this light that his pleas for educational development should be seen (BSN, 1976, 471).

---

*For this term see Appendix I.

The second stage of his career, which resulted in the establishment of the Nur movement, was shaped in the 1920s. The same reasons which had caused his concern in the nineteenth century appeared once more, but with a narrower focus. He was now deeply disturbed by the fear that Turkish society would disintegrate if the republican government abandoned Islam as a foundation stone for social organization and intellectual activity, and gave way to the "inroads of materialism." In a sense this materialism, fostered by the republican regime, was simply the continuation and extension of the secularizing moves initiated during the *Tanzimat*. By the early 20th century the input of Western intellectual influence from Büchner (1890s) to Bergson (1920s) was shaping Turkish intellectual life. This cultural penetration was a continuation of the whittling away of Islamic culture which in the 1890s had alerted Bediüzzaman to the decline of Islamic civilization. By the 1920s Said Nursi himself had become a cause for concern to some of the founders of the Turkish Republic. They had seen him take part in the politics of the so-called Second Constitutional Period (1908–1918), and feared he represented a danger for their new secularist policies. He was, therefore, exiled to a hamlet in western Turkey, where his activities were closely watched (Feb.-March 1925). His attempts to win a following for his religious views in this setting were countered by persecution, imprisonment, and displacement to other places where he was kept in enforced residence.

With the advent of a multi-party government in the 1950s, the *Nur* movement was able to expand freely. Eventually, in the 1960s, the influence of Said Nursi as charismatic leader and inspired teacher was widened by the impact of his books and his commentaries on the *Qur'ān*. This replacement of the person by the message is a feature which belongs to our age. It constitutes a striking departure from the pattern used for the propagation of the lore of the reformed Sufi order which stood in Said Nursi's background. In the latter context, initiation still depended on the guidance of a person, a mentor, a *pir* or *mürşid*.

Another aspect of the development of the *Nur* movement towards what may be described as a more open communications system has been its attempt to explain the message of the *Qur'ān* to large audiences, a feature which already appears in the 1920s. Here we encounter a number of contradictory trends, but the central direction is, nevertheless, clear. To popularize the *Qur'ān*, Said Nursi had first to transcend a language barrier; he had to explain the *Qur'ān* in Turkish. The attempt was not new, but Said Nursi's aim had a new totalistic, ideological quality: this was more than instruction; it was mobilization. Bediüzzaman's literary style remained, nevertheless, allusive and metaphorical, a feature one would not usually associate with a mobilizational stance.

Said's special idiom has complex origins. Part of it reflected the style of the *medrese*, the importance given to solving complex conundrums, the emphasis on the many layers of meaning contained in the *Qur'ān*. Part of the effect was unintended: Said only learned Turkish after the age of twenty, and his style in Turkish is extremely convoluted. It is often obvious that this results from his use of a syntax which is inappropriate to Turkish. Finally, the teachings of some of his mentors must have referred to the texts of mystics such as Ibn al-'Arabī, whose writings are both elliptic and dense. Although Said often dismisses mysticism as irrelevant to the most pressing problems of modern Islam, his own style keeps reflecting the allusive style of the mystics. In a country where rural Islam was swathed in a layer of metaphors, the obscurity of Said's style was not without a hypnotic power. Despite these contradictory aspects of his religious idiom, his effort to bring an understanding to the *Qur'ān* to a widened audience stands out. This audience seems to have consisted primarily of persons from the provincial periphery who were seeking a means of coming to terms with the disenchantment of the world, and who had a perception of the new world, even though through the prism of their provincial Muslim culture.

The two characteristics in Said Nursi's message which I have described, i.e., the written text replacing the instructions of the charismatic leader and the attempt to make the central truths of the *Qur'ān* intelligible to a wide audience, paralleled a Western development in making culture more accessible. This shows that we should look at Said Nursi as more than a messiah preaching a return to tradition: once again Bediüzzaman's message was shaped by the modernizing world into which he was thrust. Scholars have stated repeatedly that revitalization movements do not consist simply of a revival of tradition; new ideas, views and values are added. In Said Nursi's case, an innovation such as the propagation of a clear understanding of the foundations of Islam to the masses was a "coming to terms" with a world-historical process which went beyond the tradition he had inherited. His involvement with Young Turk politics in 1909 had given him a further understanding of what he could take from the West, particularly the uses of social mobilization. This appears for instance in his view of the new means available for the propagation of the message of the *Qur'ān*. His attempt to bring an understanding of the basic themes of the *Qur'ān* to a large portion of the population was clearly due to a realization of the role played by mass media in the propagation of ideas in the West. In his own words: "Thank God the radio is a complete *ḥafīẓ* [*Qur'ān* reader] with a million tongues which is meant to make all of humanity listen to the *Qur'ān*" (BSN, 1976, 352).

In the contemporary world, two outstanding developments have made the world-communications picture, which overlaps with Nursi's intellectual activities in so many areas, more complex. The first one of these new characteristics, is that the communications revolution has become truly a "world" revolution. Second, the world-wide disorientation of the individual and anomie have been added to the variables that subtly affect the *Nur* movement.

The world communications revolution, by its cross-cultural influences, by its imposition of certain communications forms which are becoming increasingly standardized for all cultures, works to diminish the individualized content of the specific characteristics of a movement of spiritual revitalization such as that of Said Nursi. The world-wide concern for social organization which has also affected Turkey in the era of post-nationalism marks movements such as the one we are studying, similarly, by shifting its focus away from the sacred and onto the social. Recently, a new emphasis has appeared in *Nurcu* splinter groups which cannot by any means be described as one which denies the primacy of the *Qur'ān,* but which, nevertheless, gives increasing consideration to problems of social and political organization, cultural integrity, psychological balance and flexible interpersonal relations. The direction of gradual change is from man in his relations with God, to man in his relations with a new entity: Society.

Such elements were adumbrated in the intellectual climate which became dominant at the time of Said Nursi's first appearance on the Ottoman scene in the 1890's. During the nineteenth century, Ottoman publications—newspapers and periodicals in particular—increasingly began to use such terms as "human society" (*cemiyet-i beşeriye*), which gave a new focus to thinking about collectivities. In the past, in the works of almost all Islamic publicists, human collectivities would have been seen as religious collectivities.

Western currents of thought have a direct as well as a more subterranean and diffuse impact on traditional cultures; these work together simultaneously and cumulatively. The formation of a Western intelligentsia in the Ottoman Empire, with its adoption of Western literary genres, can be cited as an example of the direct effect. A somewhat more subtle process which worked through a more indirect trickle effect can be seen in Said Nursi's incorporation of ideas originating in the philosophy of the Enlightenment.

These reappeared in modified form in Western positivist thinking and from there filtered to Istanbul in the late 19th century, where they were picked up by Bediüzzaman.

Modernity, the System of Nature and Politics

By the end of the nineteenth century, the rural population of Anatolia had a special conception of Islamic exemplary conduct: outstanding Islamic personalities such as the Prophet Muḥammad, the Caliph 'Ali, mythical hero Abū Muslim and the legends associated with them, provided the pious Muslims model for Islamic ethics. Said Nursi, by contrast, seems to have been deeply affected by the philosophical questions which were posed by Ottoman positivists at the end of the 19th century. These questions were related not to persons, but to the operation of a *system* of nature. In particular, a system of nature where the creator was either nonexistent or consisted of an impersonal force.

Eventually, this centrality of the system of nature as it appeared in materialism was reflected in Said's ideas but with one important difference: in Said's ideas, not "matter" but God appears the undeniable creator of the laws of nature. This emphasis, in turn, has helped today's *nurcus* to place a modernist stamp on their ideas about the system of nature. Today their religion has been steered away from simple exemplary models into more complex ones where Said Nursi, the leader, still figures prominently, but where the study of the laws of nature has become a quasi-religious obligation. The adoption by the new entrants into the *Nur* group of such an outlook means that their personalistic attachment to a charismatic leader has imperceptibly been transformed into a more universalistic conception. This new stance fits in well with the idea of laws of nature which are taught in Republican schools (even though it cannot be claimed that the curriculum of the latter provides no niche whatsoever for the cult of personality).

All of this occurs at a moment when much of the younger clientele of the *Nur* movement is better educated than before and can boast of a primary or secondary school diploma. University professors also begin to appear in *nurcu* ranks. There is a gradual intellectualization of the order's concern which stems from its efforts to penetrate the intellectual establishment at large and to fight it with its own weapons. A number of *nurcu* intellectuals are beginning to underline the harmony that prevails in the physical universe; both astronomy and modern biology are involved to this end. A series of small guides to the complexities of celestial bodies and the intricacies of physiological processes have thus appeared which presage a more deistic understanding of the *Nur* message (Demirkıran, 1978; Şimşek, 1979; Songar, 1979). This, as we know, was one aspect of the intellectual history of modern Europe, and is related to the printing of books and the spread of literacy.

The recent shift in emphasis of the *Nur* group from religion to current political and social issues has been gradually proceeding since the 1950s. It has involved their daily, the *Yeni Nesil*, in current discussions concerned with Turkish society, and that is also an important change as compared to their attitude two decades ago. Does this mean that Bediüzzaman's decision to withdraw totally from politics—a decision taken in the 1920s—has been reversed? Much of the answer to this question depends on one's definition of politics. Bediüzzaman's decision had already been modified when a political party appeared after 1950 which seemed sympathetic to the expression of religiosity and which did consider the free exercise of Islam to be a fundamental right of the Turks. This party, the Demokrat Party, was supported by Bediüzzaman in its years in power—between 1950 and 1960. *Yeni Nesil* today could be described as a paper which directly takes political sides in the sense in which it supports the Justice Party (1987). A better description of the present setting is that a concept of *citizenship* has emerged which brings the *nurcu* columnist into a new debate and a new arena, that of the public. This is a new domain the limits of which are different from that of the Muslim community or *umma*. Which one of these two spheres will prove to have greater force as a stamp on the Nur movement is as yet unclear. But that Said Nursi's accent on the *umma*—on the Community of Believers—has been metamorphosed by the wider scope of political communications is clear.

Nurcu proselytizing among Turkish guest workers in Europe functions partly within this modernist frame which sets boundaries to its traditional Islamic content but also enables it to propel itself into new clusters of meaning. Yet, while the ideas of positive science have been welcomed by the *nurcu*s, some of the symbolic content of Islam has been vigorously reaffirmed. Among the latter, the special place ascribed to women, the underscoring of Islamic sexual ethics and the separation of sexes have been items on which they have been uncompromising; these ideas have gone against the values promoted by the secular civil code of Turkey.

The present options of the *Nur* movement, then, both in terms of the involvement of its following and of the ideological constraints within which it operates, are somewhat different from what they were at its inception. That the *Nur* movement, objectively analyzed, has carved its own, idiosyncratic niche in the broad, ill-defined and somewhat ambiguous process which has been labelled modernization, would nevertheless be strongly contested by the present day Turkish Marxist, Kemalist or "liberal" intelligentsia. All of these groups have combatted the *Nur* as one of the most dangerous forms of reaction and obscurantism encountered in the Turkish republic, a characterization the *Nur* movement shares with the *Nakşibendi* religious order. There are credible reasons why this antagonistic view is so vehemently held. The first and most obvious is that the secularism of the Kemalist republic by definition excludes a movement which aims to give a religious foundation to social life—and possibly—to political systems. Secondly, the *Nur* movement attacks materialism and to that extent undermines the positivistic philosophical bases of Kemalism.

The out-of-hand rejection of the *Nur* movement by intellectuals has led to a paradox: while the intelligentsia underline the dangers of the movement for the Republican-secular regime, it has made no attempt to understand its sociological dynamic. Kemalists are conspicuous among those adopting such a simplistic stance. There is, therefore, no study of the ability of the *Nur* movement to operate over an objectively determinable field.

CHAPTER II

Life

SAID NURSI WAS born in the village of Nurs,* township of İsparit, sub-province of Hizan, province of Bitlis. Like today's Turkish citizens whose idenity cards record their place of birth according to such administrative sub-divisions, Said was thereby drawn into a pattern of territorial rationalization whose origins dated back to the French Revolution: it was then that the French territory had been divided into *départements*. The reforming Ottoman statesmen of the nineteenth century had adopted a similar scheme as part of their project of modernization for the Ottoman Empire.

Between 1864–1871 the Empire adopted a system of provincial administration copied on the model of the French Second Empire. The administration of the provinces was thereby made to revolve around the office of governor (*vali*), which was to be filled by an appointed career official who acted as the transmission belt for directives emanating from the capital. A movement in the reverse direction bringing demands of the administered to the center did, also, exist based on the partly representative local councils (Provincial law as amended in 1871. See Young, 1905–6, I, 49). In Bitlis (made into a province in 1878, Birken, 1976, 184) the council consisted of the governor, the *müftü*, the president of the civil and religious tribunal, the head accountant, the secretary general, two Muslim and two Christian notables and the Armenian Gregorian bishop. The notables were elected (Cuinet, II, 1891, 525–26). The main direction of the flow of policy was

---

*Detractors have pointed out that the name of the village is pronounced "Nors" and that Said Nursi used "Nurs" to be able to use the similarity with "Nur" (light), which is a key concept in his speculations. Said Nursi's biographer gives 1876 as his birthdate (Şahiner, 1977, 22).

nevertheless from center to periphery, often due to the precarious balance of local groups (Young, 1905–1906). The attempt to make the governor the sole legitimate fountainhead of government authority in the provinces was the culmination of the efforts of the *Tanzimat* statesmen to introduce a centralized administrative system into the Empire. *Vali*s had existed before the *Tanzimat* but not as cogs within a centralized administrative machine, with their powers precisely defined and limited. The *Tanzimat* statesmen hoped that by using effective administrative machinery to promote reform they would bring the Empire around to a basic pattern of modernized institutions, gradually imposed from the center. They also hoped to facilitate the collection of taxes, a process which had been badly disorganized during the decline of the Empire. This ambitious scheme was not immediately successful. A number of sources agree that in the Bitlis region, for instance, central administration only became effective toward the end of the nineteenth century. In 1891, Mrs. Isabella Bird Bishop, who visited the town—then a provincial capital—made her own pithy summary of the aims and achievements of the administration: "Bitlis is one of the roughest and most fanatical and turbulent of Turkish cities, but the present governor, Rauf Paşa, is a man of energy and has reduced the town and neighbourhood to some degree of order" (Bishop, 1891, 352).

Bitlis itself was part of a wider region which, at the time, comprised the *vilayets* (provinces) of Erzurum, Van and Bitlis. Bitlis was a territory roughly delimited by the province of Erzurum in the north, Mamuret ül-Aziz in the west, the province of Diyarbakır in the south and Van in the east. At the time the Ottomans conquered these regions—in the 16th century—they had granted considerable autonomy to local Kurdish rulers, and the loose ties of authority thus established with the center had only been tightened with the inception of the *Tanzimat* ("Kurds", *E.I.*[1], IV, 1132–1155; *E.I.*[2], V, 462). The whole area was still a crazy-quilt pattern of tribes, loose tribal federations, ethnic units and religious groups, a feature which is directly relevant to Said Nursi's career.

The primary structural cleavage in the population of Bitlis Vilayet was that between nomads and a settled population of villagers in the more fertile plains and valleys. Whether the settled population of the fertile regions worked in conditions close to serfdom as sharecroppers on the estates of large landholders or owned their own land, it was in their confrontation with tribal leaders that many local issues had their origin. Patterns differing from the above did also exist; one example would be that of the mountain village where land was owned by independent peasants. "Nomads" is also too general a term, which may cover true nomads as well as transhuman groups both of which existed here. True nomads, however, were a relatively small group (40,000 "*aşiret*" in a total population of 398,000; Cuinet, I, 1891, 528; cf. *Blue Books, Turkey*, No. 10, p. 1150). A process of settlement of tribes had begun shortly before the Ottomans established direct rule in the region. After 1842, in the Muş region, strictly Kurdish villages side by side with Armenian villages—a new pattern of settlement—replaced the earlier symbiotic arrangement in which local tribes had been spending winters in Armenian villages. In the society into which Said Nursi was born some of the main sources of social conflict centered around cleavages between nomads and settled peasantry, between city notables and tribal chiefs, and between individual tribes. These are primary features of Bitlis society which, therefore, have to be underlined.

The type of social organization that prevailed in Bitlis is roughly comparable to that which has been studied in detail among the Pathans (Ahmed, 1980). There, the contrast was between an economy of mountain tribal groups which was that of reciprocity and autonomous family production, and a "distributional" economy where an "asymmetrical patron-relationship defines and binds the landlord and his tenant in a feudal and hierarchical order" (Ahmed, 1976, 72). A third variant of economic organization is also present in this type of social structure, i.e., a market or "modern" economy of towns. In Bitlis in the 1880s the economy of the town was supported by a special type of symbiotic relation with the state: the expenses of the garrison of 2,500 men (Bishop, 1891, 352).

This external impetus to the economy was, no doubt, important in activating local economic development. It perpetuated a form of dependency on state purchases, the fluctuating of which Istanbul artisans had known for centuries. But now, the rationalization of the military establishment and the bureaucratizations of the commissary enabled local producers to rely on this source of enrichment. Later, during the twentieth century, having a military contingent continued to be a blessing for Turkish provincial towns.

The upgrading of the town of Bitlis to the rank of provincial capital followed the Russo-Turkish war of 1877–78, during which the inhabitants of Bitlis showed great valor in engagements against the Russians (Allen and Muratoff, 1953). Many local *şeyh*s had already volunteered to fight theRussians during the Crimean War.

One characteristic of Bitlis was the composition of its population. Within the territorial limits of the provincial capital itself (i.e. the *sancak* of Bitlis), Cuinet, in a survey carried out in 1889 (and published in 1891), gives the figures of 254,000 Muslims, 130,000 + Armenians, 6,000 + Syrian Jacobites, 2,600 Chaldean Catholics, 3,862 Yezidi or "Devil worshippers," 210 Greek Orthodox and 372 Copts (Cuinet, II, 1891, 526). Some of the outstanding features of this demographic pattern were that the Turks who lived in towns made up part of the notable class and constituted the near totality of the bureaucracy. Armenians were both town notables and villagers, and Kurdish-speakers made up the tribal and village population. A smaller proportion were townspeople. Such a demographic composition alerts us to the mosaic-like structure of the area. Here ethnic and religious groups lived side by side, even though they had widely divergent cultures. In a region east of Bitlis, a French traveller who was on a fact-gathering mission for the French Ministry of Education described the situation in the countryside as follows:

> All these hamlets are made up of families of the same religious sect grouped together and forming a unit entirely distinct from the neighbouring hamlet in terms of mores, types and language: Armenians, Chaldeans, Kurds, Nestorians have each a completely different way of life. (Binder, 1887, 152)

This plural ethnic composition was one of the important structural features of the clashes which became endemic in the last half of the nineteenth century. Fragmentation was cross-cut by another cleavage in the social structure: by the contrast between the lives of the townspeople whatever their ethnic origin, and those of tribesmen.

Turkish was the language of administration and of city notables, Kurdish and Armenian—or a patois in which they overlapped—were the two prevailing languages of the local population. From information provided by the French geographer Cuinet, we learn that Bitlis had one *müftü*, or Ottoman official, in charge of religious affairs of the Islamic community of the region, four *kadı*s or religious justices of the peace, five Armenian Gregorian, two Armenian Catholic, one Chaldean Catholic and one Nestorian bishops and the Dominican Mission (Cuinet, II 1891, 525). Armenian Catholicism was a somewhat late development: it was the fruit borne by Catholic missionary work undertaken during the seventeenth and eighteenth century and may be cited as a prime example of the slow, gradual and mediated penetration of Western influences into the region. The city's communications links were more with Erzurum than with Diyarbekir (Cuinet, II, 1891, 526), and it was reported to have had a sizeable population of Christian migratory labor (Cuinet, II, 1891, 527) which worked in coastal towns. For many centuries Bitlis had functioned as a gateway for the commerce of silk, and had never been, therefore, as isolated as its mountainous configuration would lead one to believe. The local pattern was one where communications between neighboring villages might be extremely bad, whereas communications from village to provincial center and from provincial center to Syria or present-day Iraq were often easier. The telegraph office in Başkale near Van dealt with 100 telegrams a day in 1885–1887 (Binder, 1887, 118). It is this "niche" structure, created by the isolation of many communities, which allowed many of the dissimilar groups to live peacefully together, although, before the *Tanzimat*, the presence of strong local rulers interested in the welfare of productive citizens was possibly an even greater factor for community harmony.

Bitlis, described in idyllic terms by some of the European travellers of the nineteenth century ("Bitlis", *I.A.*, 660), had been spared some of the strongest blows of the industrial revolution. The missionary Mrs. Isabella Bird Bishop, who visited Bitlis in 1891, wrote of it as of "the most romantically-situated city I have seen in Western Asia. . . . " (Bishop, 1891, 350). The competition of cheap foreign goods began to be felt gradually towards the end of the nineteenth century (van Bruinessen, 1978, 27, note 12), and Mrs. Bishop had already seen "Mankester" wares on sale at the market (Bishop, 1891, 359). Yet it has also been stated that at the end of the nineteenth century its dye factories were still active ("Bitlis", 660). Mrs. Bishop said: "Remote as Bitlis seems, and is, its markets are among the busiest in Turkey and its caravan traffic is enormous for seven or eight months of the year. Its altitude is only 4,700 feet. . . . Bitlis produces a very coarse, heavy cotton cloth which after being dyed madder red or dark blue is exported. . . . It also exports loupes, the walnut whorls . . . oak galls, wax, wool and manna, chiefly collected from the oak . . ." (Bishop, 1891, 351). The education resources of Bitlis "town" consisted of three *rüşdiyes*, or secular middle schools, and five *medreses*, or Muslim "seminaries," which place it in an enviable position compared to Diyarbekir to the south (Cuinet, 1891, 534). In 1891 a military *rüşdiye* was added to its schools. It also had a local offical "gazette" by the late 1880s, as well as a cafe where "newspapers are read" (Cuinet, II, 1891, 562) and offices of the Ottoman Public Debt and the Tobacco "Régie." At least four important developments which heavily marked the region during the nineteenth century, and directly affected Bitlis, constitute the background of Said Nursi's youth and early years as an aspirant cleric. These developments continued to shape important issues in the years 1908–1918 and particularly affected the educated or semi-educated Ottomans of the time who lived in the Eastern provinces of Anatolia. They consisted in the elimination of the local ruling dynasties, the activities of the Protestant missionaries in the area, the spread of the *Nakşibendi* order around Bitlis during the nineteenth century, and the involvement of Ottoman Armenians in separatist activities towards the end of the century. The creation of an independent Armenia in the region of Van, contiguous to Bitlis, was the final goal of Armenian revolutionary "committees" such as the Hınçak or Taşnak (Hunchakian and Dashnaktsuthiun in the original Armenian) which were organized in the 1880s and 1890s. This had a momentous effect on all Ottoman citizens living in the Bitlis-Van region.

Local Dynasties

Sultan Mahmud II (1808–1839) had been the first reforming Ottoman sultan to opt for strong measures of centralization. By the end of the eighteenth century Ottoman provincial notables had established effective control over local affairs in many of the peripheral areas of the Empire. The sultan brought the powerful Anatolian notables to heel by 1817; direct Ottoman rule over the Arab provinces also began to be established at this time (Shaw and Shaw, 1977, II, 15–16).

Attempts by local leaders to break away from Ottoman rule had arisen somewhat late in relation to the similar rise of *âyâns* (notables) in other parts of the Empire. In the area which interests us these movements crystallized at the beginning of the nineteenth century. The Ottoman drive to establish central control over the same area spanned the years 1834–1847. One local leader, Mir Mehmed of Rawendiz (present day Iraq), had acceded to the leadership of the "impoverished emirate of Soran" in 1814 (van Bruinessen, 1978). In two decades he had extended his rule to all of Northern Iraq, then part of the Ottoman Empire. The Ottoman government's reaction was a clear instance of the strategy which had characterized Ottoman rule in the more remote parts of the Empire.

> The Vali of Baghdad, not capable of stopping the mir, recognized his conquests and granted him the title of Pasha—in the vain hope of thus retaining recognition as his superior. Only when the mir sent troops in the direction of Nesibin and Mardin . . . the Sultan sent Reshid Muhammed Pasha against him. The Valis of Mosul and Baghdad received orders to assist in the punitive campaign. [The mir] . . . surrendered on conditions very favourable to him: he was to remain governor of Riwandiz, but had to assert his submission to the Sultan (1835). He was sent to Istanbul where the Sultan bestowed many honours upon him: on the return voyage, however, he mysteriously disappeared. His brother Resul then was governor of Riwandiz for a few years, until, in 1847, the Vali of Baghdad expelled him. That was the end of the Soran emirate: from then on Riwandiz was governed by the Turkish officals (van Bruinessen, 1978, 221–22).

The same fate overtook Bedirhan Bey, *mir* of Botan, a "principality" which, in 1846, extended from Diyarbekır to Rawendiz. In a series of campaigns waged by the Ottoman forces between 1836 and 1847 he was subjugated and forced to surrender. He and his relatives were brought to the Ottoman capital, he was exiled to Varna and members of his family were dispatched to other parts of the Empire. During the Crimean War (1854–56) the Bedirhans were released in order to get them to participate in the action against the Russians on the Ottoman Eastern front. Their name next appears among persons who were working in the area for a resurgence of a Kurdish entity—as yet ill-defined politically—while collaborating in Young Turk conspiracies against the sultan (1895 onwards) (Safrastian, 1948, 60). In Bitlis proper, the rule of local princes, which has been described by Turkish scholars as "totally free" ("*serazad*"; "Bitlis," 660), came to an end in 1849 when the local ruler, Şerif Bey, was defeated. But the prestige of the princely families had not disappeared. In a report on Erzurum and Bitlis dated 1885, a British consul declared: ". . . the good old times of the Kurdish Begs are not only spoken of but are fresh in the memory of every middle-aged man, and though the form of government has disappeared, the habits, customs and associations remain" (Duguid, 1979, 155 note 22).

While the destruction of the old principalities did not completely erase the influence of local leaders, it nevertheless shifted the role of leadership from princes to tribal leaders and religious *şeyh*s. Some of the most important of the tribal leaders were also given a renewed lease on leadership when Sultan Abdülhamid II co-opted them to lead local militias in the early 1890's. But from 1850 on, there existed a state of partial anarchy in the region as well as a power vacuum (van Bruinessen, 1978, 227).

In 1880 in a region lying east of Bitlis, Şeyh Ubeydullah of Şemdinli (at present a town in the Province of Hakkâri) rallied tribal leaders around him and occupied the Persian town of Urmia. He tied down both Iranian and Ottoman forces for a long time. As late as 1913, Seyyid Ali, the *şeyh* of Hizan, the sub-province to which Said's village was attached, occupied the city of Bitlis for a week (Safrastian, 1948, 72–74). Said Nursi relates how he refused to take part in this rebellion, which, according to him, was led by "religious persons" and caused by a revulsion against the "atheism" of Turkish military commanders of the area (*Şualar*, 302). Altogether, then, Hizan, the sub-province of origin of Said was an area characterized by social unrest at the time our story begins.

The structural features behind this turbulence have to be underlined once more:

> "The structure fell apart into many quarrelling tribes led by petty chieftains who were all equally eager to fill in as much as possible of the power vacuum left by the departure of the mirs. The harsh but reliable rule of the mirs made place for lawlessness and insecurity. The entire country became haunted by feuds and tribal disputes. The Ottoman administration was as yet not capable of restoring equilibrium: chieftains resented its presence, and for commoners it was too much of a foreign institution to be trusted. . . . In such periods of crisis and anomie an understandable common response of the people is to return to religion in order to find there peace and security that is so lacking in worldly daily life." (van Bruinessen, 1978, 290)

But while it is true that local sects and their charismatic leaders assumed a new role in the nineteenth century, they seem to have worked for more than a conciliation between tribes. A restructuring of the bases of Muslim power throughout the Muslim world would be one way to describe this expanded framework of the sect leaders' purposes. At the time Said Nursi studied in local seminars such a spirit dominated the pedagogy of his teachers.

In the 1880s, when Said had reached adolescence, the Ottoman government had scored a relative success in bringing some measure of peace to these regions, in part by pitting the notables who were in control of the cities against the *ağa*s (village notables) and tribal leaders of the peripheral areas (Duguid, *passim*). This enabled the "*müceddidî* (*mujeddīdī* or "renewalist") *Nakşibendi* dervishes to underline the pan-Islamic or, better, revitalizing aspect of their world-view which had lain dormant but which had already scored some success in the Caucasus in 1785–1790 and also 1830s when *Nakşibendis* had taken the lead in opposing Russian inroads into that region.

Bitlis and the Bitlis Region

In the 1890s in Bitlis the population of towns, and particularly of larger towns, consisted of Turkish and Armenian artisans as well as of Turkish and Armenian notables. Some of these notables were descendants of distinguished families, among which figured the "citified" remnants of the Rojeki tribal elite. Some notables were traders and some *'ulema*. Both Muslims and Christians were represented on municipal councils, which had an authority in the towns which they shared with the governor. The composition of the population in areas surrounding towns was different. It consisted of a number of tribes as well as settled Armenian peasants and villages of various other ethnic groups, including Yezidis or "devil worshippers," a heterodox sect which kept no real links with Islam. The Armenian peasants were clients—in some cases slaves—of the more powerful and wealthy tribal leaders. Before the local arrangements had been disturbed by the *Tanzimat*, the Armenian peasants were relatively prosperous, since they were extended the protection of their patrons. With the disappearance of the *mirs*, the Armenians had become prey to small bands of local tribesmen which the government did not have the power to restrain. Thus arose notorious brigands such as Musa Bey, whom the Porte treated with what can only be labelled extreme circumspection, despite his well-attested feats of rapine and murder. A good description of the region is given by the British consul [to Van], Col. Chermside.

Col. Chermside underlined two aspects of the local conditions both of which are of considerable importance in understanding the background of Said Nursi as well as the political frame in which his proposals for reform originated. One of these was the extent to which locals were excluded from positions of influence in the bureaucracy in the governor and sub-governor offices.

> In the course of an extended tour I only came across two Kurdish functionaries in the executive branch of Government. It seems a matter of regret for political reasons that the Turks do not pay more attention to the Kurds. They are a strong, warlike, hardy race and in the time of their Beys, mosques, medressehs, schools, bridges etc., existed in many districts where such evidence of civilization now only remain in ruins.

> The descendants of the Beys are, as a rule, illiterate and lead idle, purposeless lives, occupied in their tribal and family quarrels, and exacting all they can from their own clansmen and Christian rayahs.
>
> Very few are decorated or made much of, or employed in the executive function of the Government, nor are they fit for such employ. It would, however, seem well worth the while of the Turks to educate the rising generation and employ them in the civil and military administration in Kurdistan. (Great Britain, State Papers, Turkey, 42, 1890, p.20)

Soon thereafter, Sultan Abdülhamid II was to start organizing some of the local tribes into a militia led by their own leaders. He was also to bring sons of tribal chiefs to be educated in a "Tribes School" in the capital. Said Nursi's proposal of 1896 (?) to establish a *medrese*, a religious seminary on the shores of Lake Van that would educate tribesmen into becoming a fully-fledged Ottoman citizens, echoes Col. Chermside's concern.

The Consul's second series of remarks were concerned with some of the consequences of a policy which had been engineered by the sultan even though he had acted with extreme circumspection.

> The policy of the present reign has been consistently to develop the Moslem feelings of self-reliance, and to bring home to Moslems the expediency of being a self-supporting community.
>
> Thus Moslems are trained as engineers, doctors, and in the professions of various other departments, in these branches are gradually replacing the native or alien Christian employees.
>
> The fostering of the exclusive spirit of Islam combined with the great jealousy of Moslems at the material prosperity of such a large number of their Christian fellow-subjects, have stimulated that bitter feeling against Christians which so strongly pervades the Moslems throughout the Empire . . . . (Great Britain, State Papers, Turkey, 45. Vol. 42. [1890] p.19)

The Şeyhs

The title of *Şeyh* (*Shaykh*), which appears in the names of some of the local leaders whom we have had occasion to mention, refers to a peculiarity of political and social structure of the area which has survived into our time. In the middle of the nineteenth century this aspect of the area was beginning to acquire the outline which can still be discerned in the politics of the eastern regions of Turkey today.

The position of *şeyh* is a "set of roles" (van Bruinessen, 1978, 258) which comprises those of *seyyid*, (i.e., descendant of the Prophet Muhammad), doctor of Islamic law, (i.e., *âlim,* holder of a diploma of religious studies), *molla* (mulla) or village priest (in the special sense in which this word is used for the Eastern regions) and sometimes even *mahdi* or God-appointed leader (van Bruinessen, 1978, 253).

Two strands can be distinguished in the title. The first is concerned with establishing an affiliation with the religious hierarchy through the confirmation by a teacher of one's competence as a religious specialist. The Ottoman state had some control over this aspect of the legitimation of religious status, but the diploma of religious studies was not of one single type. The diplomas of provincial institutions of learning were considered to confer less prestige than those of the Great *Medreses* of Istanbul. A diploma of religious studies could also be obtained in villages around Bitlis where teaching was carried by leaders of the *Nakşibendi* sect. But even these diplomas were graded in the sense that they allowed all or only some of the subjects on which the master had specialized to be taught by the licentiate. It is not clear which type of diploma Said received at the end of his studies, although he cites a long list of books of the contents of which he claims to have been fully cognizant (Şahiner, 1979, 55).

A minimum of study was all that simple village prayer leaders ever achieved, and some could be extremely ignorant of Islamic theology. "*Şeyh*", in the Bitlis context, could mean a man of religion with some training in religious sciences on whom hung another quality which possibly conferred even greater prestige: *keramet* (*karāmā*) or "gifted spiritual powers" (Trimingham, 1973, 26). These powers legitimized qualities of wisdom and leadership. Another example of this would be a cleric who held a teaching certificate, but whose prestige was enhanced because he was a descendant of the prophet. A third variant would be a learned sect leader who also trained aspirants in the religious sciences.

Many of the persons who had risen to become leaders of "mystical" orders were attributed charismatic powers. Some of them were originators of a line of hereditary charisma: their descendants carried the divine spark. In most cases this quality had to be confirmed by the actions of the descendant as a person with influence and power as well as charisma, although their learning might be minimal. Tribal chiefs who took a religious mission upon themselves also could figure among the chosen who partook of a divine spark on the emanation of the divine. As van Bruinessen points out, during the nineteenth century, local political leadership devolved increasingly to the *şeyhs*. This was a novel feature of local politics. The change was due both to the elimination of the earlier princely structure and—at a later stage—to the Islamic horizons which the *şeyh*s' leadership activated and which Sultan Abdülhamid supported. The earlier, less complex, development is exemplified by the case of the Berzenci and then the Barzani family. In this case the two qualities of political leader and that of charisma-bearer were mutually reinforcing. Another variant is the conjunction of *şeyh* leadership and nationalist ambitions is seen in the case of the Şeyh Said Rebellion in Turkey (van Bruinessen, 1978, 383; and for the Pathans, Ahmed, 1976, 55). Said Nursi's career may be seen as an exercise in transcending tribal allegiances and building units of allegiance with wider boundaries as is clear in his early life.

In relation to the "roles" of the *şeyh*s mentioned, van Bruinessen states:

> All of the roles mentioned above have, at one time or another, been played by Sheikhs. Their primary roles are, however, that of holy man, object of popular devotion, and that of leader-instructor in mystical brotherhoods . . . It is because they are the object of a devotion that sometimes borders on worship that the roles of Prophet, Mahdi . . . were . . .easily adopted by them or even forced upon them by their followers. Because of the respect they enjoy, they are ideal mediators in conflicts (which gives them political leverage). Through the Dervish orders they are in contact with devoted dervishes all over Kurdistan and are therefore potentially capable of mobilizing large masses. Many dervish orders exist in the Islamic world, but in Kurdistan only two are present: the Qadiri and the Nakşibendi orders. (van Bruinessen, 1978, 258–259; cf. Beşikçi, 1969, 202–203)

It is interesting that although van Bruinessen mentions *şeyh*s as having gained their new power in inter-tribal disputes, there is no indication of this role in the detailed book on tribes by Ziya Gökalp (Gökalp, 1975). Although on one occasion we see Said Nursi assuming the mantle of an arbitrator, it is in Biro, much further south than Bitlis, and the tribes concerned are Arab tribes. This, as well as Said Nursi's foray into city politics, makes one suspect that in the 1890s the provincial town was becoming an arena for political conflict where local issues were being linked to Empire-wide concerns, and that it was this arena that promised the most desirable status to ambitious clerics on the move such as Said Nursi. The state by its very penetration was creating new economic, judicial and-educational networks, and the issues which arose within the frame of these networks were being settled in cities. It would seem as if this new urban activity also drew in well-established *şeyh*s, as we shall see below.

Bitlis was an environment in which orthodox Islam was just as prominent as the more specialized discipline of the *Nakşibendi* orders: at the time of the nadir of the Ottoman Empire the town was considered to be, if not the leading urban intellectual center of Eastern Anatolia, certainly one with outstanding prestige ("Bitlis," 664), and this pre-eminence had left its mark even in the nineteenth century. One the other hand, already before the nineteenth century, Bitlis had been a region where the *Nakşibendi* order had established its influence. Developments occurred at that time which further strengthened the position of the *Nakşibendi*. One of these was the spread of the influence of Mevlana Halid and his renewalist (*müceddidi*) doctrine.

The *Nakşibendi* Order

The *Nakşibendi* religious order had been one of the most influential in the Ottoman Empire. Among the personalities who propagated its teachings figure Abdullah Ilahi of Simav (d. 1490), who founded the first *Nakşibendi* "lodge" in Istanbul and then went on to spread the *Nakşibendi* teaching in Rumelia. Lami Çelebi (d. 1532)—also known for his poetic work— established the order in Bursa and Şeyh Muhammad Murad Buharī, who died in Istanbul in 1729 established a "lodge" in the Nişancı Paşa district of Eyüb. The latter became the "fountainhead" of a form of *Nakşibendi* pietism which is directly relevant to this study. The roots of this renewalist *Nakşibendi* movement went back to the 17th century and to *Nakşibendi* sages who operated in the Indian environment (Algar, 1985).

Ahmad Faruqi al-Sirhindi (1563–1624) was fighting the ecclecticism which was an outcome of the Mughal emperor Akbar's experiments with religious syncretism. He felt that the tolerance of this court for Indian civilization and religion was sweeping away the distinguishing characteristics of Islam, that it was duping the Muslims into becoming idol worshippers with little Islamic substance in their belief. To counter this dilution, he started a movement of spiritual renewal which became known as "Muceddidî" or renewalist. Sirhindi's self-appointed role as the "renewer" took its force from the Muslim tradition that God would "send to his community on the eve of every century a man to renew its 'din' " (Friedmann, 1970, 13). Thus a reformed spiritual tradition came into existence "which played a prominent role in keeping the threads of the community together in the political and social chaos that followed the decay of Mughal power" (Fazlur Rahman, 1977, cf. Schimmel, 1985, 216 f., and Friedman, 1971, 74).

The *Nakşibendi* order had, from its very inception in the 12th century, emphasized the inner world as opposed to an outer show of devotion. Possibly this was a means of bringing under control the ecstatic shamanistic practices of the Turks of Central Asia, whose pre-Islamic practices did not sit easily with mainstream Sunni beliefs (Trimingham, 1970, 58, 92). Time and again Ottoman rulers had had to grapple with heterodox antinomian currents (İnalcık, 181–193; cf. Hourani, 1972, 91 with Köprülü, 1976, 116, and note 52). Earlier, the *Nakşibendi* had found a way of directing this stress on mystical trance into orthodox channels by its rigid insistence on the orthodox interpretation of religious obligation and the unicity of God which did, indeed, shape the commitment of its votaries. Now it was its ability to shape the esoteric with the exoteric which gave it the force to overcome syncretist tendencies in Islam's Indian environment. The "renewalist" tradition also provided a sounding board for those who sought support in "middle of the road" Sufism.

The relation of the *Nakşibendi* order to centers of political power was complex. Bahā' ad-dīn Nakshband (d. 1389), an eponymous figure in the early history of the order had "kept his distance from the courts of rulers because power emmeshes the heart in the affairs of the world and turns it away from God. In his early life he had a certain experience of public affairs but [later] . . . turned away from things of the world" (Hourani, 1972, 91). He may well be one of the influences in the life of Said Nursi, who mentioned "Şah-ı Nakşibend" as one of his sources of inspiration. Like Bahaeddin, Said eventually turned away from politics and tried to find a new spring for his activities in a complete immersion in the inspiration of the *Qur'ān*.

Although the specific form of Sirhindi's own involvement in politics is still controversial, two aspects of his thought provided strong incentives for a form of Muslim religious activism. The first of these is the synthesis he devised concerning the *Nakşibendi*'s attitude towards Sufism. According to this view, dissolving one's earthly moorings by the experience of ecstacy is only one aspect of the right path. The true believer has also to come to grips with the realities of the world. In Said Nursi this appears as a suspicion of Sufi activities and a dedication to wordly problems encountered by religious revitalizers. The very stance propagated by Sirhindi of a constant recollection of God's presence while "in" the world established a sense of immiment intervention of divine forces on behalf of Islam. Said Nursi used a similar strategy when he exhorted Muslims to ulterly immerse themselves in their identity as Muslims, this stance, in itself being sufficient, in his view, to produce political results that favored the Muslim community.

A second contribution of Sirhindi, more directly related to an activation of the Muslim community was his theory of the two "*mims*". According to the records of Sirhindi's correspondence, *The Mektubat*,

> [the Prophet] "Muhammad had in his lifetime two individuations (*ta'ayyun*) the bodily-human and the spiritual-angelic. These two individuations were symbolized by the loops of the two *mims* of his name. The bodily individuation guaranteed the uninterrupted relationship between the Prophet and his community and consequently ensured its spiritual well-being. The spiritual one, on the other hand, directed itself toward the Divine and received the continuous flow of inspiration emanating from that source. A proper balance was thus maintained between the wordly and the spiritual aspects of Muhammed's personality, and the Islamic community was continuously under guidance both prophetic and divine. Since the Prophet's death, however, his human individuation has been gradually weakening while the spiritual one has been steadily gaining strengh. Within a thousand years the human individuation disappeared alltogether. Its symbol the first *mim* of Muhammad, disappeared along with it and was replaced by an alif standing for divinity (*ulūhiyat*). Muhammad came to be Ahmad. He was transformed into a purely spiritual being, no longer interested in the affairs of the world. The disappearance of his human attributes . . . had . . . an adverse impact on his community which lost the lights of prophetic guidance emanating from Muhammad's human aspect . . . Sirhindi . . . agrees that the ideal prophetic period was followed by a gradual decline caused by the growing inbalance in the performance of the prophetic tasks. . . ." (Friedmann, 1971, 15–16)

The process is now to be reversed and on the eve of every century a "renewer" is to revive the *şeriat*.

The revitalization of the inner spring of Muslims was to take a more active, external form in the case of Shāh Walī Allāh of Delhi (1703–1762; Trimingham, 1973, 128), the spiritual successor of Sirhindi.

Walī Allāh also had a more extensive political program. He attacked "the social and economic injustices prevailing in society, criticized the heavy taxes to which the peasantry was subjected and called upon the Muslims to build a territorial state which might be integrated into an international Muslim super-state" (Fazlur Rahman, 1977, 638–39). Both Sirhindi and Walī Allāh stressed combat with the world-negating influences of earlier mystic orders (*Ibid.*, 639). They tried to reform society through the reinforcement of the moral fibre of society by recalling the vigor of early Islam and by a "return to pristine Islam in terms of the Qur'an and the Sunna of the Prophet" (*Ibid.*).

Activism emphasized a new set of attitudes towards one's religious calling, but it did not do away with the basic philosophy of *Nakşibendis* which stressed the need "for a life wholly turned towards God: lived in His presence, filled with love towards Him, directed to worshipping Him without distraction of mediation, and without earthly reward, even that of praise" (Hourani, 1972, 91). Another aspect of activism which already had many predecents in *Nakşibendi* history was the view that the strict path of the Prophet (*sunna*) should be revived, that "bad innovations" should be checked (Abu Manneh, 1982, 13), and that rulers should be required to adhere strictly to religious law. In a number of cases this placed *Nakşibendi* leaders in the center of the political process: the "renewalist" Mevlana Halid's influenced filtered through his close relation with the Şeyhülislâm Mustafa Asım Efendi (1773–1846)) and spread to the most important urban centers in Anatolia.

Mevlana Halid (1776–77/1827), also known as Mevlana Halid Baghdadi, was the last—and the most important link—between Sirhindi and modern *Nakşibendi* activism. He was born in the district of Şehrizor near Süleymaniye (in the Ottoman province of Musul). This district was at the time ruled by the Baban family (Hourani, 1972, 94). He traveled extensively during his lifetime, went to India and studied there with a *Nakşibendi* teacher. It was at this time that he was initiated into the *müceddidî* view of the world.

During the nineteenth century, facilitation for activism which had evolved since Sirhindi's time acquired a new impetus: Mevlana Halid's stamp was more clearly mobilizational in nature than that of his predecessors. We now can begin to describe his stance as a strategy for the mobilization of Muslims. For one Halid described his teachings as a "politics of guidance" (*siyasat al-irshād*) (Algar, 1989).

The *Nakşibendi* thereafter established themselves in the center of political processes, especially in their fight against imitative Westernization and Western imperialism. Halidism became a force which confronted the expansion of Russia in the Caucasus in the 1830s. It was to find a similarly anti-Imperialistic foundation in Indonesia and in Central Asia. The tradition started by Mevlana Halid was after him to be known as the "*Halidi*" tradition.

Until Mevlana Halid's time, the *Kadiri* religious order has been most influential in Eastern Turkey (van Bruinessen, 1978, 277). Halid tried to propagate the ideas of his own "revivalist" *Nakşibendism* both in Syria and in Eastern regions of the Ottoman Empire.

> He succeeded in uniting into a more unified *tariqa* cluster various branches in Syria, Iraq and eastern Turkey. His attempt did not succeed in that after his death his *Khalifas* regarded their groups in Aleppo, Istanbul and other towns as fully independent organizations.
>
> Shaikh Khalid's propaganda was successful in causing members of important Qadiri families in Kurdistan to change over to the Naqshabandiyya, with considerable effect upon the subsequent history of Kurdish nationalism. " 'Abdallāh, son of a prominent Molla Ṣāliḥ, having become Naqshabandī, made Nehrī his centre and the family came to wield temporal power, especially under 'Ubaidallah (1870–83), who imposed his authority over a wide area. He was at enmity with another family, the Barzānī. One of Khālid's *khalīfas* called Tāj ad-dīn had established himself at Barzān a Kurdish area in Northern Iraq, and his line became an important factor in Kurdish nationalism . . . ." (Trimingham, 1973, 124, cf. van Bruinessen, 1985, 112 who thinks this influence was more extensive)

We have already encountered Şeyh Ubeydullah ('Ubaidallāh), the leader who was defeated only through the concerted efforts of Ottomans and Persians in 1880. It seems that, paradoxically, the looseness of the *Nakşibendi* order which enabled its lodges (*tekke*) to emerge as autonomous centers of teaching was also the cause of the long range success of the *Halidi*s.

The extensive spread of the *Kadiri* order, on the other hand, was hampered by the fact that authoritative delegation for the establishment of lodges was difficult for persons who were not in a designated line of succession to leadership (van Bruinessen, 1978, 285). At a time when the interactive process was accelerating, *Nakşibendi* advantage cumulated.

The influence of *Nakşibendi-Halidi* communities and lodges spread from Nehri, west of Lake Urmia, to Hizan, the sub-province into which Said Nursi was born, and then to Bitlis, Nursin and Muş. These were places where Said Nursi was to study with *Nakşibendi şeyh*s, some of whom were carrying on the *Halidi* tradition. The spread of the lodges occurred at a time when the services of lodge-leaders as mediators or symbols of an ordered society were needed by much of the population. The *tarikat*, the religious orders, provided the structural framework into which community problems as well as political issues could be brought to a head. Şeyh Fehmi, a *Nakşibendi Halidi şeyh* who was the leader of the order in Erzincan in the 1850's, was "not averse to being considered the *Sultân-i 'Ulamâ' bi'llâh*, that spiritual Khalifa who manifests himself once in every generation" (*E.I.*^{2}, II, 878).

One person who had a splendid opportunity to witness the working of these lodges in Eastern Anatolia somewhat earlier—in the years immediately following the Crimean War—is "*Aşçıdede*" Halil Ibrahim, whose memoirs give us considerable information on the subject. He seems to have gone through a series of infatuations with *tarikat* and their spiritual leaders. The region he describes is Erzincan and Erzurum, located to the northwest and north of Bitlis. According to him, a large majority of the city dwellers in Erzincan were *Halidi*s, whereas Erzurum was in the *Kadiri* "camp." (The first *Halidi şeyh* in Erzincan had died in 1848 (*E.I.*^{2}, II, 878). Halil related how the local *şeyh*s took up the protection of interest of lower class persons against Ottoman officials. The fact that such remonstration sometimes has little effect shows how the closed realm of bureaucracy set the popular classes—in alliance with the *Nakşibendi tarikat*—in an opposition to officialdom. This split between the local population and the officials, who represented Ottoman government in the area, was one of the major social cleavages in Bitlis.

The *Halidi*s had found an audience ready to accept revivalist ideals in Istanbul in the 1820s when the Empire was taking stock of its decline (Abu Manneh, 1982, 23–25). Turkish officialdom had always been suspicious of the activities of charismatic leaders and self-appointed messiahs who had caused considerable trouble in Anatolia for centuries. Possibly, the fact that Mevlana Halid himself had clashed with the representatives of state-supported religion, the doctors of Islamic law, in Süleymaniye (Hourani, 1971, 97) had alerted the authorities in the capital to the subversive potential of the order. At any rate, the sultan was not pleased with their popularity, and Mevlana Halid's deputies were banished from Istanbul on several occasions (Abu-Manneh, 1982, 25). They were also pursued in Syria.

The Ottoman officials had been correct in their fears. The first attempt at a conspiracy to unseat the government, which followed the granting of fundamental rights to non-Muslims in 1856, the so-called Kuleli Rebellion of 1859, which has for many years puzzled students of Ottoman reform, was, one finds, stirred up by a *Halidi şeyh* (Kuntay, 1949, 689).

In a society such as that in which Said Nursi had been born, to accede to the local cluster of *şeyhly* power was one of the important sources of social mobility open to persons of lower social background. Indeed, Bediüzzaman's adolescence seems to have been spent in such activities, aiming to wrest such a mantle for himself. Said Nursi was deeply influenced by the example of Sirhindi. Later in his life came to believe that his own achievements, showing special spiritual powers, reached back to Sirhindi's spiritual influence manifested across the centuries.

Said Nursi mentions both Sirhindi and Mevlana Halid as persons who influenced him. But the more direct influence seems to be that of Sirhindi (known in Turkey as *İmam-ı Rabbanî*). Both Said Nursi's insistence that he was not simply a *Nakşibendi* but also a *Kadiri* and his frequent references to *İmam-ı Rabbanî* lead one to think that by skipping lightly over the *Halidi* link in his spiritual ancestry he was trying to justify the novelty and the distinguishing characteristics of his own movement.

Only in the long run did Bediüzzaman choose the high road to Islamic reform which has become parochialized in the seminars of *Nakşibendi şeyhs* in the Eastern setting. The orthodoxy of the *Nakşibendi tarikat*, the reaffirmation of the tenets of pristine Islam and the slowly emerging internationalist character of *Halidi* reformism were eventually more influential in shaping his behavior than local factors.

Long before pan-Islam provided an inspiration for Ottoman statesmen, the *Nakşibendi*s, as was pointed out, had begun activities which extended the influence of the order from India to Mecca, to Indonesia, to the Caucasus and to Central Asia (Trimingham, 1973, 122, 127), and it is in the reports of these successes that Said Nursi found an inspiration that remained a leitmotif of his policies. Possibly, also, the manipulation of local conflict was becoming a less attractive option for an ambitious young man, and taking sides with the centralist Ottoman state was beginning to be seen as a positive step. But the new polarization of Muslims and Christians which had produced cohesion in the Muslim population of Bitlis also provided the opportunity to underline a novel dimension of Islam. The call to regroup under the flag of Islam was an alternative to the call to gather around tribal chiefs, a form of proto-nationalism which had already caused concern to the Ottomans. Said eventually opted for the Islamic solution, although he was to lend his assistance to the Kurdish autonomists who were working in the Ottoman capital immediately following the Young Turk coup of 1908.

One final element in Said Nursi's propensity to set himself up as a fearless propagator of new ideas may have been his *Şafii* (*Shāfi'i*) *mezhep* (*madhhab*). This branch of Islam had not followed the *Hanefi*s, (*Hanafī*s), the main Ottoman *mezhep* (school of law) in its supine attitude towards the state (Communication of Hamit Bozarslan, December 1985).

The Armenian Question

The *Cihannumâ* of Kâtip Çelebi (1609–1657), an Ottoman world-geography, reported a number of Armenians in the town of Bitlis ("Bitlis," 659). As to the Muslim-Christian balance, estimates for Bitlis in the early nineteenth century seem to vary between half and two-thirds Muslim. Educated guesses at the end of the century are closer to two-thirds Muslim. Regardless of these proportions, it is clear that the economy of the region was dependent upon a symbiotic arrangement between Turks filling the official functions, the richer merchants (primarily Armenians?) establishing commercial links, the artisanate consisting of Armenians and Turks with part of the remaining population in local towns in the role of unskilled laborers.

In traditional times, most Christians—what is meant here are cultivators—have been said to have been "politically dominated and exploited by tribal *ağa*s [leaders]" (van Bruinessen, 1978, 119). Some symbiotic arrangements between Armenian cultivators and nomads also existed (*Ibid.*). The attitude of the overlord toward Armenian peasants is expressed in an incisive statement by van Bruinessen: "Tribesmen are warriors and do not toil, non-tribals are thought as unfit to fight and it is only natural that their lords should exploit their labor" (van Bruinessen, 1978, 117). Yet there were limits to exploitation which were set by the interests of the exploiters; the *mirs* (the princes) were interested in the prosperity of all of their subjects.

The Christian population of the Ottoman Empire became a target of missionary activity quite early. The rivalry between the Catholics and the Protestant missionaries had for long been a subject of considerable concern to Ottoman statesmen, who looked at the entire proceedings with a jaundiced eye. The Armenian Protestant community had been recognized as a corporate entity before the law and thereby as a politically autonomous unit in 1850 (Shaw and Shaw, II, 1977, 126). The fact that there existed 200 Protestants in Bitlis (town) at the end of the century was a sign of the relative success of the Protestant mission in Bitlis, which had been established in 1858 (Stone, 1984, 120).

The Protestant Armenians had a "substantial Church edifice with a congregation of about 400 and a large boarding school for boys and girls" (Bishop, 1891, 354). American missionaries had a school for girls with fifty boarders and fifty day students. In 1870 Misses Charlotte and Mary Ely opened "the Mount Holyoke Girls Seminary for Kurdistan" (*Ibid.*, 121). A network of schools went out from this center as far as the outlying towns and villages of Bitlis (*Ibid.*, 122). Ottoman officials had feared the "opening up" of the area to missionary activities because they were aware of the outcome of earlier, similar developments. When the Ottomans had opened the way for missionary presence following the suppression of local rulers the following had occurred:

> Muslim-Christian relations in Kurdistan now grew rapidly worse. In 1843 Kurds of the Botan Emirate invaded the Tiyari district (populated by tribal Nestorian Christians) killed nearly 10,000 men and carried many women and children away as slaves. As even Layard admitted, this massacre was at least partly provoked by the construction of a fortress-like school and boarding house by American missionaries. But Layard blamed especially for the anti-Christian feeling, among the Kurds of Botan, the Fanatical Sex̄ Taha who lived at the court of Bedr x̄an Beg, the emir of Botan. (van Bruinessen, 1978, 291)

To Bediüzzaman, penetration by the Protestants meant the decline of Islam. In fact, the Boy's Academy was directed by an Armenian and one of the local missionaries was expelled by Ottoman authorities for his role in inciting Armenian revolutionaries (Stone, 1984, 122).

Armenian Revolutionary Activities

Armenian revolutionary activity had started as early as 1862 (Nalbandian, 1963, 67). In 1881, an underground society called The Protectors of the Fatherland was established in Erzurum and was uncovered by the Ottomans (*Ibid.*, 85). In 1882 Mekertitch Portugalian established the "Central Gymnasium" in Van, the largest town in the vicinity of Bitlis. This was an attempt to revive Armenian culture. The first Armenian revolutionary party was also founded in Van in 1885 by his students (*Ibid.*, 1963, 90). The school in Van was closed the same year. Portugalian thereafter left for France and established the Armenian Patriotic Union. In May 1889 three members of the Union left Persia for Van; they were intercepted by the Turkish police and killed in a fierce encounter. In 1887 Armenian students who had left Russia to study in Western Europe established the Hunchakian Revolutionary Party in Geneva. Leaders were sent to a number of towns in Anatolia. Among its aims were the "political and national independence of . . . Armenia" (*Ibid.*, 108). Its methods of propaganda, agitation and terror were inspired by the Russian *Narodnaya Volya* party. In

July 1890, it organized the Kumkapı demonstration in Istanbul. In 1892 and 1893 placards were posted in a number of cities in Turkey addressed to all Muslims encouraging them to rebel against "oppressors." In 1890, a new party working for Armenian independence, the Dasknaktsiuthun was established in Tiflis (*Ibid.*, 151).

> Rumours and fears that the European powers (mainly Britain, France and Russia) whose great influence on the Ottoman administration did not pass unnoticed, were allying themselves with the local Christian groups against the Muslims, led inevitably to an exacerbation of the tension between Kurds and the Christian groups. . . . (van Bruinessen, 1978, 289)

Some of the Ottoman fears had materialized during the Russo-Turkish War of 1877–78 when the Russians had appointed officers and administrators of Armenian origin to serve on the Ottoman eastern front (Allen and Muratoff, 1953, 111). At the peace negotiations, the Armenian Patriarch Nerses, who lived in Russia, had tried to gain support for the creation of an Armenian state in eastern Turkey (Shaw & Shaw, 1977, II, 202). Following the Congress of Berlin which ratified the agreements reached after the war, Armenian revolutionary societies had, as we saw, greatly increased their revolutionary activity in the Ottoman Empire. At the end of the war, the Ottoman Empire had been obliged to cede the territories of Kars, Ardahan and Batum to Russia (Shaw & Shaw, 1977, II, 191). Because the breakdown of law and order in the eastern Turkish territories, with its important Christian minority population, was well known, the issue of the Christian inhabitants of the area was one which figured prominently in the negotiations for a peace treaty. A British reform proposal had been accepted by the Ottomans in 1879. It provided for a European-organized "gendarmerie" and inspectors of the judiciary (Duguid, 1973, 141) in areas settled by Armenian minorities. Because of the scattered settlement of the Armenians and the resulting ineffectiveness of the revolutionaries, as well as the negative response they caused among Armenian notables, the revolutionaries employed terrorist tactics both against the Ottoman government and against Ottoman Armenians (Shaw and Shaw, 1977, II, 202–203). The sultan retaliated by establishing a new local militia made up of Kurds and Turcoman tribes (1891).

> The cavalry was formed first in the nomadic areas adjacent to the Russian border in the provinces of Van, Bitlis and Erzurum, with some 50,000 men being called to service and grouped into regiments . . . Arms were supposed to be provided only when they were engaged in combat, but in fact most of

> them managed to keep their traditional arms . . . The regiments were commanded by tribal chiefs, but regular army officers also went to train the men. (*Ibid.*, 1977, II, 246)

Armenian revolutionary activity surfaced clearly in 1893–1894, showing "signs of obvious planning and co-ordination" (Duguid, 1973, 147). One incident in particular, in Sason—a sub-province of Bitlis—took many lives (August 1894; Duguid, 1973, 148). The Armenians had refused to pay tribute to the Kurds and had repulsed them with arms. They also feared the solidarity that was beginning to build up among local tribes because of the "propaganda of the Sheikhs" (Nalbandian, 1963, 120). The immediate effect of the Sason incident was to bring about a dramatic increase in the activity of the local Muslim population.

> The government was making attempts to control the Kurds throughout the fall and winter of 1894, but these attempts did little towards lowering the level of tension in the area. . . . All the consuls noted that the dominant split in the cities was rapidly becoming a Muslim-Christian one. This had been true to some extent since the early 1870's, but there had remained a great deal of cordiality and cooperation between Armenian and Kurdish peasants, Armenian and Turkish merchants and artisans, and among the notables in the cities. By 1894 this was rapidly changing as the Armenians came to be seen as a threat . . . the Muslim population was convinced that all Europeans were in league with the revolutionaries and were interested only in presiding over the disintegration of the Empire. (Duguid, 1973, 149)

By September 1895 there were reports of secret organizations of Muslims which, in the tradition of the rebellion of 1859, were pledged to oppose by force reforms introduced solely for the benefit of Christians (Duguid, 1973, 150). These consular reports mentioned "lower class officials and religious Sheikhs" (*Ibid.*). Russia, England and France warned Turkey that she should carry out reform in the provinces of Erzurum, Bitlis, Van, Sivas, Mamuret ül-Aziz and Diyarbakır (Nalbandian, 1963, 122). On September 30th, 1895 there was a Huntchak demonstration in Istanbul, with riots against the Armenians and much bloodshed, particularly by migrants from Eastern provinces.

When it was announced on October 21, 1895 that the Ottomans had agreed to implement a British reform proposal, the first reaction came from Bitlis. On October 25 there was a panic riot in Bitlis in which 200 Armenians were killed. Much graver incidents with many killed occurred in

Istanbul following an Armenian demonstration on August 24, 1896. A few months thereafter, Said Nursi left for Istanbul with eastern region reform proposals which he hoped to submit to the sultan.

Said Nursi: Early Life

Even though the social history of Bitlis provides a backdrop for the extraneous influences which were impinging on Said's life, this backdrop did not explain his reaction to his life circumstances. Indeed, Said shows an attitude towards these events which singles him out from among his contemporaries and which in some measure explains his later success as a propagator of his religious views. Bediüzzaman's very special approach to the revitalization of Islam—which shows similarities with the opinions which some Muslim intellectuals were developing in the far-away Ottoman capital—can partly be explained as a function of an internal psychological dynamic. This dynamic is much more difficult to reconstitute than the social background of his early activities. What seems to have been happening here is that a somewhat raw expression of vitality slowly assumed a more coherent form as his youthful exuberance was channelled by his encounters with the social reality of Bitlis. Still more fundamental changes seem to have occurred after the First World War.

Among the threads of his personality that emerge at an early age appears a strongheadedness reminiscent of the character traits that have been attributed to Luther by E. Erikson. His childhood wilfulness, as depicted in his authorized biography, serves to underline the very early age at which his vocation appeared and may, therefore, be classified as "hagiographic," but his own insistence on aspects of his life that are related to conflict, to strife, to betrayal by his peers, to lack of understanding by his teachers provide us with a clue that is important in reconstructing some of the deeper, possibly subconscious, sources of his motivation. This is a theme which continues to appear later in his life. His self-confessed extreme misanthropy (*Emirdağ Lâhikası*, 1959, 60) gives us another dimension of internal turmoil.

Said Nursi was born in a "clerical" family, his father being an impoverished village *molla* with seven children and with a small holding of land. That there was some drive for status in the family appears from the title of *mirza*, which was used by his father and which could be an attribute of noble descent. His grandmother is stated to have been a relative of Alişan Paşa, a regional notable, and Said traced her ancestry to the family of the Prophet Muhammad (Şahiner, 1979, 45). It is clear that he had a very strong attachment to his mother. On a number of occasions, Said Nursi refers to what he considers to be his low social status and underlines his identification with persons of a similarly modest background, while in one case he also expresses strictures against the bourgeoisie.

During Said Nursi's childhood the population of the Nurs area were clients of a *Nakşibendi şeyh*, Seyyid Sibgatullah Efendi, known as the "pole" (*Gavs*) of Hizan (van Bruinessen, 1978, 350; Şahiner, 1979, 47). Said Nursi told his disciples much later that while his relatives were all *Nakşibendi*, already at the age of "8 to 9" (*Sikke-i Tasdik-i Gaybî*, 116) he courageously took sides against them and against the people in the surroundings by becoming a follower of Abdülkadir Ceylanî ('Abd al-Qādir al-Jīlānī) the founder of the *Kadiri* order. This may be a slice of biography that Said Nursi later added to his life events. Its function would have been to underline the idea that Said Nursi had brought so many new elements to *Halidi* teachings that he deserved to be seen as the founder of a new branch. Such a claim of originality and Said's practice of citing Sirhindi more often than Mevlana Halid confirm this stance.

Said remained in his father's house until the age of nine. At that time he began his education and one of the first schools which he attended was that of Molla Mehmed Emin Efendi in the village of Tag. Şeyh Abdurrahman Tagi—who was also the first person in the vicinity of Bitlis admitted by the latter's spiritual successor to spread the message of Mevlana Halid (van Bruinessen, 1978, 351)—was the resident sage in that village. Describing the teaching of his master, Şeyh Abdurrahman Tagi, with whom he studied intermittently in the following years, Said explains:

> He trained many students and preachers and learned men, and when all . . . began to sing his praises, I, immersed in scientific disputations of a high calibre and placed within a wide circle of science and *tarikat*, was convinced that these preachers were about to conquer the earth.
>
> When the famous *'ulema* and the saints *(evliya)* and learned men and *kutb*s were mentioned, I, nine or ten years old, would listen with rapt attention. My heart felt as if these students, then men of learning, had made extensive conquests in the field of religion.
>
> If a student showed some sign of superior intelligence he would be accorded great importance. If someone scored a success in a debate around a problem he would be made much of. I was struck by the fact that I became animated with the same feelings. There was, in fact, an extraordinarily competitive spirit among the *şeyh*s at the level of township, sub-province and province. (*Emirdağ Lâhikası*, 1959, 53)

The competitiveness that was encouraged by this mode of teaching is not necessarily related to the type of conflict that was encouraged by tribal society; rather, it appears to be the end-product of a particularity of cultures of oral learning and transmission in Islamic society. In a setting where manuscripts are rare and expensive the most efficient way to record knowledge is to consign it to memory. This explains the great number of rhymed textbooks used by Ottoman pedagogues. But another means of keeping a tradition or a set of answers to questions lively is to keep discussing the point and the set answers provided. K. G. Ghurye has underlined this feature of traditional societies by pointing out that "the knowledge that is acquired from books and not received from a teacher does not shine in deliberate assembly, i.e. is not operative and fruitful" (Ghurye in Goody, 1968, 13). However, deliberate assemblies could become more contentious in the tribal area because of the underlying pattern of conflict.

The ubiquitous tribal formations in Bitlis and the turbulence which prevailed in his time made for a tough, male-dominated frontier society. Individuals carved their reputations by feats of courage or by their ability to show extreme endurance or to undergo superlative tests of physical privation. A man's holiness could emerge as a result of his depth of learning or wisdom, but it was the sum of these qualities of physical and moral steadfastness which determined personal influence. As we have seen, contentiousness was not excluded in the sub-society made up by the teachers of religion; Said assumed such a contentious role early in life. His official biography states that even at this tender age he could not bear the smallest remark made with a commanding tone. This led him to leave school and return to his village where he continued his studies (BSN, 31).

The harsh set of values which were imposed on local mountaineers seems to have clashed with something in himself which rejected them:

> When I was ten years old I had an attitude of self-esteem (*iftihar*) and self-praise (*temedduh*). I was acting as if I were doing important things which required heroic deeds, even though this went against my grain. I would say to myself, "you are not worth five *para*; why do you show this self-assurance, and particularly why are you so keen to appear courageous?" The villagers in my village of Nurs, as is quite well known to my students and village friends, loved to shine and show off and test their courage . . . . (*Emirdağ Lahikası*, 1959, 52–53)

An insistence that his own view of the world should be given precedence over received wisdom emerges as a striking personality trait at an early age and continued to mark his attitudes throughout his life. This was compounded by the activism contained in *Halidi* teachings and by the values prevailing in the Eastern setting. One cannot but recollect in this connection that the activist puritanism of the Wahhabis emerged in a similarly tribal background. But a universal dimension could only be acquired by this activism when it joined a stream which emerged from the West. A condensed heading for this new dynamic frame might be the "acceleration of history," an expression Daniel Halevy used to describe the effect of what we know as "modernization" (Halevy, 1948).

In his village, Said studied with his elder brother, who had already been in the same educational stream for some time. Later, he moved to Pirmis and then to Hizan, another center to which Mevlana Halid's influence had spread (BSN, 31). There he sat at the feet of Seyyid Nur Muhammed Efendi, the grandson of the second person in the chain of authorized successors of Mevlana Halid (BSN, 31; van Bruinessen, 1978, 351). He speaks of this figure as his *Nakşibendi üstad* or master (*Şualar*, n.d., 370). Said did not get along with the students in the *medrese* who looked for occasions to pick a fight with him, but he was able to show his teacher that he was not at fault and that he had been set upon. He remained in this *medrese* for a time, and then left for the plateau of Şeyhan with his brother, who was already studying theology. When he questioned the authority of his old teacher Mehmed Emin Efendi, stating that his powers were derived from the *medrese* founder Şeyh Abdurrahman, Said had once more to leave. He seems to have been unable to continue his *medrese* career at this juncture and therefore returned to his village. He had a dream at this time, in which he was admitted to see the Prophet Muhammad (BSN, 32); the vision gave him renewed strength to pursue his studies. Gradually, then, Said was moving towards a rejection of the *şeyhly* social structure into which he was born and was gathering strength from sources which were part of that world but which hovered above the existing set of social relations controlled by *şeyh*s. But once more, during this second stint of school attendance he was at loggerheads with a number of teachers including Mehmed Emin Efendi and had to withdraw. There followed another series of tentative affiliations with *medreses* ending with a three-month course in Doğu Bayezit with Şeyh Mehmed Celali. Again, we get a clue as to the reasons for his inability to settle in any *medrese*. "The treasures (of learning) you control," he said to Şeyh Mehmed "are in a strongbox. You have its key. What I need is a clue to its contents. I will choose whichever I find appropriate." It is doubtful that Said could actually have used such direct language, but his intentions are clear: he was finding the entire long-drawn curriculum too cumbersome.

This was a remarkably modern perception. The psychological process underlying this change of perceptions in the mind of a peasant boy born in a village of twenty houses cannot be recaptured, but the process is clearly both personal and has to do with Said's generation. This generation had the benefit of some of the early reforms of the *Tanzimat*, such as acquaintance with the Istanbul press. The new bureaucracy penetrating into the provinces was another regular source of information on the happenings in the capital. It is interesting that similar thoughts about the cumbersome weight of religious studies as they were set in the syllabus of religious teaching had occurred to and entirely different person who made his career in Western Turkey two decades earlier. This was Ali Suavi, the Young Ottoman who had been trained in the *medrese*. Possibly, the fact that a much larger proportion of the citizenship had to be educated to implement the institutions of the new society was a new feature which was perceived by sensitive persons in the religious educational stream as a gap in the existing institutions of religious education. The *Tanzimat* statesmen had used their innovative 3–4 year *rüşdiye* to provide the greater number of functionaries who were necessary to implement reform. A similar type of "middle range" education was necessary to mobilize the literate population within an Islamic frame. Said perceived that in the world which had been initiated by the reforms of the *Tanzimat*, an acceleration of history, a more dense interaction between individuals—brought about by an extension of communications networks—would require a recasting of religious studies. Much later, he was to state that his understanding of the need to simplify religious studies was a divine inspiration which enabled the *Nur* sect to make up for the suppression of religious studies by the Turkish Republic (BSN, 34, note 2). His authorized biography highlights his insistence on simplification, pointing out he thus caused "faith" to be spread to "millions" (*Ibid.*). It underlines that while still an adolescent he covered in three months an education which usually lasted twenty years (*Sikke-i Tasdik-i Gaybî*, 143). According to Şahiner (1979, 55), Bediüzzaman obtained his diploma around 1888 at the age of fifteen, a remarkable achievement. Because of the variety of Sufi diplomas available, we are not sure what this "graduation" meant, but certainly in time he became extremely knowledgeable on religious matters, and, especially, on *hadis* (*ḥadīth*).

It is at this time that Said came across a strain of Islamic thinking which was later to become a constant theme in his religious imagery and a central fulcrum of this theories, the theme of light or illumination. (Interview with Şahiner, September 1984). The school of mysticism known as the *ishrāqī*—or illuminists—believed that a complete knowledge of God could be attained by striving to reach him through contemplation and asceticism but that this knowledge could only be achieved in a flash of illumination. Said also discovered this direction, and this time engaged upon a regime of mortification and "*zühd*" (*zuhd*) or world denial while living in the mausoleum of the celebrated seventeenth century Kurdish writer Ahmed Hani. Two aspects of Said Nursi's thought explain the role illuminism played in his thinking. For one, illumination was a road to knowledge of God which bypassed the academicism of his teachers and could surmount their charisma as *Halidi* leaders. Secondly, the concept of God as Light of Light, as an emanation from His Being, which was reflected in all aspects of being, was one which he seems to have used in preference to the *Nakşibendi*'s strict monism at this time. Illuminism, in fact, had a potential for a more populistic vision of the Godhead, and one eminently suited to his goal of making the idea of the divine comprehensible to persons, who, like himself, did not have time to waste in complex and time-consuming intellectual initiation. The backdrop of mysticism of Anatolian Islam predisposed a message based on the idea of emanation to meet with a sympathetic response: Anatolia had been thoroughly suffused by beliefs in metempsychosis which appeared in widely disseminated poetry. Poetry itself was not simply literature but also a link to the divine. Said's own writings, later, may be seen as an attempt to fuse this inward-looking aspect of Anatolian Islam with a new sense of destiny.

Anatolian mysticism had found an elective affinity in the ideas of the mystic Ibn al-'Arābī, who established no sect but whose influence in Anatolia was pervasive (see *E.I.*[2], III, 707–11). It is interesting that though there is little evidence of the direct influence of Ibn al-'Arabī on Said (Said mostly gives him lukewarm praise), Ibn al-'Arābī's idea that the world is the field and man is the locus where the attributes of God materialize (Fazlur Rahman, 1979, 146), can also be found at a number of places in Bediüzzaman's writings. Like Ibn al-'Arābī, and like many Islamic renovators, Said was later to regard his early activities as a time of *cahiliye*, (*jāhilīya*) a period of incomprehension of the true message of God. He thought that this truth was to be revealed to him in a vision, once more, a well-known Islamic source of legitimation for new ideas.

Another sign of his perceptiveness was the populism of his proposals, and his denial of the authority structure established by the *şeyhs*. Like his explicit model for behavior, the Muslim theologian al-Ghazālī (*E.I.*[2], III, 1038–41), Said accused the hierarchy of *şeyhs* of using their charisma for worldly purposes and of not being content with community support of their minimal needs. According to him, these leaders had imposed additional *zekât* (*zakāt*), or religious dues, on their votaries (BSN, 32), which he considered sheer exploitation.

Nevertheless, Said—as is apparent from his activities already described—gladly joined in the fray where a contest for prestige was concerned. The opportunity to mobilize large groups of supporters which had already involved Mevlana Halid in a truly political battle was not one which he avoided. For in Said's time, too, the extent to which part of the population would follow a *şeyh* was a basic political datum. Behind this allegiance could be distinguished the special role that *şeyhs* had assumed as the voices of community grievances, even though charisma, *baraka*, an emanation which only the elect would possess, was also part of the forces working for those seeking to achieve a position of authority. The power dimension of "lodge" activity overflowed into both the rivalry between orders and the political struggles which a novice with ambitions of leadership had to face. Last, but not least, the Ottoman provincial town, linked to the center by communications as well as by a new administrative network, with its contingent of city notables as intermediaries between the government and the people, was acquiring a new importance: it was now part of the centralist network of the *Tanzimat*. Town politics had a place for *şeyhs* just as tribal politics did.

Shortly after his graduation Said Nursi decided to visit a number of famous local *'ulema* to widen his horizons. Dressed in dervish clothes, he roamed in the uplands, making his way towards Bitlis. Once more we see him as a student of Mehmed Emin Efendi. Once more, however, he moved to Siirt to the *medrese* of a new teacher Molla Fethullah (1889). The latter is stated to have been highly impressed by Said's abilities. This perceived brilliance led Molla Fethullah to organize a special debate in which his star pupil was to answer questions asked him by learned doctors of Islamic law. His success in the interrogation is reported to have caused jealousy among his fellow-students and *'ulema*, an outcome with which Said Nursi was already familiar. Conspiracies began to be organized against him, and Said was saved from bodily harm by that part of the population of Siirt which had sided with him in the fracas following the examination. These quarrels, which now involved part of the population of Siirt, alarmed the governor-delegate in residence in the town—the *mutasarrıf*—who is stated to have offered him assistance, which Said rejected (BSN. 37).

After the fracas died down, Said announced that he was ready to take on anyone who wanted to engage in a physical or intellectual contest. Shortly thereafter he departed for Bitlis. Possibly, the sub-Governor had decided that Siirt would be calmer without Said's presence.

In Bitlis, Said took upon himself to give counsels of moderation to local families of *şeyh*s who were loggerheads with one another and to students in seminaries who were opposing their teachers (BSN, 37). This seems to be the first instance when he assumed a conciliating role, a role which clearly underlined his ambitions as a religious—and in that setting—a political leader. His presumption led the religious notables to complain to Mehmed Emin Efendi, presumably the one person which still had the greatest influence with him. The latter could only assure them that these forays by Said were no more than those of youthful mischief. It is reported that his master availed himself of this opportunity to test his knowledge once more. Said, who it is said, successfully surmounted this obstacle, then went on to preach in the Kureyş mosque in Bitlis. The new role provided him with a set of followers in the town who were now aligned with him against his detractors. The governor of the province stepped in at this juncture and asked Said to leave town. Said went to Şirvan (BSN, 38), south of Bitlis. Once more the pressures of political strife sent Said on to a retreat and into religious contemplation.

He took refuge in the hamlet of Tillo, (between Şirvan and Siirt), a place where the 18th century Ottoman encyclopaedist and mystic İbrahim Hakkı had studied for a time. Some of Said's concerns with the disintegration of Eastern society surface in clues which one may find in sections of his authorized biography which cover the Tillo period. His admiration of the organization shown by the ants living around İbrahim Hakkı's tomb were a reminder of his sensitivity to the upheavals which were surrounding him. Here too, Said saw in a dream the founder of the *Kadiri* order 'Abd al-Qādir al-Jīlānī (BSN, 39). Although it was not unusual for members of orders to harken to the message of more than one *tarikat*, the intervention of this religious figure does not seem to have been a random occurrence since Said's contentiousness had pitted him against the *Nakşibendi*s, who had been competing with the *Kadiri*s for control of the region. In years to come, the figure of this sage, given the title of *Gavs-i Âzam*—the Highest Saint—by Said, was to be one of his main sources of inspiration. In the dream, 'Abd al-Qādir ordered him to stop the depredations of Mustafa Paşa, the chief of the Miran tribe.

The theater of the activities of the Miran tribe was a region which today straddles Turkey and Syria. The tribe had the reputation of being one of the strongest in the area: Bedirhan Bey had to incorporate it in his own emirate by force. Upon the defeat of the Bedirhans by the Ottomans, some Miran chiefs became contenders for the positions formerly filled by the Prince and began to extend their power at his expense (van Bruinessen, 1978, 224). It is possible that Mustafa Ağa of Miran was granted the title of "Paşa" by Sultan Abdülhamid and leader of the local militia or "Hamidiye Corps" for this reason. Mustafa Paşa, thereafter, became the "single most powerful man in the area" (*Ibid.*, 228). He took advantage of the position to establish his own petty kingdom (*Ibid.*, 236) in which Ottoman administration worked primarily through the capricious implementation of its policies by Mustafa Paşa. Mustafa Paşa also knew how to keep the Ottoman powers at bay in what he considered his hunting preserve, namely, local brigandage.

> He also took a heavy toll from passing caravans and from transporation rafts floating down the Tigris: his men raided the wide surroundings. Thus Mustafa Pasha acquired some of the powers that formerly were the mirs. There were two important differences however: 1. His power was not based on consensus, but on violence. That became clear in interior intra-tribal conflicts. These were never brought before him (as they were brought before the mir) but before one of the Shaikhs. 2. He could maintain his independence vis-a-vis the civil administration because he had powerful protection. . . . The superior and protector of the Hamidiye commanders was Zeki Pasha, commander of the 4th Army Corp at Erzincan and brother-in-law of the Sultan himself. To the great annoyance of the civil officials, Zeki Pasha removed the Hamidiye (*militia*) from under their judicial competence and always protected transgressors. (van Bruinessen, 1978, 236)

Upon receiving the saint's summons, Said immediately departed for Mustafa Paşa's encampment which was in Cizre (present province of Mardin). Mustafa Paşa was absent; when the Paşa finally appeared, he enquired as to who this stranger was and was told that he was the "celebrated Molla Said" (BSN, 39). Mustafa Paşa, apparently, did not hold much affection for the *'ulema*, but in the existing situation, with the *'ulema* still using their charismatic aura to establish their influence, it was prudent to approach this intrusion with caution. Mustafa asked Said what the reasons of his presence at the camp were. Said answered that he had arrived to make a good Muslim of Mustafa: in the event Mustafa Paşa refused, death would inevitably follow. Again, it is probable that Mustafa Paşa suspected that there was more to the presence of Said than could be seen at that instant. He took a walk outside his tent and returned, asking him once more what his business was in his camp. Upon receiving the same answer from Said, he pointed at the rusty sword which Said carried. "With this?" Eventually, it appears Mustafa Paşa was more bemused than frightened by the menaces of the young man. He too organized a "scientific" (i.e. theological) debate to test Said's mettle. Said's biography states that he was able to answer all the questions which the convened examiners posed, that Mustafa Paşa promised him to fulfill his daily prayer obligations and gave him a rifle as a present to boot.

Rifles and swords are not the usual appurtenances of *'ulema*, but in the case of Said they appear as part and parcel of his contentious attitude towards his surroundings. Even later when he was residing in the Ottoman capital, Said continued to wear the baggy pants of the tribesmen and stuck two silver daggers in his wide, cummerbund-like belt. Further features of the frontier style that he had adopted are seen in his willingness to show Mustafa Paşa his skill as a rider (BSN, 41). Although Said alternated between Mustafa Paşa's camp and that of the Arab tribesmen of Biro, he was eventually asked to leave the camp by Mustafa Paşa's son. At this stage, then, the vocation of Said as a conciliator—a task to which he expended considerable effort in his relations with the Arabs of Biro—was beginning to acquire clearer outlines. In Biro he was set upon by brigands, who nearly killed him but who desisted when they found that he had been active as a holy man. Said thereupon left for Mardin, whose *'ulema* he immediately challenged to a match of wits (1892).

An important development in his stay in Mardin was his encounter with two travellers, Muslim students who were followers of two prominent architects of the Muslim reformist tradition. The reform movement was developing in Egypt and in the Ottoman capital towards the end of the nineteenth century. Two important figures, Cemaleddin Afgani (Jamāl ad-Dīn al-Afghānī) and his follower Muḥammad 'Abdū, were attempting to recast a modernist form of Islam. Afgani was trying to get the Muslims to gather round Islam as a banner that would reinstill in them the energy that was necessary to stop their political decline. Although extremely influential in Islamic circles, he had been torn between two options which never seemed to come to a resolution: one of these was to convince individual Muslim rulers to strengthen their own country, the other was to reinvigorate and tap the deep sources of religiousity of the large masses of Muslims. This alternative was also to create one of the more difficult problems with which Said was to meet. Said's consciousness of the problem was not necessarily due to the influence of Afgani, but he was enmeshed in the same quandary as that reformer and it was one which continued to confuse issues for him until the 1920s. The second person Said met in Mardin was a student in the *Sanusi* religious order. This order had already gone a long way towards providing a religious scaffolding for the formation of a modern nation-state in Cyrenaica (BSN, 42; Şahiner, 1979, 63).

Said Nursi's official biography states that his first political life began in Mardin. What is meant by this is not entirely clear. Possibly, the remark refers to Said's first attempt to rally Muslims to work together for the greater glory of Islam. In any case, these activities got him into hot water, and the *mutasarrıf* of Mardin sent him to Bitlis under armed guard. One of the first supernatural interventions into Said Nursi's life is related as having occurred at this time. His guards had halted their march to pray and found that Said Nursi had unaccountably gotten out of his handcuffs and was also praying.

In Bitlis he joined the staff of Governor Ömer Paşa (1892–93). He was given the freedom to devote himself to his own education in exchange for teaching Ömer Paşa's children. Said remained for two years in the governor's mansion. He now began to study the Muslim classics more intensively than he had hitherto (Şahiner, 1979, 66–67) and was tutored by Şeyh Mehmed Küfrevi of a prominent family with hereditary charisma.

Said seems to have been undergoing a process of intellectual confusion and crisis at the time. He recalls the times as being characterized by an alternation of sensations of extremely acute perception and a dulling of thought processes, accompanied by a failure to understand anything that he was reading. Upon the invitation of the *vali* of Van, Hasan Paşa, Said moved to the town of Van and joined the staff of the governor. It is here that Said Nursi continued to extend his culture by adding to his Islamic learning information which he culled from the newspapers which came into the governor's office. He states that he thereby became aware of such fields of learning as history, geography, mathematics, geology, physics, chemistry and astronomy (Şahiner, 1979, 68; cf. BSN, 44–45).

This is not so absurd a statement as it might seem to be on the face of it. Van had been an early "showcase" of administrative reform ("Van", *İ.A.*, Fasc. 137, 1982, 201), and the Armenian community of the city was progressive, enlightened and only partly active in revolutionary movements. In

Istanbul the popularization of science had been proceeding since the 1870s. During the first year of Sultan Abdülhamid's reign a number of pocket libraries with series on science was published. In 1890 Said could have studied the following subjects through books and brochures (or textbooks meant for the higher schools): logarithms (*J.A.*, 7–16, 433), the telephone (7–19), cosmography (7–19, 192), industrial chemistry (7–19, 199), geometry (7–19, 200), the formation of the universe (8–13, 465), inorganic chemical analysis (8–17, 386), nutrition (8–17, 387), zootechnology (7–19, 468), natural history (8–13, 473), physical anthropology (8–17, 385). He could have read the description of human anatomy contained in *Insan* (7–19, 192), in one of the many technical treatises on physiology, or *Beşer*, a book which stated clearly the thesis that man was to be understood as a function of his biological make-up rather than his soul. He could have waded through a text on the then emerging field of atomic physics entitled *The Rules of Changes in the Movements of Atoms*. He could have found in the library of his patron some of the books which were beginning to appear on the role of women in society and one in particular entitled *Famous Islamic Women*, published by the Imperial Press (*J.A.*, 7–16, 429). He could have read a number of books on world history. He could have followed the apologetic thesis for the decline of Islam in *The Civilizational Progress of the Arabs* by Ahmet Rasim or consulted the opinions of the famous journalist Ahmed Midhat Efendi concerning *Progress*, or read his translation of Draper's *History of the Conflict between Religion and Science* or Midhat's refutation of materialism entitled *Who Am I? (Ben Kimim?)*. He could have followed Midhat Efendi's *Müdafaa* (A.H. 1300), a work complaining of missionary attempts to convert Muslims and the counter-polemic resulting from some of these publications.

As to what influence the daily press could have had on Said Nursi, one witness of his times commented:

> The tone and trend of Turkish papers is to intensify the hold of the Sovereign and Khalif on the imagination of the new "true believers," especially in lower classes, even in the outlying districts of his extensive dominions, thus directly increasing the influence and prestige of the Central Ottoman Government among the non-Ottoman tribes and nationalities. (Duguid, 1973, 140, citing G. P. Gooch and H. Temperley, *British Documents on the Origin of the War* (London, 1938), V, p. 27)

It was his contacts with the officials in the Governor's mansion which convinced him that the classical arguments which he had encountered to refute the doubts of unbelievers (i.e., the Westernized *Tanzimat* intellectuals) were worthless (BSN. 44) and that a study of secular sciences (*funûn*) was necessary to refurbish these arguments.

Said Nursi's official biography states that it is at this time that he was given the sobriquet of "Bediüzzaman" ('nonpareil' of the times) because of the speed with which he had mastered the new secular sciences. His familiarization with these subjects must indeed have involved some feat of superior intelligence, for up to that time he had only been fluent in Kurdish and he had just begun to learn Turkish (BSN, 46). His first statement of principles, which was to be the basis for the *Risale-i Nur*, was written in Arabic (*circa*, 1920).

Bediüzzaman's experience with these new subjects convinced him that he should "enlighten his students by demonstrating the truths of religion in the manner most appropriate to the understanding of that century" (BSN, 45). Too much time was spent in detailed investigations of theology, while the real target should have been to win over the "hearts" of people, and kindness (*şefkat-shafaqa*) and fellow-feeling had to replace the thrill that the Sufi spoke of as love for God (*aşk-'ishq*). This characteristic reference to the "hearts" of the community of believers alerts us to a similarity with the vocabulary of a movement, much removed in space, which also had stressed that salvation was a function of faith rather than of learning, namely Methodism. That two faiths separated not only by distance but by dogmatic differences should have converged on a similar style of address to the faithful is a remarkable feature most probably due to more than a coincidence. In both cases, the changes which had occurred in society made an appeal for active participation to the hitherto passive masses.

In the case of Methodism, it was the population uprooted by the industrial revolution which was seen as constituting the shock batallions of a revived Christianity (Wilson, 1970, 48). In their state of uprootedness and spiritual disarray, a direct appeal, a mobilizing thrust were the means of recapturing them for an increasingly activist society. In the Muslim setting "aşk" (love) was the means by which the Sufi lost his earthly moorings; but, for Said Nursi, as for Sirhindi and many of his intellectual heirs, Islam had to be brought back into this world. The ecstatic practices of Sufism as well as the mystics' theory of the "unity of being" were of no use in solving the contemporary problems of Muslims. In the Ottoman Empire the stagnation of the traditional structure of religiosity and accelerated social change also made it incumbent upon religious leaders to elicit a religious mobilization.

Said continued to fight against what he considered the greed of his colleagues while acting as religious attaché in the office of the governor of Van. He served the authorities as a conciliator in tribal disputes. Newspapers were regularly received in the office of the governor, and it is in a news dispatch from London that Said Nursi states he received the first great shock that urged him to adopt a crusading spirit in the cause of Islam. The date was 1895 (Şahiner, 1979, 72). A fracas with Armenians in Istanbul had aggravated the Armenian problem. Europe was in arms against the Muslim Ottoman "barbarians." The British secretary of the colonies had made a speech stating that Muslims never would become civilized unless the *Qur'ān* was wrested away from them. Said Nursi reacted violently, pledging to show the world that the *Qur'ān* was "unextinguishable." It was the very same type of shock which was leading the Young Turks of the capital to post placards against the rule of Sultan Abdülhamid II.

Said Nursi's fiery defense of Islam must have reached the ears of Yahya Nüzhet Paşa, the *mutasarrıf* of Zor (in present day Syria, Deir el-Zor) a newly created sub-province which had a problem of nomad pacification. Yahya Nüzhet Paşa was one of the trusted advisers of the palace and presumably was aware of the elaboration of pan-Islamic propaganda which was taking place in the immediate circle of the sultan through consultation with various *şeyh*s (Gündüz, 1984, 225; Trimingham, 1973, 126–127; Abu Manneh, 1979). Nüzhet Paşa met Bediüzzaman in Erzincan. He must have felt that Said was a suitable element to add to the select group of advisers that the sultan was using. He thus gave a letter of recommendation to Said, commending him to Abdülhamid's Imperial "Birdkeeper," Kuşçubaşı Mustafa Bey. It was through such trusted aides rather than through the formal governmental structure that the sultan carried out his more secret policies. The son of Mustafa Bey, Eşref Sencer Kuşçubaşı was later to become a leading figure in the Secret Service of the Young Turks, the so-called *Teşkilat-ı Mahsusa*, and was a good friend of Said Nursi. It was he who was to implement the pan-Islamic propaganda of the Young Turks during the First World War to which Said Nursi also contributed.

Said remained in the mansion of Mustafa Bey for a year and a half, more or less on call to the sultan. His talent, presumably, did not impress the sultan, because he eventually returned to Van (1899; Şahiner, 1979, 77).

There now follows an interlude of about a decade in which we hear nothing of Said in his authorized biography. He appears in the Ottoman capital once more in 1907, moving into a *han* or hotel which catered to the Muslim intelligentsia of the capital. This was a place where Mehmed Akif, the poet, who was also a theoretician of an Islamic cultural revival for the Ottoman Empire, could be found, as well as a host of other eminent literateurs.

We do not know what prompted Said to move to the capital at that date. Perhaps the deterioration of economic conditions throughout the Ottoman Empire and especially in the east gave a new urgency to his desire to present the sultan with a reform proposal which he did eventually submit.

The following is a contemporary description of the impression that he created when he moved into the "Sweetmakers" (*Şekerci*) Han:

> It was about the time of the Second Constitutional Period. I was studying in the Fatih Medrese. I heard that a young man by the name of Bediüzzaman had arrived in Istanbul and had hung the following sign on his door: "Here any problem is solved, all questions are answered. But no questions are asked." I thought someone that presumptuous could only be mad. As I began to hear of the many flattering comments concerning him and the admiration expressed by the community of believers and the *'ulema* and students I was intrigued and tried to get to know him better. I decided I would make up a list of questions covering the most difficult and subtle problems of theology. I too was considered quite an expert on such questions at the time. Finally, one day I went to visit him. I presented him with my problems. The answers I received were extremely original and showed great depth. He had answered the questions as if he had been at my side when I had prepared them on the preceding night. I was completely satisfied with his performance and came to the conclusion that his knowledge was not like ours acquired (*kesbi*) but inspired (*vehbi*). (Başoğlu, in *Nurculuk*, 355–356)

Said Nursi indicates that through prescience (luck?) he had re-read the previous evening all the books that he needed to answer the questions posed.

Through his connections in the palace Bediüzzaman found the way to present the sultan with a petition. The date of this event is not clear, but the petition was reprinted in a newspaper entitled *The East and Kurdistan* (November 19, 1908; Şahiner, 1979, 85) following the Young Turk Revolution of 1908. In his petition Said stated that although some new schools had been established in the Eastern area, the local population could not take advantage of these because the teachers sent by the government knew no Kurdish. Said Nursi proposed that the government take up a policy of what has since been called "reverse-discrimination" in minority studies of our time. According to him it was incumbent upon the Ottoman government that it sponsor and support a contingent of Kurdish speakers in order that they be educated in the Ottoman secular school system. In the existing system they could only be educated in the *medreses*, because the language used there was Kurdish. The availability of a more varied educational fare as well as the opportunity to study in Turkish would eliminate internal factional strife among the tribes and make them into good Ottoman citizens. This enterprise could then be capped by establishing an eastern "university" which would train the local graduates of these secular schools. The university would be built on the model of al-Azhar, the Arab center for higher theological studies in Cairo. Indeed, at the turn of the century, the Azhar was being gradually modernized to serve a function similar to that which Said had in mind. The sultan had already given some thought to the problem, and had established a special palace school for training the sons of tribal chiefs.

The option of upgrading existing religious educational establishments versus their replacement by the type of secular school introduced by the *Tanzimat* had already made the substance of an extensive debate in the Ottoman Empire. Said opted for the first of these solutions. Bediüzzaman was convinced that a compromise solution could be reached in which the conflict between "religious sciences" and "philosophical sciences" was eliminated and the clash between *medrese* graduates, *tekke* graduates and secular school graduates would become irrelevant (BSN, 46).

As he stated on another occasion:

> I had seen the miserable state of the tribes in the Eastern provinces. I understood that what earthly happiness we could attain would be in one respect through modern science, and a lively channel to establish these sciences would be the *'ulema* and *medrese*, for the *'ulema* would thus acquire an understanding of these sciences. Everyone knows that in those provinces the fate of the seminomadic citizens (*vantandaş*) is in the hands of the *'ulema*. And it is this which led me to come to the capital. . . (BSN, 66).

A proposal for enlightening the rural masses had already been prepared in the 1870s by a *Nakşibendi şeyh* of Erzincan (Gündüz, 1984, 221). At the time he presented his petition to the sultan, Bediüzzaman is said to have reminded the ruler of the similar petition which the Central Asian pan-Islamist Abdürreşid Ibrahim had already given the Ottoman ruler.

Persons present at the audience have testified to Said's great courage in exposing his proposals to the sultan and criticizing his passivity as caliph and leader of the Muslims (Şahiner, 1979, 88). It is this unheard-of behavior which led the sultan's officials to wonder whether Said was mentally deranged. He was, therefore, sent to the Toptaşı asylum for observation, but during his interrogation it became evident that he was sane. He explained that outspokenness was a characteristic of the mountain culture in which he had originated and that the convention of Ottoman politeness current in the capital could not be used to judge his behavior. His attitude was also an outcome of his rebellion against the current apathy which he had found in the capital, for he had dedicated himself to service to the nation (*millet*; *milla*), religion (*din*; *dīn*) and the state (*devlet*; *dawla*). For fifteen years—possibly since his stay in Mardin—he had been thinking of an idea, "*Qur'ānic* freedom" (*hürriyet-i şer'iyye*), and now this idea was in danger of being swamped by an impending revolution by which he presumably meant the Young Turk conspiracies (Şahiner, 1979, 90–91).

As to his bizarre mountaineer clothing, Said explained it as a means of drawing attention to the contentiousness with which he wanted to approach Ottoman society as it existed. His continuous criticism of the *'ulema* was due to the stagnation into which he felt religious studies had fallen. He proposed a complete recasting of these.

If the Ottomans had been unable to achieve advances in science it was due to the existence of three divergent streams of education in Turkey: the *medrese*, the *tekke* (the "lodge" of the Sufi orders) and the secular school (*Ibid.*, 93). The only way to bring back creativity was to reintroduce religious studies in the secular schools, to add the study of science to the program of the *medrese* and to bring competent *'ulema* into the *tekke*.

This was quite an impressive argumentation. The proposition that the elimination of religion as a philosophical underpinning of studies had led to sterility in the new schools had already been advanced by Cemaleddin Afgani. Afgani believed that education as imitation and without a base of philosophy or ethics was condemned to bear no fruit: graduates of Egyptian schools were only superficially aware of the meaning of Western civilization because they did understand its philosophical underpinning. The argument is still being used in our day by such eminent thinkers as Ali Shariati, who built up secular support for the Islamic revolution in Iran, and by contemporary Turkish thinkers such as Cemil Meriç. Said Nursi also pointed out once more that at a time like the one he was living through, marked as it was by increased scepticism, asserting the truth of Islam was no longer sufficient to impress people. It was a time when "a tendency to investigate the truthfulness of a statement has awakened among all," (Şahiner, 1979, 94). The person who advanced a claim had to prove it and convince his opposite. This meant also that people could not "retreat in the corners of old times" and use the ornate classical Ottoman rhetoric. The new era demanded that one speak words "in tune with [changing] conditions and time" (*Ibid.*).

Said was disappointed by what he found in the Ottoman capital. In his own words, which possibly also refer to his voyage of 1896, he stated:

> I had grown up in the mountains of Kurdistan. I was imagining the seat of the Caliphate to be a beautiful place. I arrived in Istanbul and saw that the hatred which persons nourished against one another made them all into well-dressed savages. I understood that the reason for the disease was this hypocrisy. They called me crazy. But I saw this bitter truth: I saw and understood that Islam was behind, far behind the civilization of our times . . . There were three culprits of this decline: the Doctors of Islamic law, those who had not understood Europe and the members of mystic orders (*tekke*). (Kutay, 1966 (2), 214)

We next see Said in Salonika, the center where the preparations for a *coup* against Abdülhamid were the most intense. We do not know how long he stayed in that town before the Young Turk revolution, but his authorized biography provides us with the text of a speech which he is supposed to have delivered in Salonika following the success of the Young Turk insurrection of July 3rd 1908. The sultan's proclamation that the Ottoman Constitution of 1876 was, once more, in force (Shaw and Shaw, 1977, II, 266–267) had followed this successful coup.

In his speech, Budiüzzaman described himself as a "nomad whom freedom had awakened" (for the speech see BSN, 51 f.) and went on to state:

> O, oppressed sons of the fatherland let us enter the doors of progress and civilization (*medeniyet*). The first door is that of participating in the common stream of the *şeriat*, the second is love of one's nation, the third education, the fourth human labor, the fifth the adandonment of debauched morals. (BSN, 51–52)

Here also appeared an unusual imagery where technology was made to serve the ends of religion. Such hybrid metaphors continued thereafter to characterize his style. He went on: "With the assistance of the miracle of prophethood, God willing, we shall leave behind us more than a century of lag in the race for progress and step onto the railroad of the basic laws of the *şeriat*, bodily, and mount the prophetic steed of consultation based on religious law, intellectually" (BSN, 52).

In practice, equality, too, was more than a function of Young Turks' virtue (*fazilet*) and honor. It was a term that had reference to the law and to the "higher law" or which the law rested. As to the non-Muslims, their place in society was a secondary one; they were not to occupy the slots at the summit of Islamic society (BSN, 76).

That the Young Turks had something different in mind than Said when they spoke about freedom was to become apparent in the months that followed. As heirs to the mantle of the Ottoman state they had just as little patience with uncontrolled religious currents as had the sultans who had preceded them. Yet the autonomous flowering of religion was one of the most striking developments that followed upon the revolution. In particular, they had to take a serious view of pan-Islamic currents which found support in part of the Ottoman press. Abdürreşid İbrahim, the Siberian *molla* who had travelled throughout the Islamic world and was to produce a two-volume work on the *World of Islam* was prominent among those who demanded assistance from the Ottomans for the Islamic World. He was one of the publishers of a review which appeared in Istanbul; in it he wrote an open letter to Bediüzzaman. He had read and agreed with the latter's *Speech* given in Salonika, but what was really necessary was to devise a common policy for all Islamic people (Kutay, 1967 (5), 206).

While in Salonika, Bediüzzaman was on good terms with leading Young Turk figures. He had participated in social gatherings organized in the house of the future minister of justice Manyasizâde Refik Bey. Young Turk leaders such as Talat (Paşa), Dr. Nazım, and Ali Fethi Bey had been present. Talat asked him to accompany him to Istanbul (Kutay, 1977, 345), but this did not prevent Said from being arrested by the new administration even before he had departed for Istanbul. The Young Turks must have been suspicious of his activities as a religious leader riding on the new wave of freedom.

I have already tried to show how Islam operated in the Eastern provinces as an autonomous political structure encouraged but not entirely controlled by the state. I have also indicated that factions which formed within the framework of popular Islamic institutions were important building blocks of provincial politics even during the reign of Sultan Abdülhamid II. While these activities continued, a somewhat new phenomenon was also emerging: Islam was becoming a channel through which persons who had failed to become integrated into the secular system of the *Tanzimat* were engaged in their own project of boundary expansion, and search for freedom. Said Nursi's protest against the rigidity of religious studies provides us with an example of how this was being done.

It is clear that the Young Turks, who were rather good at political manipulation, could not understand that this was a movement which replicated their own search for greater freedom, although in a different form. In the various associations with an Islamic coloring which were formed after the revolution of 1908 they saw only clusters of political opposition in which Islam was used as a banner by cynical manipulators who wanted to seize power. It is true that in the eastern provinces Islamic institutions were placing their stamp on community life and in that sense escaped Young Turk control. Also, there did exist many cynical notables who were ready to use Islam for their own narrow political purposes. Nevertheless, the Islamic component of political behavior in the Ottoman Empire was somewhat more complex than could be derived from the model which the Young Turks had learned to invoke when they were in Europe, namely that of the Catholic Church seen as an insidious force undermining the secularism of the French Third Republic. This image reinforced traditional suspicions which Ottoman statesmen had always harbored with regard to localistic religiosity. The Young Turks did appreciate the mobilizing dimension of pan-Islam and had no qualms in using them, but they were not ready to share power with groups which had a deeper commitment than their own to Islam, and used it to shape their own model of an ideal society.

A consequence of this Young Turk attitude towards social movements which, in their opinion, "endangered" the revolution, was their increasing persecution of formations which they perceived as traitorous and which others perceived as simply incipent political parties with a right to exist. The reactionary outbreak of March 31st 1909 seemed to justify their fears.

Said Nursi was a founder of the Muslim association known as the *İttihad-ı Muhammedî* (The Muslim Union). The association was established a week before the military rebellion in Istanbul which has acquired notoriety in Turkish history as the "incident of March 31st" (1909). The rebellious group consisted of privates led by non-commissioned officers. The mouthpiece of the *İttihad-ı Muhammedî*, the *Volkan*, immediately became a leading voice among the opposition to the Young Turks. It accused the latter of a policy intimidation based on terrorism and, at the same time, of attacking Islamic institutions. Because the "incident" was a reactionary, populist outbreak demanding a return to the *şeriat*, the association was inculpated in the rebellion. Its most popular writer, Derviş Vahdetî, was hanged. Said Nursi disculpates himself of complicity in the outbreak. He states that he harangued the Eastern porters of Istanbul so that they would abandon any ideas they might have harbored of joining the rebellion.

The founders of the *İttihad-ı Muhammedî* seem to have been *'ulema* of middling and lower social status representing the central Orthodox (but provincial) Ottoman Muslim tradition. The group had a special attraction for provincial *'ulema*. The association termed itself a "party" (*fırka*) (Tunaya, 1952, 261; 1984, I, 183). Both its self-image and the sources of discontent to which it appealed are important in establishing the setting for Said Nursi's life history. For one, the creation of this party showed considerable understanding of the workings of voluntary associations. The self-image of the "Party" which likened itself to "Anarchists," "Jesuits," or "Missionaries" showed that it also understood the role of world-revolutionary or mobilizing organizations. On the other hand, it had a substantive Islamic content. It saw itself as different from political parties in the sense that it was not the representive of a group but the carrier of an ideology slated to "awaken Muslim political and social thought" (Tunaya, 1952, I, 270) in all states where Muslims were in "political slavery." Its leader was "the Prophet Muhammad" (*Ibid.*, 27). One of its primary aims was to make the *şeriat* the fountainhead of Parliamentary legislation. Here we have already an adumbration of the populist Islamic revolution that was to shake Iran in our time. In a sense, then, the elements of social and political mobilization which brought about these developments were more directly linked to the expanding communications frame of Muslims and to the clash between Islamic and Western culture than to the short-term political circumstances preceeding the outbreaks.

Said Nursi's familiarity with the terminology of nineteenth century liberalism emerges clearly in connection with the speech that he pronounced on the occasion of the re-establishment of the Constitution in 1908 (Bediüzzaman, 1326), a speech of a later date than the Salonika speech. Freedom, he states on this occasion, is so powerful a force that it has been able to awaken even a "Kurd like him" steeped in ignorance. If freedom had not appeared, the *millet* would have remained in the prison of slavery (*Ibid.*, 4). Here the term *millet*, which up to that time meant clearly the Muslim *nation*, begins to acquire connotations of the Ottoman *nation*. Furthermore, if the nation uses freedom as a guide, this will enable it to progress (*terakki*). Freedom also demands us to love our nation (*muhabbet-i-milliye*) (*Ibid.*); it has opened the doors of progress and civilization (*medeniyet*). The time has come when social bonds (*revabıt-i içtimaî*) and the need for sustenance (*lüzum-u taayyüş*) have increased to such an extent that the nation can only be governed by a national assembly. Nevertheless, the newly acquired freedom is described once more as "*Şer'i*": it should not be used for "indulgence in rake-like dissipation" (*sefahat*) or to achieve "illegitimate pleasures" (*Ibid*., 5). Science should be gladly accepted from the foreigners, but this must be done in such a way as to preserve our national customs (*adat-i milliye*) (*Ibid*., 9). This is what the Japanese have done, and they should be an example to the Ottomans. The new government is based on "public opinion" (*Ibid*., 10) and actions undermining this newly won solidarity should be shunned. The old times were also times when savagery (*vahşet*) was dominant and force and compulsion ruled, but in the times of civilization it is science and learning which rule. In olden times men were so circumscribed in their action that they were no different from animals. On the other hand, if the Ottoman Empire has declined, this is due to the neglect of the *şeriat*, as much as it is due to autocracy. It is also the result of being misled by appearance and of slavish imitation of Europe.

All of these are not very original statements of political theory, but they do show that Said had begun to use the liberal-constitutionalist terminology which figures prominently among the intellectual baggage of the Young Turks. Somewhat more striking is the stress he places in one of his later speeches on poverty, ignorance and anarchy as the three main enemies of the Ottomans. To eliminate these enemies Said advised national union (*ittihad-ı millî*), human exertion (*sây-ı insanî*), and national solidarity (*muhabbet-i millî*) (*Ibid*., 20). There is nothing in these sources to justify the later accusation levelled against him by most of his modern Turkish critics that he was a Kurdish nationalist. It is true that by 1910 his message to the inhabitants of the Diyarbakır region was that they should be in control of the region (G. Lowther to E. Grey, Constantinople, January 22, 1911, *F.O.*, V, 225). In the perspective of Said's later career it is fair to evaluate this attitude as that of an "Ottoman" demanding cultural and administrative autonomy. Before the Turkish Republic this attitude would not have been misunderstood by many Ottoman officials, who saw the Empire as a *consociation* of ethnic groups.

A second point of theoretical importance concerns the ethic of exertion that Said continuously invokes in these years. This ethic may not be the full equivalent of a puritan ethic, but it certainly was an activism which preachers of his time were only beginning to use as a social value with the widest application. However, the source of this activism has to be sought even earlier, for the *Nakşibendi* order had acquired this stance long before the confrontation with the West to which Ottoman activism is usually attributed.

An additional point would be that Said Nursi's movement, just as that of the *Nakşibendi*, had nothing to it that can be described as millenarian. It was pre-millenarian in the sense of being in line with orthodox expectations as to the future prospects of the Muslim community.

Said moved from Van to Urfa and Diyarbakır. There he met Ziya Gökalp, a person who was shortly to become a major Young Turk theoretician and who had had similarly intense religious experiences during his youth (Şahiner, 1979, 134–136). At the time Gökalp was slowly adopting the viewpoint of European positivism and solidarism. Bediüzzaman seems to have by then established his prestige in the area as an important *şeyh*, since he was a guest of the most important notable, Mustafa Bey.

In the winter of 1911 Bediüzzaman arrived in Damascus (Şahiner, 1979, 136). This may have been a spiritual pilgrimage to a center where *müceddidî Nakşibendi*sm had been established by the Muradi family (Hourani, 1972, 94). He is purported to have given a long sermon in the Umayyad Mosque in which the main themes were those that Muslims advocating a revival of Islam had already been developing: while adopting the technology of the West, Muslims should not let themselves be overwhelmed by hopelessness. They should find means of reinforcing the cohesion of Muslim society: Islam provided a superior spiritual basis for social cohesion. This Islamic social cement was so strong that, if it were activated, Islam would spill into the rest of the world and bring it under its sway (BSN, 83–85).

Said thereafter returned to Istanbul. Sultan Abdülhamid had been deposed and replaced by the kindly and rather ineffective Sultan Mehmed Reşad. The sultan was known to have had an affiliation with the *Mevlevi* order. Perhaps this is what made him take sympathetic notice of the petition which Said Nursi presented him: in it he repeated what he had already asked in his petition to Sultan Abdülhamid. When the sultan undertook a journey through the Balkan provinces of the Ottoman Empire, Said was co-opted into his personal staff. Taking advantage of the government's laying the foundations of a new university in Kosovo, Said obtained an allocation of similar funds for a university in Van (BSN, 254). Returning to Van, he personally selected a place for the university and saw that the foundations for this institution were laid. Turkey, however, had by then become embroiled in the Balkan War, and the project was abandoned. The Turkish regular army suffered a series of reverses during this war, which came to an end in July 1913. The Ottoman inhabitants of the capital were severely shaken, and desperate schemes began to be proposed in order to assure the survival of the Empire. The entry of the Ottoman Empire into the First World War on the side of the Central Powers was one of these moves.

Said had once more returned to Van and Bitlis to teach in the Horhor Medrese. It might have been at this time that he was approached by a number of local personalities who were preparing an insurrection against the Young Turks:

> Those Chiefs and clans who had benefited under the fallen Sultan were being incited by reactionary circles in the capital to make trouble in outlying provinces and create difficulties for the revolutionary party in power. Widespread robberies in isolated valleys and out-of-the-way districts and the raiding of flocks of defenceless peasants increased in proportion to the Turkish defeats in the Balkans.
>
> There also was a political aspect to it: "Kurdistan for the Kurds" a new password was being whispered from *tekké* (a shrine or hostel) to *tekké* of the Sheikhs who were convinced that the Ottoman Empire had suffered the great disaster of 1912–13 because the Young Turks were godless and *Farmason* (Masons). (Safrastian, 1948, 72; also Şahiner, 1979, 167)

One person involved in the movement was *şeyh* Şahabettin, son of Said's teacher, *Nur* Mehmed Efendi (van Bruinessen, 1978, 350).

In 1913 an ill-advised *vali* of Bitlis who tried to collect taxes due to the government was faced by a full-scale rebellion. In July 1913, the *şeyh* who was leading the insurrection occupied Bitlis. Ottoman troops took the city back within a week (Safrastian, 1948, 73–74). Bediüzzaman seems to have joined the Young Turk secret service soon after this event. He participated in the drafting of the five *Cihad Fetva* proclaimed by the Young Turks upon their entrance into the First War on the side of the Central Powers (for the text see Albayrak, 1975, 86; for Young Turk propaganda see Green, 1978, 223).

We have a remarkable explanation of Said Nursi's affiliation with the Young Turks, who after all had not accorded him the gentlest treatment. For him the Young Turks represented the last chance of using the Ottoman armed might to good avail. With the disintegration of the army during the First World War this opportunity had also disappeared. Said states that all that was left for him to do then was to reintegrate into his role of the new Said, the Said who appealed to the religious faith of the community rather than the Said who worked through political structures.

In 1915 Said went to Tripoli by submarine, being sent by the Young Turks to encourage the *Sanusi* to resistance against the Italian occupiers of Tripolitania (Şahiner, 1979, 153). By August of 1915 he had returned to

Turkey and was fighting on the Anatolian eastern front in the local militia (Şahiner ed., 1978, 234). The collaboration of some of the Armenians of the Anatolian regions with the Russians made the struggle a particularly bitter one.

Said was taken prisoner by the Russians while defending Bitlis (Şahiner, 1979, 172). In Russia he was sent to a prisoner-of-war camp in Kostroma, where he spent two and a half years. He must have been impressed by the attitude of his jailers, for he was later to state that while the Russians allowed him to gather a congregation for prayer in the camp, the Turkish Republic had refused him the same right. He lived through the Russian Revolution and escaped in the spring of 1917. He returned to Turkey via Petersburg, Warsaw, Berlin, and Vienna (BSN, 104). He later stated that he had also taken a trip to Switzerland to study how people of different religious and ethnic stock had been able to make up a modern state. The Young Turk leaders were still in power when he returned but were to flee upon the signing of the Armistice in October 1918.

Moves were immediately initiated to make the Young Turk administration answer for its actions in involving Turkey in the War. The *şeyhülislâm* Musa Kâzım Efendi, who was accused of having helped the secularizing moves of the Young Turks, was placed on trial. On the other hand, some measures in the spirit of Said's proposals were carried out in order to modernize the *medrese* structure. One of these was the *Dâr ül-Hikmet il-İslâmiye*, an embryonic academy of higher Islamic studies. Bediüzzaman was appointed to this body (Albayrak, 1973).

A flood of commentary on the religious and cultural policies of the Young Turks began to appear in the press. Said joined in the debate, writing a number of pamphlets in which he tried to explain the causes of the Ottoman debacle. According to him one of the deep causes of the defeat had been the inability of the Young Turks to integrate Islam into their ideology. *Sunuhat* (1920), *Hakikat Çekirdekleri* (1920), *Nokta* (1921), Rümuz (1922), *Işarat* (1923) made up this series. Cenap Şahabettin, a prominent Turkish author (1870–1934), had published an article in the daily *Peyam-ı Sabah* stating that he did not see how Islam was going to be preserved through a tightening of control over the observance of religion; rather, he believed it was through the opening up of the door of *içtihad* (*ijtihād*; interpretation) that Islam could be integrated into modern life. It was in this way that aspects of Islam restricting participation in modern life, such as the interdiction of the drawing of the human figure, could be avoided. It was in this way, too, that polygamy could be made a thing of the past (Şahiner, 1979, 230). Said Nursi's answers in such pamphlets as *Tuluat*, *Lemaat* and *Hubab* replicated those which had already been used by the school of Islamic reformists in Egypt, the Salafiyya. He stated that there were two aspects of *Qur'ānic* injunctions. Some were fixed, and no amount of liberalization could change their meaning. Others were amenable to change through *içtihad*. This was a somewhat oblique statement but one which has often constituted the gist of an answer to requests for the opening of the gate of *içtihad*. What Said Nursi seems to have offered in the place of *içtihad* was a means of finding new applications for old principles. He thus advised that the bookishness which had crept into the pedagogy of the *medrese* be replaced by teaching based on a new educational philosophy (Şahiner, 1979, 92–93). Each *medrese* student also should choose a specialization for themselves in the non-religious sciences. This seems to be the meaning of his use of *fen* in referring to the field of specialization (*Ibid.*).

Some time after the Armistice, a Society for the Promotion of Kurds, *Kürdistan Teali Cemiyeti*, erroneously known as "*Kürt Teali*" (Tunaya, 1986, II, 186) was formed. It seemed to promote primarily cultural goals (van Bruinessen, 1985, p. 131) even though some members had more radical aims than others, and the Diyarbakır association branch was for outright Kurdish nationalism. Said Nursi is said to have figured among the founders of this association. But a number of points have to be taken into account here, which, in fact, absolve Said from the accusation of being a separatist. Said does not figure among the directorate elected at the first general meeting of the society. He is not mentioned as a founder by the scholar who has collected the most extensive information about the association (Tunaya, II, 1986, 186f.). He claims that he was always opposed to nationalism, which he considered an evil doctrine because it had created divisions among the followers of Islam (*Mektubat*, 59). In addition, the person who was selected to head the association, Abdülkadir, the son of the rebellious Şeyh Ubeydullah of the 1880s, was a supporter of Kurdish autonomy, not of independence. He was the head of the Ottoman Senate and was considered an Ottoman agent by his own community.

Crisis of Conscience

A turning point in Said Nursi's life was the "Crisis of Conscience" which he experienced following his return from Russia. The Young Turk triumvirate had fled in the fall of 1918. In February 1919 an Allied fleet anchored in Istanbul, and General Franchet d'Esperay rode into the city on a white horse, a gift of the Greek community. The new sultan, Vahdettin, had dissolved the Chamber of Deputies and appointed a grand vizier known for his conservative leanings. Tendencies opposed to the radicalism of the Young Turks were emerging. The Young Turks had given a fair share of attention to religious issues but in the long run a secularist pattern could be seen to emerge from their solicitude for Islam. Much of family law, for example, had been taken out of the jurisdiction of religious courts in their time (Bouvat, 1921).

Now a more truly religious experiment, aiming to salvage and reinforce Islamic institutions, was being attempted.

Mustafa Sabri Efendi, known for his conservatism, became *şeyhülislâm*. The year he was appointed his refutation to the liberal approach to Islam appeared entitled *The Scientific Values of the New Interpreters of Islam (Yeni İslâm Müçtehitlerinin Kıymet-i İlmiyyesi)* (Berkes, 1964, note 3, 434). In it, Sabri criticized the reformist approach of Musa Carullah, a Muslim religious thinker from Russia. Mustafa Sabri claimed that the idea of freedom of conscience had no Islamic base. We do not know what Said thought of the debate at the time. At a later date he stated that both Mustafa Sabri and Musa Carullah had adopted extreme positions.

In the Ottoman capital, Said was given a position in the newly established Islamic Academy, the *Dâr ül-Hikmet il-Islâmiye* (BSN, 112–117). He writes of these years as being ones during which he was extremely happy. He lived in Çamlıca, on the Bosphorus, and shared his lodgings with his nephew Abdurrahman, who acted as his secretary. Despite these happy associations, the years he spent in Istanbul (1919–1921) were also a time of crisis for the Ottoman Empire, and he could not but share in the burden of defeat and occupation by enemy troops. These were also years during which a crisis of conscience was to change his views radically. His years at the Islamic Academy were marked by repeated breakdowns in health (Albayrak, 1973, 188). Since an early age Said had been in the center of provincial and later national politics, now he had to turn away from political involvement and work at the grass roots level. This transformation occurred relatively slowly and culminated with his exile in 1925, a development which Said considered to be a sign of his new vocation.

The crisis of 1921 was precipitated by what he describes as a totally unexpected betrayal by one of his close friends (*Lem'alar*, 225). A feeling of helplessness, reinforced by the realization that he had passed the prime of life, began to dawn. All of this plunged him into dark thoughts followed by complete despair. His own description of this crisis is quite clear:

> With the stark recognition (*intibah*) that resulted from old age (*ihtiyarlık*) I first saw the mortality (*fanilik*) of the ephemeral things in which I was interested. At that time, my soul, which was seeking permanence and which became fixated on the impermanent believing it was permanent, forcefully impressed on me the following: Since my body is mortal, what can I gain from these ephemeral things. Since I am powerless, what good can come from the powerless. I must find an ever-lasting protector (*Baki-i Sermedî*) an eternal power (*Kadir-i Ezelî*). (*Lem'alar*, 225)

Bediüzzaman described the changes which he experienced in a series of brochures published in Arabic in 1921 (*Lem'alar*, 104). The starting point of his spiritual voyage was the discovery that he had been captivated by the philosophical sciences (*Ulûm-u Felsefe*) (Lem'alar, 225) and had given them weight equal to that of religion (*Ulûm-u İslamiye*). These philosophical sciences had muddied his soul and become an obstacle to his moral progress. The pessimism that philosophy generated resulted in his soul being "strangled" by the Universe. A sudden flash originating in his reading of the *Qur'ān* impressed upon him the idea that there was no God but Allah (*Lā ilāha illā hu*) and "cleaned out all those impurities." His own recollection of the intellectual change he experienced is as follows:

> Forty or fifty years ago, Old Said who had been steeped too deeply in intellectual and philosophical sciences (*Ulûm-u akliyye ve felsefiye*) tried to find the ultimate truth among the followers of mystic orders *tarikat* and the investigators of ultimate reality (*ehl-i tarikat*, *ehl-i hakikat*). He could not be satisfied like most of the followers of *tarikat* with an impetus coming from the heart because his intellectual faculties carried the wound of philosophical discourse. He had to be cured. He then tried to follow some of the investigators who had combined heart and mind. Every one of them had a different attraction. He was confused as to which one to follow. The İmam-ı Rabbanî [Sirhindi] transmitted to him a hidden message (*gaybi*) which carried the meaning of "unify your *kibla*" or, in other words, find a single master. This deeply wounded heart of the old Said who then thought: 'The true master (*ustad*) is the *Qur'ān*. Finding a single master will be only possible with that one.' Thus, following the guidance of this divine master, his heart and his soul began to rise up in a strange way. His selfhood (*nefs-i emmaresi*) with its own failings (*sükuk ve sübehatiyle*) forced him to a spiritual and intellectual confrontation. But not with his eyes closed; he journeyed with his eyes open just as the İmam-i Gazzalî, Mevlânâ Celaleddin and the İmam-ı Rabbanî had

> journeyed with the eyes of their heart, soul and wisdom open in the same places where the absent minded had closed their mind's eye. Praise be to God . . . he found a path to truth through the lesson, the guidance of the *Qur'ān*.
> (*Mesnevi-i Nuriye*, 1977, 7)

The process by which Said's reasoning self was convinced of the central importance of the unicity of God was one in which he put to a critical test what he knew about biology and botany. Prior to the flash of illumination he had believed that natural phenomena were to be explained by natural causes: the tree produced the fruit (*Lem'alar*, 226). The new insight he received was that effects (*the fruit*) as well as causes (*the trees*) were the product of the direct unmediated intervention of God. If one were to survey the processes which took place in the fruit, one would find that they were no less complex than those taking place in the tree. But if the product (or effect) was infinitely complex, there was no possible way of correlating this complexity with that of the cause (tree). Also, since something could not arise of nothing, the tissues, and other complex biological entities which appeared in the full-grown plant existed as a potential in some location before the maturation of the plant, yet they could not be observed anywhere before this maturation. Therefore, the structure of the plant could only be attributed to a divine plan, particularly since every species went through its appointed paces without a deviation from the plan, without a mistake ever occurring.

Said Nursi's concentration on "final causes" was a natural outcome of the fashion in which philosophical debates had been carried by the Ottoman intellectuals of his time. Both agnostics and conservatives had chosen biology, life and creation as the arena in which to wage the war of materialism against spiritualism. The same debate had also marked European intellectual history in the nineteenth century, but in that context, creation could still be seen as a remote event which had set the universe in motion. The laws of physics were the means by which the creator had enabled the dynamic of creation to be perpetuated. Muslim, *Ash'arī,* philosophy had always accorded a more direct role to God, who was conceived as recreating the world at every instant. The doctrine of "emanation" which saw the events of the world as an emanation from the being of God was the mystic's somewhat different explanation of the primal force.

The reason Said Nursi had fastened on biology in his refutation was related to the peculiarities of the spread of Western science in the Ottoman Empire in the nineteenth century. In the Ottoman Empire the sciences of life—biology, botany, physiology—had developed quite early through their incorporation into the program of the medical schools. It is on this ground that scepticism had grown, for in the medical school life processes were shown to have a physical or chemical origin. This was the breeding ground for scepticism, and it must have been that upon which Said focused his attention. His later writings constantly take up the processes of biology and botany as proofs of the creative force of divinity.

Said states that the works which helped him clear the way to a resolution of his own confusion were the *Mektubat* of Sirhindi and the *Futūḥ al-Ghayb* or sermons of 'Abd al-Qādır al-Jīlānī (for these sources, Trimingham, 1973, 41), the sternness and soberness of which (Schimmel, 1978, 247) seems to have given him a cathartic jolt.

It is probable in this latter source that he found the inspiration for another idea which was to reappear in his own work—but which is a main theme of Islamic reformism—that of the unicity of God as a guiding principle. Said Nursi gained from the idea of the unicity of God an internal confirmation of belief which was also to effect his strategy of revivalism. This internal turmoil made him view the circumstances of his day-to-day life in Istanbul with disgust, which led him to return to Van (1920–1921). Here he found the *medrese* where he had taught in the past, the Horhor Medrese, in ruins, its students dispersed and both the Armenian and the Muslim quarters of Bitlis gutted by the war.

He felt abandoned by all; his nephew and secretary, Abdurrahman, had left, and, although he eventually received some news from him, Abdurrahman died shortly thereafter. This loss shook Said Nursi. He states that one half of his private world had disappeared with the death of his mother; Abdurrahman's death meant the loss of the remaining half of his private universe. Abdurrahman's death was shortly thereafter to be compensated for by another young man who dedicated himself to Said's service and to the propagation of his writings (*Lem'alar*, 232).

Bediüzzaman had published a brochure (Şahiner, 1979, 226) in which he attacked the Greek occupation of Western Anatolia and the British policy which had made this occupation possible. He also protested at the *fetva* of the *şeyhülislâm* Dürrizâde Abdullah (April 11, 1920) which proclaimed Mustafa Kemal to be an outlaw (Şahiner, 1979, 236). The Ankara government formed in opposition to that of the sultan seems to have been impressed and invited him to join the movement. Bediüzzaman arrived in the summer of 1922 (Şahiner, 1979, 240). In one passage of the *Emirdağ Lahikası* (1959, 10) he states that Mustafa Kemal asked him to perform a function similar to that which the *Sanusi* leaders had performed for Lybia, a unification of the population by providing a religious focus of allegiance. Mustafa Kemal had himself been in charge in 1916 of an army corps which was to have rescued Bitlis, but he had arrived too late (Allen & Muratoff, 1953); he therefore was aware of Said Nursi's heroism on that occasion.

The Grand National Assembly allocated 150,000 liras for a university in Van (BSN, 254). However, in January of 1923 Said Nursi was already circulating in parliament a broadsheet which pointed out that it was through God's grace that the Turkish War of Independence had been won, and yet nothing had been done to bring Turkey to a more Muslim way of life. He was now warning the deputies of the Grand National Assembly that he feared a dangerous wave of destructive secularism would submerge Turkey.

> The instrument of your victory and the body which recognize your services are one, they are the community of believers, and in particular the lower classes who are solid Muslims. . . . And it is therefore incumbent upon you to act in accordance with *Qur'ānic* injunctions. To prefer the pitiable, rootless (*milliyetsiz* = nationless), Europe-worshipping imitators of Frankish customs who are detaching themselves from Islam to the masses of the Muslim people (*avam*) is against Islamic custom and will lead the world of Islam to direct its gaze in another direction and request assistance from others. (BSN, 126)

Bediüzzaman still believed that the Turks should make use of the forces of Islam throughout the world, a policy which the Young Turks had also followed. At the same time, this was just before the government's move toward secularization of March 3rd, 1924, which abolished the caliphate. He must have had an inkling of the way the wind was blowing in the immediate circle around Mustafa Kemal since he also made the point that the religious legitimation derived from the caliphate placed the ruler of Turkey in an unusually strong position in an age when community ties of religion were acquiring an enhanced value. He returned to Van in the spring of 1923, where he remained until February–March 1925. The uprising of Şeyh Said was now in full swing, and Said Nursi was accused of having links with its perpetrators (van Bruinessen, 1978, 380). Bediüzzaman himself denies this and states that he tried to prevent the rebellion (BSN, 135); at any rate, he was arrested with a number of other local notables and herded into a school building in Van. The group was directed to Antalya, from where Said was sent to Burdur and İsparta (Şahiner, 1979, 260–61; and compare with *Son Şahitler,* II, 212 which gives the first place as

İsparta). At İsparta he continued to teach in a *medrese*, but the crowds he attracted forced the governor to move him to the village of Barla (*Son Şahitler*, II, 212).

The circumstances which now pitted Said Nursi against the Turkish authorities constitute one of the most colorful episodes in his life. They also underline the type of fear which Said Nursi inspired in the authorities. Finally, they show that later, in the 1950s, after the defeat of Turkish Jacobin secularism, the Turkish judiciary gave a creditable performance of impartiality in cases in which the basic charge was the undermining of the constitutional principle of laicism or secularism. This principle was defined by a series of statutes which made up its substantive content. Among these figured the law abolishing the *medrese* and the *'ulema* hierarchy, the adoption of the Swiss Civil Code and the disestablishment of Islam. In 1932 the Arabic call to prayer was made illegal. In July of the same year Said Nursi was arrested for having given the call in Arabic in the village where he resided. Somebody must have been waiting for the occasion because the law was not as yet being strictly applied. Nothing seems to have come of this particular accusation against him. In 1934 he was transferred from Barla to İsparta (Şahiner, 1979, 297). By that time, the number of persons who were spreading the message contained in the many lectures he had written was increasing. It is this accumulation of followers and disciples acquiring increasing renown as the "students of *Nur*" which seems to have alerted the government. Bediüzzaman was transferred to Eskişehir under military escort and placed in the town jail (1935). The conditions in which the prisoners lived seem to have been particularly bad. Said Nursi was eventually condemned to eleven months in jail as the author of the pamphlets which had been found in the houses of his disciples. Fifteen of his followers were condemned to six months in jail and 105 were acquitted.

In his defense, Said Nursi stated that whatever writings he had written, he, nevertheless, had not published anything that would be counter to the new secular laws. He also pointed out that reading the brochures, the totality of which were now called the *Risale-i Nur* (*The Epistle of Light*), was a means of shoring up law and order, not of undermining it. He was not trying to set up a new *tarikat* and this for a simple reason: many people who were not members of a religious order had been able to go to paradise but none who lacked faith had been able to achieve this. The point, then, was to encourage faith, not to spread religious orders. One of the questions he asked was the following: taking someone like himself who had shown his mettle in the defense of Turkish national goals, would it be dangerous to have some Turks establish a bond of "brotherhood in the hereafter" (*ahret kardeşi*) with him? "I am before all else a Muslim . . . ," he argued, "but I did serve the Turks and of all the services I rendered, ninety-nine percent were to the Turks." He added: "In Asia it is religion which is the dominant force. There can be no doubt that the Republican regime which may be seen as the commanding force in Asia will try to take advantage of this force." Said was arguing that his teachings constituted a force for good in two respects: as a support for law and order inside Turkey, and also as a means of eliciting the sympathy of the other Asian nations. Again, this was a point at which Said Nursi showed remarkable perspicacity.

In 1936 Bediüzzaman was released. He was sent to Kastamonu under a gendarme escort. He remained there for seven years. He had retained contacts with İsparta, in particular with the villages of Bedre, İlema, Kuleönü, İslamköy, Sav and Atabey (Şahiner, 1979, 310). These were villages where veritable rural printing presses had sprung up and where his works were being copied for distribution. One person in this network, known as the "*Nur* Exchange" was the *imam* of the village of Bedre, Sabri Efendi, who made thousands of duplicates of the letters which Said sent to followers. It is stated that 60,000 copies of the various chapters of what was to become the *Risale-i Nur* were distributed at this time (*Ibid.*). This figure is obviously exaggerated but that his message was beginning to be heard in the surrounding area is clear.

In Kastamonu the same activity continued. To the lycée students who came to him because they stated they had been given no knowledge about God (Şahiner, 1979, 314), he answered:

> All of the sciences which you are studying proclaim the name of God in their own terms and testify to the name of a creator. (Şahiner, 1979, 314 and for confirmation, Abdullah Yeğin in *Aydınlar Konuşuyor*, 245)

In 1943 Bediüzzaman was again arrested and taken to Ankara. He was thereafter exiled to Denizli. All of his followers, a total of 126, gathered from İsparta, Kastamonu and other towns, were arrested. A jury made up of experts on religion were given the task of looking through his writings. They came to the conclusion that these were concerned with faith and religion and that there was no evidence that they constituted the ideology of a secret religious society. In 1944 he and his students were acquitted by the

Denizli higher court. Said was ordered to establish obligatory residence in Emirdağ near Afyon, where he was under constant observation.

In 1948 (Şahiner, 1979, 347) Said once again was accused of establishing a secret society with political goals. It is quite clear that this time his followers were very badly treated while in prison under arrest. In December 1948 he was condemned to 20 months in jail; one of his followers was condemned to 18 months, and twenty to six months each. Said Nursi was being kept in the Denizli prison in preventive detention while his case was being judged. He was released when a general amnesty was proclaimed by the new Demokrat administration in May 1950. After a stay of two years in Emirdağ he moved to Eskişehir; in 1951 he went to İsparta. In 1952, the public prosecutor in Istanbul once more opened a case against him for illegal religious propaganda because of a book entitled *Guide to Youth* which had just been published (in Latin characters since only these were legal since 1928).

Said Nursi's trial became a public event of huge proportions. Now an old man, Said Nursi entered the courtroom supported by university students. He was wearing a black frock and the officially proscribed turban. By the second session of the case—one month later—a large crowd, partly made up of university students, was in attendance in the courtroom and filled the streets. Said Nursi was acquitted. He was once more acquitted in a trial in 1953.

By 1956, with a government somewhat more sympathetic to Islam in office since 1950, Said Nursi announced that it was incumbent upon his followers to support the new Demokrat Party. Thus began a third phase in his life in which he kept personally aloof from politics while encouraging his followers to take part in it. In 1957, for instance, he encouraged his followers to vote for Dr. Tahsin Tola, a Demokrat Party candidate who later edited Bediüzzaman's authorized biography. In 1952, Tola had been tried by his own party for anti-secular (anti-*laic*) activities together with another representative from İsparta, Said Bilgiç.

A letter which Said Nursi wrote to his followers at that time clarifies his stand. To a self-posed question as to why for a time he had given up politics he answered: "I did not engage in politics, because at some point the individual had to sacrifice his desires to the good of the community. It is this common good that the *Risale-i Nur* tries to proclaim." To a second question: "Why do you speak of contemporary 'civilization' as a civilization that has nothing civil in it? Had you not attempted to convince the Nomads of the advantages of civilization and progress?" he answered:

> Because Western civilization as it stands today has contravened the divine fundamental laws, its evils have proved greater than its benefits. The real goals of civilization which are general well-being and happiness in this world have been subverted. Instead of economy and abstemiousness (*kanaat*) we have waste and debauchery, instead of work and service we have laziness and sloth. Thus humanity has simultaneously become very poor and very lazy. The fundamental law of the *Qur'ān*, which originated in the firmament (*semavi*), is that the happiness in life of humanity is in economy and in concentration on work and it is around this principle that the masses and the elite can come together. And to explain this principle which is already in the *Risale-i Nur* let me add one or two points.
>
> First: In the state of nomadism people only needed three or four things. And those who could not obtain these three or four products were two out of ten. The present oppressive Western civilization in consequence of its consumption and waste and the stimulation of its appetites has brought nonessentials to become essentials and because of mores and habituation this so-called civilized man instead of four has twenty needs. And yet he can only obtain two of these twenty. He still needs eighteen. Therefore, contemporary civilization impoverishes man very much . . .
>
> Second: As the *Risale-i Nur* points out, while the radio is a great boon (*nimet*), which has partly been used for social purposes (and, therefore, should elicit our gratefulness) on the other hand, four fifths of it is being devoted to fancy, to superficial matters. . . .

Said concluded that contemporary civilization had reached this impasse because it had diverged from the path of heavenly religion (meaning monotheistic religion—*semavi dinler*).

Said, as is clear from the foregoing, often had to face accusations that he wanted to re-establish the rule of the *şeriat* in Turkey. In fact, the steps by which he believed Islam could be revitalized show a progression which allowed him to argue that he was not, in his own lifetime, engaged in undermining the secular laws of the Turkish Republic. In one of his works, the *Sikke-i Tasdik-i Gaybî*, which is in part an analysis of the signs confirming his divine selection for the task to which he had devoted his life since the 1920s, he emphasized that some of his followers had gone too far, and offered them a clarification of the place of his own contributions to Islam.

The primary duty of the unnamed person (or persons), for whose appearance "sometime in the future" (*ahir zaman*) the Islamic community had been waiting, would be to strengthen faith. The spiritual message which would shape this revitalization had been in process of formation for many centuries. In fact, the Caliph 'Ālī, Sirhindi and Halid had all contributed to it. (There is no particular *Shi'ite* emphasis in this enumeration; for Said, *Shi'ites* were mistaken but retrievable into the bosom of Islam.) Bediüzzaman was one link in this chain. The second duty of the elect of God would be to apply the *şeriat* integrally. This demanded a very great material force and sovereign power which the *Nur* movement could not begin to claim since it had just begun working on the first stage of the program. The third stage was the unification of the Islamic world. He believed his work, the *Risale-i Nur*, would make the *Shi'ites* join forces with the *Sunni*. Bediüzzaman consigned steps two and three to an indefinite future. He advised his followers not to come to the erroneous conclusion that the time was ripe for their implementation.

On the occasion of Turkey's adherence to CENTO, he again pointed out his own support of Muslim union. For him, the true nationality—among others of Turks and Arabs—was Islam (Şahiner, 1979, 389).

Said Nursi was also quite sanguine, now, about the possibilities opened up for the spread of Islam throughout the world:

> The paroxysm of cruelty and oppression of this last World War, with its pitiless destruction and with the misery it imposed upon hundreds for the sake of one enemy; the awesome crushed spirit of the defeated, the indecent haste of the victors and their attempts to shore up their authority, the enormousness of their remorse deriving from their inability to repair the wanton destruction they have wrought, the fact that life on earth is, in any case, ephemeral and transitory and the general perception that the superficial froth of civilization is misleading and anaesthetizing, the fact that the humanitarian aspect of man's higher dispositions has received a tremendous blow, the tumultuous awakening of the feeling for the eternal and the naturally humane inclinations of Man, the smashing by the diamond sword of the *Qur'ān* of the worship for nature, most stupid and treasonable, the unmasking of politics as the deluding, stifling and most widespread face of stupidity and treason, as the result of the manifestation of its true countenance, ugly and oppressive, will, without any doubt whatsoever, lead mankind, as is already apparent in the West and in America, to seek with all its energy its true love and quest which is the life that remains forever (*baki*). And no doubt, the miracle of the declaration of the *Qur'ān* which, in a span of 1,360 years has gathered 350 million students in every country, whose every truth and goal millions of believers in truth have confirmed and sealed with their signature, which is a sacred presence in the hearts of millions of *Qur'ān* readers every minute, whose language provides lessons for humanity and the good news of continuing life and eternal happiness and treats the wounds of mankind in ways unequalled, who through its thousands of vessels . . . backed by unshakeable

> proof, possibly tens of thousands of times, will if humanity does not completely lose its head, be sought by Sweden, Norway, Finland, and England whose celebrated orators are trying to get the *Qur'ān* accepted as well as by the very important American association whose goal is to find the right religion (*din-i hak*), and having understood its proofs will cling to it with all the might of their soul and life. (*Sikke-i Tasdik-i Gaybî*, 6–7)

Until 1956, the *Risale-i Nur* could still be prosecuted because it was published in Arabic characters. Tahsin Tola, obtained permission for it to be published in Latin characters. A second important publication was the authorized biography of Said Nursi which was printed in 1958 and began to sell at a relatively high price for the time.

In the last months of 1959 Said Nursi visited a number of provincial towns, everywhere attracting huge crowds. That part of the press which saw itself as a protector of the principle of laicism began to sound the alarm. Even in his last writings Said Nursi continued to stress the theme of altruism and dedication. It was these qualities, he said, which would triumph against egoism, self-centeredness, the qualities which modern civilization fostered. But there was an ambiguity in Said's demand of dedication. Was it dedication so that common social goals could be attained, or was it dedication to the *Nur* community which was in the process of dawning? This question had not been resolved when he died. In January 1960 Said Nursi's followers in Ankara decided to invite him to the capital. Said was now in residence at Emirdağ in the vicinity of Afyon. He set out for Ankara but was stopped by the police and sent back to Emirdağ; he was forbidden to move from the city.

Said Nursi died and was buried in Urfa. Three months later a military coup overthrew the Demokrat Party. In July 1960 he was disinterred and his bones were transported by military plane to the vicinity of Isparta, where he was buried in an unknown place in the mountains. This seemed to be a fitting end to the brilliant little mountain boy who had appeared more than eighty years before out of nowhere with a new view of the uses to which Islam should be placed.

Possibly the most interesting aspect of the writings of Said Nursi is that those which appeared after 1925 do not mention the caliphate as a central Muslim institution. This may be linked to his belief that the caliphate should be fused with the corporate personality of representative institutions (Mürsel, 1976, 273). The focus of his discourse is the believer in his interaction with his fellow believers. This shift of emphasis from the leader of Islam to the Islamic community as such was only to be gradually accepted in other Islamic societies. That Said Nursi should have dispensed with it so easily may well be an additional proof of a theme which appears again and again in his life history: the need to mobilize Muslims as *individuals* and as members of a *community* but not as *subjects* of a political order. This denial of the primacy of politics and the stress he placed on social mobilization is, possibly, that aspect of his theories which caused the greatest apprehension for the rulers of the Republic.

CHAPTER III

Religion, Ideology and Consciousness in the Ottoman Empire at the End of the Nineteenth Century

> It is hardly possible to exaggerate the evil influence of the Turkish newspapers. The old "storytellers" of the bazaars and cafes have given place to the newspaper reader, the arrival of the mail is watched for, and the reader at the cafe is surrounded by listeners who carry away to their villages such versions of politics as is contained in the articles of 'Vakit', 'Hakikat' and other papers. The hostile feeling against England has been entirely created in this manner. Arabi Pasha is looked upon as a champion of Islam. . . .
>
> Lt. Col. Wilson to [Lord] Duffries, August 25, 1882 (Farooqi, 1983).

The pluralization of social life-worlds has a very important effect in the area of religion. Through most empirically available human history, religion has played a vital role in providing the overarching canopy of symbols for the meaningful integration of society. The various meanings, values and beliefs operative in a society were ultimately 'held together' in a comprehensive interpretation of reality that related human life to the cosmos as a whole. Indeed, from a sociological and socio-psychological point of view, religion can be defined as a cognitive and normative structure that makes it possible for man to feel 'at home' in the universe. This age-old function of religion is seriously threatened by pluralization. Different sectors of social life now come to be governed by widely discrepant meanings and meaning systems. Not only does it become increasingly difficult for religious traditions, and for the institutions that embody these, to integrate this plurality of social life-worlds in one overarching and comprehensive world view, but even more basically, the plausibility of religious definitions of reality is threatened from within, that is, within the subjective consciousness of the individual. (Berger, Berger and Kellner, 1973)

SAID NURSI WAS born in a region of Turkey which exhibited a particular structure, that of a semi-tribal society in which figure both nomadic and sedentary groups. His mature thought, however, was the product of a confrontation with a process of Ottoman modernization and secularization which had begun far away from his birthplace. This process had been initiated in the Ottoman capital and had been proceeding since the 1840s, raising such issues as the permissible extent of secularization in an Islamic society. Said Nursi had to face both these developments and their repercussions three times during his lifetime. In the first instance he had become aware that large scale changes had taken place in the Muslim definition of administration through his contact with Ottoman administrative institutions during his early years in Bitlis and Van. In the second instance, he eagerly participated in the subdued discussions and controversies concerning Islam, culture and progress that were current in the capital during his stay there in 1896–98. The experience recurred and took a much larger scope after the Young Turk revolution, and during his residence in the capital in 1918–21. But what he had to face were not only debates concerning the applicability of "modernity" in the Ottoman Empire. He had to confront the structural consequences of the modernization policy that had been followed since the middle of the nineteenth century. For instance, a consequence of these policies had been an increasing gap between persons educated in the new educational institutions established by the reformers and the population which still owed its educational formation to the *medrese* system. His preaching was partly addressed to those who had been left out of the modern stream. He also had to work with an ideologization of Islam which had taken shape after 1870. These various outcomes of the *Tanzimat* reforms which confronted Said Nursi should also be placed in the context of an asymptotic convergence toward the ideal-typical Weberian model of a rationalized, bureaucratized, disenchanted society. The following is a description of this historical process. It is only remembering that Said Nursi's proposals were formulated within such an "immersion" into historical developments that we can make sense of them. In the following chapter I try to pinpoint the extent of the religious change to which he had become an heir.

Islam: Stability and Change

Often, words mislead by their implied promise of stable, unchanging meanings. Thus the word "Islam" is used to describe the dominant religion in the Ottoman Empire both at the beginning and at the end of the nineteenth century. In fact, Islam was a different sort of enterprise at each one of these moments. Were "Islam" to be used purely in the context of early nineteenth century Ottoman history, it would still be misleading since it would refer to two divergent realities: on the one hand, state-supported, orthodox religion, on the other, folk Islam, a force shaped by more elusive and subterranean forces operating at the grass roots level. Matters became more complex during the nineteenth century. A process of differentiation brought about the gradual separation of the sphere of religion from politics, and the leadership of the political elite began to look askance at the Islamic component of Ottoman culture. The Muslim lower classes did not follow the rulers in this secular stance, and the cleavage between the governing elite and the governed, which had always existed, became starker and now refocused on a religious axis. Paradoxically, this was a time when the elite was becoming increasingly dependent upon the masses: the program of modernization of Ottoman institutions could succeed only if it obtained the acquiescence and support of a plurality of the population. Participation was a much more central aspect of the new system that the Ottoman reformist statesmen were sponsoring than it had been of the traditional Ottoman system. The architects of the *Tanzimat* realized their need to rely on participation, but they saw this as a purely economic concern on the one hand, and as one of a consociation of religious groups on the other. Neither did they realize the ideological backlash of modernization: in the 1840s modernism meant a carefully controlled, nevertheless clearly discernible program of secularization, but already in the 1860s and 1870s educated Turks were rediscovering the use of religion as a social cement. A more detailed picture of these institutional and ideological development follows. In the most general sense, the ideologization of religion brought with it a rigidity which contrasted with the relative tolerance, the adaptability to local circumstances of the antecedent system.

The Religious Hierarchy

The corps of doctors of Islamic law was one of the central institutions regulating the functioning of Ottoman society. Its vital role can best be understand in function of the occupations it controlled. Before the *Tanzimat,* judges and jurists, professors and teachers, doctors and healers, priests and mystics, mathematicians and logicians, astronomers and astrologists, musicologists and librarians and, to a much lesser degree, administrators and officials originated almost exclusively in the so-called "learned institution," the *ilmiyye*.

At the beginning of the *Tanzimat* a number of groups could be discerned among the *'ulema*. These groups were also strata within a hierarchically organized institution where prestige and power clustered towards the top. At the apex of the pyramid figures a well-heeled "patriciate", the members of which occupied the higher positions in the judiciary. In theory, these posts could only be filled by persons who had graduated from institutions of higher learning which capped the entire religious edifice. In fact, long before the 19th century, persons who belonged to the influential families of *molla*s (incumbents in the position of superior court justices) were given special consideration, and the examination for the post was a mere formality in their case (Repp, 1971, 31). Often the judicial post to which the *molla* was appointed was farmed out to *naib*s (substitute judges), who were sometimes illiterate ("Naip", *I.A.*, IX, p.50).

Yet the *kadı*, the magistrate, to whom fell most of the responsibility for the day-to-day administration and distribution of justice before the *Tanzimat*, had always been a mainstay of Ottoman administration. *Kadı*s had relatively low subsidies, although these seem to have been higher than those granted to the teaching profession. Due to the overcrowding of the profession, the term of office of the *kadı* had eventually shrunk to 12 months. After this term, they were shifted to inactive duty and had to wait for another appointment to receive a full salary. The temptation to recoup one's losses during the short term of office was overwhelming and resulted in the corruption of the judiciary (Karal, *Tarih*, VI, 138; "Ilmiyye" *E.I.*[2], III, 1152–1154). At the bottom of this hierarchical pyramid of the learned institution could be found students living off the endowments of pious foundations and *medreses*.

The Ottoman reform movement which had preceded the *Tanzimat* had begun by establishing a new army and by trying to uncover new sources of taxations to support the creation of a standing army. It was extended after 1839 with the creation of a new administrative, judicial and educational network. The reform movement had originated in the higher ranks of the emerging Ottoman bureaucracy. This corps, whose ancestry was the staff of officials trained in the Palace School, had a much more secular cast than the body of *'ulema* trained in *medreses*. The early reform of the army was not a direct threat to the *'ulema*. In fact, some higher ranking *'ulema* had collaborated with the reforms of Selim III (1789–1807) and Mahmud II (1808–

1839). It was only with the gradual westernization of Ottoman institutions that their position was undermined. Progressively eased out of the central processes of government, they were also denied all but marginal roles in administration, in the judiciary and in the educational system. When the deeper basis of their power—their legitimizing role—was questioned, then only did they raise a more or less organized protest.

To recapture the complex set of attitudes one discerns among the religious personnel of the Ottoman Empire during the nineteenth century one has also to remember that at the beginning of the nineteenth century, religion and religious institutions were still part of the Ottoman governmental and administrative machine. It is familiarity with political roles and issues which enabled some eighteenth and nineteenth century *'ulema*—admittedly a minority among them—to place the preservation of the Ottoman state through modernizing reform at the head of their priorities. This also explains why some of them collaborated with the Ottoman reformist statesmen of the *Tanzimat* (1839–1976). The secularizing policies of the men of the *Tanzimat* gradually deprived the higher *'ulema* of their share in the preparation, elaboration and execution of state policy. Religion was gradually segregated from judicial and administrative affairs, and educational institutions were secularized. Many of the official positions which demanded statesmanly behavior as well as theological learning from incumbents were severed from the sources of power. An example may be provided in the changes which occurred in the composition of the Imperial Council, the Divan, in 1837. The two chief justices (*kazasker*) sitting on the council were turned over to the office of the *şeyhülislâm*, the highest religious authority in the Empire. "Thus the latter's office, which was originally only for interpretation and consultation on religious-legal matters concerning temporal affairs, became the highest office of the judiciary regarded as "religious" and having jurisdiction only over Muslims, and believed to remain beyond the scope of reform" (Berkes, 1964, 98). More important, even, had been the decision which turned the administration of pious foundations over to a new ministry established (1826) for that purpose, the Ministry of *Evkaf* (*E.I.*^{2}, III, 1153; Unat, 1964, 2). Later the income of pious foundations was siphoned away by various budgetary changes ("Vakıf," *I.A.*, fasc. 137, 1982, 184). It is true that in the *Tanzimat* era a number of *'ulema* were nominated to government posts, either after they had agreed to be "defrocked" or even when they maintained their positions as clerics, but this was different from the institutionally legitimized, politically influential positions they had enjoyed before the *Tanzimat*.

The strains introduced among the *'ulema* by the secularization of the judicial and educational system were of two types. On the one hand, the *'ulema* had been relegated to a narrow field of political influence; on the other, their occupational opportunities were narrowed. They had to relinquish control of a number of occupational slots which they had almost monopolized in the past. Thus the position of imperial physician (*hekimbaşı*) which was filled by Abdülhak Molla (1786–1865), was turned over to the civil branch of government after 1836 ("Hakīm-Bashī", *E.I.*[2], III, 339–340). The effect of this transformation was to be seen somewhat late because at the beginning of the reform movement personnel with modern training were unavailable and the positions continued to be filled by old style incumbents with religious training.

The changes introduced into the judicial system, the establishment of a system of secular courts parallel to the religious courts, also, did not require the judicial personnel to abandon their posts at once; the change was gradual. Here, turbaned (i.e. religious) personnel continued to fill the position of judge for a long time. Many of the new secular positions had to be staffed by *'ulema*. Also, special schools were established to train competent *kadı*s and, later, to teach the new skills of advocate of public prosecutor as well as matters of procedure to those candidates who were still considering a career in the *şer'i* courts. But few *âlim*s took advantage of this olive branch.

Public instruction was placed in a new secular frame in an uncompromising manner by the creation in 1846 of a Ministry of Public Instruction (Unat, 1964, 19). In 1847 the state took hold of primary education by replacing the old system of neighborhood schools financed by charitable grants or private support by a system of state financed primary schools (Unat, 1964, 38). The program of primary schools was also modified. Prior to the *Tanzimat*, primary instruction had consisted in learning the *Qur'ān* by rote together with reading, writing and elementary notions of arithmetic. Some of the better primary schools concentrated on non-*Qur'ānic* education, but the majority emphasized *Qur'ānic* recitation. Now, extra-*Qurānic* learning was given increased weight ("Mektep", *I.A.*, 652–659, here 656; Unat, 1964, 2–3). In the 1850s and the 1860s a new system of post-primary education began to spread throughout Turkey. This major educational achievement of the *Tanzimat* was the *rüşdiye*, the capstone of the *Tanzimat*'s policy for general education and the training of cadres. It created a pool of persons who could be recruited to government offices and who could fill in the personnel needs of the reformers. The spread of the *rüşdiye* was followed by a wave of lycée building inspired by the program of French lycée. Between 1882 and 1900 Ottoman provincial capitals each gradually acquired a lycée (Unat, 1964, 45). The secularization of education had continued even earlier with the establishment of educational institutions of university level. The French *grandes écoles* provided the model here. One of the earliest of these was the School of Political Science (1859) (Unat, 1964, 70). Beginning with the 1880s, executive posts in the administration were increasingly staffed by graduates of these schools. A new, secular law school began to function in the terminal classes of the lycée of Galatasaray in 1875. Galatasaray itself had been founded in 1868 as an experiment in French education on Turkish soil (Davison, 1963, 246–248). A secular faculty of law was founded in 1880 (Mardin, 1946, 238; Unat, 1964, 74).

Nevertheless, the attempt to establish a university in 1869 failed. The *'ulema* objected to a lecture which showed that some of the basic concepts of Islam could be interpreted from a perspective which echoed a controversial "gnostic" intepretation of the role of prophethood. (The position of the *nabī* as contrasted with that of the *walī;* Berkes, 1964, 185–187, compare with Schimmel, 1980 for a better insight into the problem.) As in the case of the dispute involving the draft of a civil code, which had occurred in the late 1860s, this reaction pointed to a new hardening of attitude among the *'ulema.* Their sensitivity stood at the confluence of a number of currents which seemed to meet in the 1860s. First, one could notice a stronger stand against Western cultural penetration. This had begun with the riots that followed the edict of 1856, a document which had gone a long way to making Ottoman Muslims and non-Muslims equal under the law.

At the beginning of the *Tanzimat,* when the *'ulema* still constituted the main reservoir of the educated, the new secular schools such as the Military Academy had to a large extent to be staffed by them. In 1853, when twenty-five new middle-schools (*rüşdiye*) were opened up, even though teachers graduated from the new normal school were available, it was still an *âlim,* Vehbi Molla, who became the director of *rüşdiye* education at the Ministry of Public Instruction (Unat, 1964, 43). Often, even the student body of the schools had to be siphoned from the *medrese.*

Because of this overlap of personnel and clientele between the old and new educational system, the inception of reforms did not produce fewer, but more jobs for *'ulema* who were willing to seize this opportunity. The situation gradually changed in the 1870s, when newly trained secular personnel became available as students graduated from new schools.

Reform of the Medrese

The reform of the learned institutions, and, in particular, of the *medrese* system was a subject which *Tanzimat* statesmen would have preferred to ignore. Throughout the nineteenth century, the option of letting the *medrese* system decay further was one which a number of statesmen chose, and this for a good reason. Kemal Efendi (1808–1888), the first Ottoman Minister of Public Instruction had attempted to tackle this issue but faced strong opposition from the *'ulema* and had to be whisked out of Turkey (Ergin, 1939–43, I, 92). The men of the *Tanzimat* were most successful in whittling down the top-heavy judicial aristocracy. By isolating *molla*s from positions of influence, by restructuring the ranks and the salaries of the entire profession, by insisting on competitive examinations for the post of *kadı* (Mardin, 1946, 27) and by creating new centers for the training of judges to acquire competence in the rules of civil procedure as well as in *şer'i* law they gradually transformed this stratum. Cevdet Paşa stated that the *Nakib ül-Eşraf* (Recorder of Descendants of the Prophet) Tahir Bey, who was the doyen of the *'ulema* and who died in A.H. 1278 (circa 1860), was the last "person to live in the style of the old judges" (Ahmet Cevdet, 1953).

By the 1860s the new liberal intelligentsia, as well as the *şeyhülislâmate,* were once more broaching the problem of the reform of the *medrese* system. In 1867, fifteen leading *'ulema* were given the task of studying the reform of the *medrese* and prepared a report on the subject. But the recommendations of the committee were concentrated on matters of form rather than content, one exception being a recommendation that students should study mathematics during their vacation (Unat, 1964, 86). The proposals of the cleric Ali Suavi, who had joined forces with the Young Ottomans, the group of intellectually inclined bureaucrats who challenged the men of the Tanzimat in the 1860s, were similar.

Ali Suavi had very precise criticism to direct against the *medrese* of which he was a product. He had studied *belagat* (*balāgha;* rhetoric), but he could neither understand a sophisticated product of traditional literature nor did he have enough confidence to compose a text according to these traditional canons. He had studied logic, but he could not apply these principles to distinguish right from wrong in his daily life. He had studied religious law (*fıkıh; fiqh*) from classical texts, but he knew no more of theology than a court assessor in Islamic courts (*naib; nā'ib*) could learn from court practice. He had studied systematic theology (*kalam; kalām*), but he had been unable to penetrate the system of thought; he had simply mastered its terminology. He had studied philosophy (*hikmet; ḥikma*), but he found that the problems analyzed by this science were irrelevant. What he had been taught in school as natural science (*hikmet-i tabiiye*) was only a distant cry from modern physics, which had been harnessed in modern times to education and industry. As to classical literature, the only thing it could inspire was immorality, drinking, lust and sensual pleasure, a criticism which was later to be replicated by the publicist Ahmed Mithat Efendi (*Muhbir*, 21 Ramazan 1283, 27 January 1867; Ergin, 1939–1943, I, 88–89). What is interesting about this statement is the extent to which the Victorian ethics of industry and the taming of the material world had become central for Suavi, and made up the substance of his criticism.

The idea of *medrese* reform was one also prompted by others and the most systematic attempt to implement these ideas was offered by Süleyman Paşa, a general who was, for a time, director of military education.

In the months that followed the deposition of Sultan Abdülaziz in 1876, an Ottoman parliament, the first ever, was convened. Parliament also took up the problem of the *'ulema*, and complaints about *âlims* who had received titles without adequate studies were heard once more. But it would appear that one of the main problems even at that time was the training of cadres for secular schools. As one of the leading deputies in the parliament and an *âlim* by profession, stated:

> Some days ago, someone read a statement to the effect that the *medrese* should be abolished. Your humble servant, however, has the following to say. I observe that since the days of the late Sultan Mahmud, many military schools and universities and the like were created. Later, middle schools and lycées were set up. Teachers are being posted to these schools. What I see, however, is that teachers of English and French still come from France and that teachers in the middle schools still come from the *medrese*. (Us, II, 210)

As late as 1892 the official historian of the Empire was lamenting that the *medrese* had not reformed to cover Western scientific subjects (Sungu, 1964, 21). The damage caused by the rift between the new secular schools of the *Tanzimat* and the *medrese* (and the *tekke*) was, as we have seen, to be a prominent theme in Bediüzzaman's ideas.

Sultan Abdülhamid II, who had seen the dethronement of his uncle Abdülaziz sanctified by the *fetva* of the *şeyhülislâm*, had also seen the part played in it by demonstrations of the students of religion who were known to constitute part of the clientèle of the Young Ottomans, who were clamouring for an Ottoman constitution. The ancient Ottoman system of mobilizing these so-called *softa*s against an unpopular government had been used once more on that occasion. The sultan was therefore extremely wary about the revitalization of the learned institution. His tactic was to let the *'ulema* sink into a morass. Only in 1898 was a section on higher religious studies (*Ulûm-u Aliyye-i Diniye*) attached to the newly created Istanbul University (Ergin, 1939–1943, I, 93). Said Nursi could not but he shocked by this attrition of religious studies, which was so different from the liveliness of the *tekke*s of his region.

But the government's policy of change and neglect had unanticipated consequences; with the increasing retrenchment of the profession, a growing number of persons in the religious estate were forced to focus on the primarily religious aspect of their vocation. Religion thus became more of a subject matter or a field of specialization than a pervasive social function. This, in turn, led a number of more intellectualistic clerics to begin to think of the role of religion in society. The trend emerged towards the end of the century and produced a mode of argumentation in defense of religion which was entirely novel.

On the other hand, *'ulema* of lower social origins, who in the past could only have risen by claims to greater moral perfection and/or charismatic powers, could now use the emerging mass media to assume the role of opinion leaders. Their effectiveness in this respect was increased by what appears to have been an emerging Muslim-Ottoman public opinion. This was not entirely a product of the educational reforms of the *Tanzimat* (or of the mass media) since an earlier form of it had existed in Muslim culture. Cevdet Paşa describes the new mode of influence of public opinion by referring to the reserve which was displayed by the congregation attending the burial services of the Grand Vizier Âli Paşa. Âli Paşa had died in 1871. As usual, his coffin was placed in the courtyard of the mosque where prayers would be said for his soul. But when the time came to ask those attending the funeral how they remembered the deceased, there was total silence instead of the usual formula which would release him from the sins committed towards those still alive. This was because of the somewhat abrupt Westernizing policies of the deceased vizier. Cevdet Paşa who had collaborated with the secular reformers on a number of policies in the first years of the *Tanzimat* states that he was careful, thereafter, to refrain from actions which "ran counter to public opinion" (Ahmet Cevdet, 1965, 44).

Cevdet traces the first emergence of public opinion to the Crimean War. It is also instructive that the posting of bills critical of the government became a method of rousing public opinion in mid-century (Ahmet

Cevdet, 1965, 23). A certain amount of propaganda seems already to have accompanied the attempted coup of 1859, which we shall recall was directed by a *Nakşibendi şeyh* (Kuntay, 1949, 687). A synthesis of old and new propaganda patterns was the use of mosque preachers' sermons for constitutionalist agitation by the Young Ottomans in the 1860s. Clearly Islam was acquiring a new "ideological" cast.

The Ottoman Bureaucracy and the Secularizing Reform of the *Tanzimat*

Although the Ottoman secular bureaucracy shared the elaboration of symbols of political legitimation with the *'ulema,* they were often in disagreement with them. Officials saw themselves as the preservers of the sultanic prerogative, a feature of Ottoman rule which had Central Asian antecedents. They had a set of values in which political necessity and reason of state predominated. It is in the light of the survival of the theory of autonomy of the state, and its reinforcement at the end of the eighteenth century by a class of emerging reforming bureaucrats, that we have to view the swiftness with which Ottoman statesmen adopted policies which displaced the *'ulema* from their influential position in government. It would be difficult, otherwise, to understand how a personality such as the statesman and minister of public instruction Saffet Paşa (1814–1883) could, in the 1870s, urge Turkey to accept the "civilization of Europe in its entirety; in short, to prove itself a "civilized state" (Berkes, 1964, 185 quoting a letter of Saffet). This statement was not part of public declaration, but Saffet Paşa did also put himself on record in similarly strong-worded public statements (Berkes, 1978, 234).

The distance travelled by Saffet in relation to his early life is quite remarkable, since he was trained in the *medrese.* The formative influence in his youth, however, was that he was very early apprentice to a bureau of the Ministry of Foreign Affairs. This was the bureau in which the careers of other reformist statesmen before him had been shaped.

The policies of the leading statesmen of second generation *Tanzimat* leaders such as Âli Paşa and Fuad Paşa show an increasing propensity to disregard the *'ulema*. Both statesmen realized that some cultural anchor for the Ottomans was necessary, but believed that good government and the development of commerce and education would fill the gap left by the gradual receding of Islam. This rationalism was shared by many future reformers of Turkey who had a similar disregard for the function of religion. In fact, the 1870s represent a point at which the pragmatism of an Ottoman bureaucracy which had allowed them to welcome reform was imperceptibly being transformed into support for a positivistic world view.

The hoary Ottoman bureaucratic tradition had, by the time the *Tanzimat* reforms were initiated, created a fund of secular legislation and legislative practice. This predisposed the builders of the *Tanzimat* to visualize statutory regulations as the lever which would ensure the implementation of their plans. The *Tanzimat* was thus characterized by a flood of statutes, regulations, laws and by-laws ("Düstur", *E.I.*^{2}, IV, 640). In the era preceding the *Tanzimat* there had been overt collisions between religious law (*şeriat*) and statute law (*kanun*), the enactment of which was controlled by officials who regarded the interests of the state as ultimately overriding all other considerations ("Ḳānūn", *E.I.*^{2}, IV, 560).

The increased volume of regulations was, by its very nature, secular. It originated in the bureaux of the Porte, and set very specific targets for the implementations of administrative, financial or educational policies. The practice was not an innovation, but new administrative rationale and regulations which had been "exceptions" in the past were becoming the core of the system. The religious law content of administrative practice was also on its way out. Central to this change was the transfer of the administrative functions of the magistrate, the kadi, to a new official, the administrative employee.

Gradually, also, as mentioned above, a system of secular courts emerged where the cases adjudicated were those which arose in the application of the new legal corpus of the *Tanzimat* (Shaw and Shaw, II, 118–119; Berkes, 1978, 170 cf., 216). The religious law, the *şeriat*, thus became more clearly a matter of private law and was relegated to the *şer'i* courts which dealt primarily with matters of personal status such as marriage and inheritance. But already in the 1860s, there appeared a reaction against this trend. As a consequence of the widespread application of the *Tanzimat* codes which had been copied from Western law codes, principles of civil law as they appeared in the Code Napoleon had begun to infiltrate Ottoman legal practice. In addition, *Tanzimat* codes had been revised on an *ad hoc* basis without a common rationale being devised. A group of Ottoman statesmen led by Kabuli Paşa now proposed that the Code Napoleon be adopted in its entirety by the Ottoman Empire. The proposal was rejected. Ahmed Cevdet Paşa, a doctor of Islamic law who had started his career by being detached from a "clerical" professorship to serve as an advisor to the leader of the reform movement Mustafa Reşid Paşa, had objected with the argument that a civil code was one of the foundation stones of a state; it therefore had to be in harmony with the general spirit animating that state. Cevdet Paşa's view received the approval of the Council of Ministers (Mardin, 1946, 66) which appointed him to chair a committee to codify Muslim law in areas corresponding to those covered by the civil code (1868). The basic document that emerged from the work of this committee, the *mecelle* (*majalla*), was drafted after years of discussion and was never completed, but it is considered a monument of Ottoman jurisprudence.

While the religious hierarchy was depoliticized and its religious role highlighted, the *'ulema* were not completely dispossessed: within two decades of the inception of the *Tanzimat*, the problem of political mobilization brought with it the question of the formula to adopt as a guideline for the reform movement. This search for a political and social formula, and a principle of legitimation, opened up a new field for *'ulema* ideological thrust and influence at a time when a new interest for religion was appearing among a younger generation of bureaucrats. Their ideas provided grist for the mill of the developing Ottoman press. Ali Suavi, an ex-*medrese* man took up the writing of provocative, politically motivated leading articles for the *Muhbir* in the 1860s. This new role potential of the *'ulema* is one of the reasons for which clerics appear in the ranks of the Young Ottomans, in these years.

By the 1860s *'ulema* and persons with a conservative religious attitude had begun to realize that a real *Kulturkampf* was in the offing and that they might be on the losing side of the battle. Here, too, Islam could not remain silent: the theme of the cultural content of Islam as a civilization was brought out and its superiority to Western civilization emphatically affirmed. The more intellectualistic of these schemes were produced by a basically secular intelligentsia—the Young Ottomans being the clearest example—working to revive Islamic cultural premises. The need to find a foundation for the Ottoman state which was more *explicit* than the traditional formula—"the state and religion are twins"—was rising. This need was the direct result of the new discourse introduced with secular schools and the secular literature which was on the way to becoming the new language of educated Turks. The newer Islam used by ideologues as a legitimizing discourse and a cultural foundation was undoubtedly different from traditional Islam. On the other hand, the *'ulema* seemed to be able to devise an Islamic populism appealing to the traditionalist masses more readily than was the case with the secular intelligentsia.

While the *Tanzimat* statesmen had scored some success in displacing the *'ulema* from administration, education and the judiciary, the mobilization of resources necessary for their plan to fully succeed could only be achieved by harnessing the energies of their subjects to a new political formula providing wider political participation for these subjects. The *Tanzimat* statesmen were wary of initiating too rash a movement in this direction, and it was left to their critics of the 1860s, the Young Ottomans, to make an issue of the matter. The latter realized that the thrust of reform was towards creating a nation-state. The viability of this state was dependent upon solidarity and support by the mass of the population, and their proposal of representative government followed from this premise.

The *Tanzimat* statesmen had tackled the problem in the light of a theory of the enlightenment which postulated the basic similarity of men. To the question "How can one make Muslim and non-Muslim subjects of the Ottoman Empire support the same political formula?" the answer of the *Tanzimat*'s advisors had been "by good government." Good government was a religiously neutral practice which for administrative purposes could bring together the religious group into which the Ottoman Empire had been traditionally divided. To the *Tanzimat* statesmen's proposal of good government framed by an enlightened despotism, their foes, the Young Ottomans, replied by their own conception of good government as defined by constitutional liberalism: for them it was *participation* in the process of government which would rally Muslims to reforms and eliminate the barriers between different religious groups. It was in this way that one could create an Ottoman patriotism which would elicit allegiance to the Ottoman state regardless of religious affiliation. But at the time the Young Ottomans first formulated their theories, in the 1860s, Patriotism had already been overtaken by a new formula, Nationalism. It emerged by fastening onto a sense of identity that had already been built up by the non-Muslim religious communities in the Empire and promoted by their churches. That this identity could often turn out to be fictitious was beside the point. An institutional boundary for a new identity was sought by non-Muslim Ottomans and, ambiguous or not, some root of identity was located by the Greeks, Serbs, Romanians, Bulgarians and Armenians in their several churches. Even the Greek-Orthodox community, which had incorporated sub-communities such as the Serbs, was split by the new national aspiration of Serbs and Bulgarians.

The Church origins of Balkan proto-nationalism shows how established the practice had been for churches to act as vessels of identity in the traditional system. This was also, therefore, a time when Muslim Ottomans similarly began to ponder on the ability of the Muslims within the Empire to re-group as Muslims. From this followed reflections on the suitability of Islam as a social cement. Pan-Islam was the international dimension of this revival of interest for Islam and was an Ottoman answer to Russia's sponsoring of pan-Slavism. There is, then, a politicizing and ideologizing of Islam which emerges as we proceed along the 19th century, in response to political developments. Said Nursi was thoroughly aware of this dimension of religion.

Structural Change and Change in Consciousness

Ottoman secularization had started with officials wresting a number of institutions away from the *'ulema* in the fourth decade of the nineteenth century. Accounts of the developments which were thus set in motion are now widely available, although it would be difficult to say that they supersede the first, brilliant, essay on the *Tanzimat* by Engelhardt (1882). These descriptions, however, only initiate an understanding of social change. In order to bring fresh understanding to a period of history now well covered by competent research, one has to try to unravel the social-structural transformation which was precipitated by the *Tanzimat*.

The first finding in this respect, is that some individuals set themselves against Ottoman reform because they had the rug pulled out from under them: the positions which they filled were given to others or eliminated (İnalcık, 1973). I have attempted to show above that this was not the main cause for the somewhat later development of a new rallying around Islam, and that the use of Islam as a *banner*, i.e., as a means to elicit the ideological-mobilizational energizing of Ottoman Muslims, was also involved. A second element in the situation was the frustration of upper and lower class Ottomans when faced with new institutions. This was not because the *Tanzimat* officials enforced reforms with bayonets, but because they had changed the rules of the practice of social relations and seemed to continue to change them as the *Tanzimat* proceeded. The desperation of those who clung to the old culture and its system of knowledge becomes clearer when we remember that knowledge is a system which has a much larger background than the individual items it subsumes. It includes "a vast body of . . . knowledge which is present and taken for granted in . . . everyday consciousness, although of course [any person] . . . does not possess this larger knowledge" (Berger, *et. al.*, 1973, 30). Effectiveness was dependent on learning the new rules of the game, comprising not only school knowledge but all kinds of attitudes to which this knowledge was linked, and the set of philosophical premises underlying them.

Another way of taking stock of popular reactions, themselves affected by the changing cast of Islam at the time, is to remember that Islam had already been transformed by the third decade of the 19th century. It had stopped being something which was lived and not questioned. Secularizing reforms had made Islam more "Islamic"; religion emerged on its own well-delineated field. A rationale had to be devised for this new religion. Soon, religion became identified with the civilization of the Arabs (Smith, 1962). For Ahmet Cevdet Paşa, the same motivation led to his painstaking elaboration of the Muslim legal code which we know as the *mecelle.* Middle-of-the-road Muslim reformers also went on to separate the cultural core of Islam from its implementation in everyday life. This postulated cultural core was now considered as important and as characteristically Islamic as the ritual side of Islam.

Thus, culture as a setting becomes increasingly important in understanding what was happening to Ottoman society at the end of the nineteenth century, and this may be observed among the religious-minded of all walks of life: *'ulema* who had not been pre-empted by the *Tanzimat* were elaborating their own theories about the superiority of Islam and its contribution to democracy or science. Clerics close to the lower classes, like Ali Suavi, on the other hand, were trying to revive what they saw as the direct democracy of pristine Islam as a way of life. As for the lower classes, a feeling that the hegemonic position of Muslims had been shaken by the reforms was accompanied by a nostalgia for the looseness of the old society, its ability to compromise at all times, its swift reversals of good fortune due to despotic caprice which could destroy the rich and the mighty at one blow.

Pre-*Tanzimat* education had focused on revelation. The pattern of revelation found in the *Qur'ān,* its symbolism, its cues as to preferred attitudes and approved conduct was the filter through which one had to work in every field of endeavor. Religion was the frame through which the common man understood his obligations of citizenship. In this sense the *Qur'ān* had had a "mythical," Malinowskian, function. Its guidelines allowed enough elasticity to take into account many different situations. Education centered on the *Qur'ān* at the primary school level provided a common ethical foundation: it was the equivalent of Western humanities.

The *Qur'ān* had been the device that enabled the various Muslim sciences to claim that they had the same religious foundation. But, in fact, this foundation did not allow for the type of permutations and combinations which were the stuff of modern Western science. The Enlightenment schema of knowledge was different at one crucial point: it rested on the conception of a universal cognitive currency which enabled combinations of items of knowledge unheard of its societies where knowledge was compartmentalized. Ernest Gellner has spoken of this as follows:

> By the common or single conceptual currency I mean that all facts are located within a single continuous logical space, that statements reporting them can be conjoined and generally related to each other, so that, in principle, one single language describes the world and is internally unitary; or on the negative side, that there are no special, privileged, insulated facts or realms, protected from contamination or contradiction by others, and living in insulated, independent logical spaces of their own. (Gellner, 1983, 21)

Mathematics as the operator of this single conceptual currency was different from Islamic mathematics which was embedded in a religious field. In fact, not only the ideas propagated by modern education but its very operation showed marks of the new conceptual currency insofar as it was rationalized and depersonalized.

One master, initiating his students into the intricacies of the classics in his own field, and, in secondary studies, one book, learned by rote, passed around from student to student, brought out of the cupboard to resolve new questions; these were the central features of the old educational system. Now, with the *rüşdiye* and the Ottoman *grandes écoles* a new system emerged: schoolbooks for all, or at least for those who had passed the entrance examinations. This was a major cultural watershed, for it replaced a system of face-to-face contacts in learning and teaching. The personalistic aspect of the old system was not different from that which prevailed throughout traditional Ottoman social relations. It was by such bonds of personal relations that this society had been structured. Even status was transacted through personal relations. Now, through the reform of the educational system, a number of modifications were working cumulatively to change this personalistic dimension of social structure.* The master was increasingly replaced by his textbooks. Encyclopedias, dictionaries (printed dictionaries replacing the rhyming dictionaries of old), manuals, novels,

*In primary school "writing" had meant "calligraphy," not the ability to write a text; now the second took over (Ergin, 1939–43, I, 70–73).

were the new fountainhead of knowledge. Mehmet Kaplan has stated that it was "book knowledge" which made the difference between the generation of the 1870s and the generation of the 1890s, which was the first to graduate from the fully operative schools of the *Tanzimat*. Among the latter, it was as if "school and book had severed their links with life" (Kaplan, 1946, 19). Speculation and projection of information culled from books opened up a Pandora's box roughly similar to that which had informed early modern criticism of the text of the Bible in Europe. But even more was afoot: young officials preparing plans for new institutions were now propelled into a realm of abstract possibilities which was beginning to seem much more real than the conglomerate of rickety frame houses, crumbling public buildings and venal officials from which they started. This ability to transcend the present and soar into the future was new for Ottoman thought: at the beginning of the *Tanzimat*, "reform" had had a much shorter conceptual span. The first reformers believed that they were doing much the same as would have been promoted by their hard-headed bureaucratic predecessors. Now, the feeling that reform meant pre-empting an inexorable, if progressively better future was creeping into reformist thought. However, the generation which had first acquired these new tools was not entirely aware of the distance it had travelled from the metaphor of the fulfillment of God's design to that of progress. This speculative, abstracting, utopian and futuristic cast of thought now separated the ignorant from the educated.

The transition from a history in which the perfectibility of man was seen within the frame of an eschatological promise to a plan for a secular utopia, and finally to the idea of "Paradise now" had been gradual. The change was partly due to the influence of Western ideas, but one of the most effective of these had been the idea of youth as the guardian of Turkey's fate. With the establishment of an education system of 11 years duration, with sub-parts fitted into one another and making up a whole, a secular student body different from the body of religious students, was now a reality, and a secular student identity followed. The process went a long way back, to the first years of the *Tanzimat:* when Sultan Mahmud II had opened the School of Military Medicine (1827), he had given a speech to the students and entrusted them with the future of the Ottoman Empire. Youth was moving in to replace the grey beards to which one would have entrusted the Empire in the past. In the 1880s, on the first day of his entrance to the School of Political Science, Ahmed İhsan, a future publisher, heard his director, the historian Abdurrahman Şeref address the students as follows:

> Gentlemen, all of the places you see on the map [which were formerly Ottoman territory] were lost because of ignorance. I consider it a special privilege to have at least fifty young men in the Empire who can understand this map when they see it. Study and apply yourselves; become the informed officials which our country needs. . . . (Tokgöz, 1930, 1, 21–22)

The young men took his words to heart and each in his own way began to make up for lost time.

Just as the *Tanzimat* educational system brought about important changes, so, too, the concept of a field of learning changed. Rather than a product of the educational system, this was more directly related to the general process of differentiation and secularization. Islamic law had covered a wide area where strictly judicial matters were not separate from Muslim ritual. Both were part of a system of religiously grounded obligation. Now Islamic law was becoming a specialty, a technique for the solution of well-delimited problems. Not only were the things that one learned in the schools different, the routines which one used to approach government or to be a useful citizen had been transformed. The Islamic canopy had provided a common language for the rulers and the ruled despite the distance that separated them. Islamic messages were still listened to with respect but had lost their old (limited but real) effectiveness in communicating with the new bureaucrats.

Differentiation had not closed the space between strata or the distance separating persons on the hierarchical ladder; it had increased it. The lazy Janissary, said many travellers to Turkey, lay on the training field and only answered diffidently to commands because there was too much familiarity between him and his officer. Drill the dunces in company formation, mould them into the cohesive pieces of a unit, separate their daily lives from that of their officers, train officers in institutes of higher education and a modern army will emerge. Indeed, at the end of this process of internalizing drill manuals, the Turkish officer looked at his recruits somewhat like the German officer in East Africa would have looked at the *askari*. The military regulation was now the uncompromising "book" which regulated military life from the company level upward. Its rationalized, legalistic spirit was made to ensure unstinting obedience: protest became a real feat of courage.

At the beginning of the *Tanzimat* there had existed an overlap of careers, an absence of systematic thinking about institutions and a set of humanizing relations which were in harmony with the patrimonial cast of the entire society. This diffuseness appeared as chaos to Western observers, but the same apparent disorder was also characterized by a tolerance for dissonances. In this respect, the so-called traditional system was more tolerant than the new system in which rationalization brought in procrustean systematization. It was because the religiously informed intellectuals of the capital and, in particular, persons in the *Mevlevi* community of Istanbul, had detected similar intolerant traits among the *Halidi Nakşibendi* that they had condemned fundamentalism which went counter to the leniency of sophisticated Muslims of the capital (Ziya, n.d., 196). But then, the new, mobilizing political and social stance of the *Nakşibendi*s was more in tune with the 19th century than the broadmindedness of the *Mevlevi*.

The Young Ottomans

The importance that religion as an ideology was acquiring in the Ottoman Empire at the time of the modernization of its institutions is exemplified by the importance that the Young Ottomans accorded to it. These young intellectuals, formed in the bureau of the Porte and widely read in Western sources, were quite aware of the decay of the *medrese* system. They were also aware that in the provinces the local Islamic hierarchy could exert a baneful influence in their capacity as local notables. Yet their leader, Namık Kemal, based the legitimation of his theory of representative government on Islamic premises. A somewhat different theory which he also adopted was that the Ottomans could not cut themselves off from what, in effect, were their basic cultural foundations. Turks could not adopt modern institutions without basing them on deeper foundations. Islam was the mold in which Islamic-Ottoman social personality had crystallized, and Namık Kemal believed this could not be neglected in a new political theory.

There were a number of contexts in which the Islamic cast of Ottoman thought was underlined by Kemal. One was that in the traditional society a kind of rough social justice had been achieved, linked to the transitoriness of political status. Second, the new constitutional system of the Ottomans had to rest on Islamic ethical foundations in order for the entire edifice to stand. Third, while Ottoman constitutionalism would take its inspiration from the *şeriat*, law-making in parliament would be once-removed from the *şeriat* and could, therefore, apply to all the religious groups in the Empire. Finally, the Young Ottomans had followed the development of pan-Slavism with some apprehension and were beginning to wonder whether it did not provide a model for the Ottomans' relations with Muslims dispersed throughout Asia and Africa. The policy would have started by tightening the bonds between the Ottoman Empire and its tributary provinces such as Egypt and Tunisia, with whom the connection had all but snapped (Mardin, 1962, 60). Namık Kemal was aware that changes in world communications had created opportunities for links to be established with other Muslim nations (Özön, 1938, 78, 91).

The true representative of the early pan-Islamist trend thus initiated was the newspaper *Basiret*, which appeared in Istanbul for a decade between 1869 and 1879 ("Ali Efendi", *Aylık Ansiklopedi,* 1929). A Polish exile, Mustafa Celaleddin, who had already begun to write about the prestigious origins of the Turks in Central Asia, was among its major contributors, as was the Young Ottoman, Ayetullah Bey. The *Basiret* had supported Germany in the Franco-Prussian War; at the end of the war, a grateful German government offered its editor, Ali Efendi, a free trip to Germany and a large grant plus a complete set of German presses. After 1876, the *Basiret* began to give increasing importance to Islamic elements in Ottoman culture and to Islamic cultures outside the Ottoman state. To what extent this was a policy still dictated by Ali Efendi's obligation to Germany is a matter for speculation. Interestingly enough, Ali Suavi, the *âlim* who had for a while collaborated with the Young Ottomans, set himself against mechanical pan-Islam in a remarkably cogent way:

> Our semi-official gazette, the *Turquie,* stated that the time has now arrived for the Porte to follow the example of Italy and Prussia, adopt the cause of nationality (*kavmiyyet*) and assemble all Muslims. It is advised that Egypt should be made into just another province like the province of Edirne. Do our ministers realize that the question of nationalities is one special to the Europeans and that we do not have a nationalities problem? Nationality questions would cause our ruin. To gather Muslims together would be at most a religious question but not a question of national origin. (Mardin, 1962, 372)

But while Ali Suavi indicated the political difficulties that were inherent for the Ottoman Empire in following a policy of nationalities, he did not object to Islam being used as a flag to rouse Muslim populations. Sultan Abdülhamid had the finesse to keep these two aspects of pan-Islam separate, and this is probably the reason why it has been difficult to retrace his own steps in the matter.

Sultan Abdülhamid's Islamic Policy

In the draft of the first Ottoman constitution of 1876 prepared by the sultan's liberal grand vizier, Midhat Paşa, there had been no mention of the office of *şeyhülislam* or of state religion. In the next draft, which was finally adopted, there were clauses which delineated the respective positions of the state and of the religious institution. Now, the sultan had executive authority with regard to the application of the *şeriat* as well as in the application of secular laws. The *şeyhülislâm* was included in the council of ministers (Karal, VIII, 303). These were clauses which, no doubt, pleased the sultan, because they provided him with the means of establishing control over the religious institution. The sultan feared the latter because of the extent to which the students of the *medrese* had been involved in the coup against his uncle Abdülaziz. The sultan also looked for an occasion to get rid of the *şeyhülislâm,* Hayrullah Efendi, who had legitimized Abdülaziz's deposition. Hayrullah was exiled to Medina and then to Taif (Gövsa, ed., 174). Thereafter, the sultan kept the *şeyhülislâmate* under strict control (Tahsin, 1931, 39). Nothing was done about a proposal dated 1877 to reform the *medrese* (Unat, 1964, 80).

The fact that some members of the sultan's family were affiliated with Sufi orders caused additional worry for the sultan. The heir to the throne, Mehmed Reşad Efendi, was a member of the *Mevlevi* order. If communication were established between Reşad Efendi and the Çelebi Efendi, the leader of the order, a cabal against the sultan could take shape. The Çelebi Efendi was, therefore, under constant surveillance, and persons who had contacts with him were taken into the sultan's net of suspicion (Tahsin, 1931, 67). During Abdülhamid's reign, meetings of students of religion were forbidden (Karal, 1983, 305). The sultan had a policy of benign neglect towards the *medrese,* one exception being his approval of the establishment of a faculty of theology at the time of the creation of the first university in 1898. But the very name of this faculty showed that the sultan was not a supporter of the *medrese* (Ergin, 1939–43, I, 93). Despite all of these internal controls, the sultan did proceed towards an Islamic policy which bore his own imprint. This was his often misunderstood policy of pan-Islam, which has to be distinguished from his policy vis-a-vis the Arab provinces of the Empire with which it overlapped.

The origins of widespread interest in pan-Islam in the 1870s were complex (Davison, 1963, 274–277), but both intellectuals and governing officials seemed to meet on this common ground. Thus, during the crisis of

1876, which had developed from a confrontation between Christians and Muslims in Bulgaria, a vizirial proclamation stated that those who wanted to destroy the Ottoman state would be faced by "the whole family of Islam" (*Ibid.*, 347) and that troops were being mobilized "in the name of Islam" (*Ibid.*). In 1877, the grand vizier Kâmil Paşa, in a somewhat different vein, was warning the sultan that Ottoman children who were in foreign missionary schools were being torn from their own culture.

The sultan believed that Western civilization could be divided into "technology" and "ideas." Technology was the door to progress, but the "ideas" of the West were poisonous (Karal, 1983, 249–250). It is in this light of Islam as culture that the question as to whether Islam could constitute the principle of internal cohesion for the Empire emerges once again after 1878. As a consequence of its signature of the Treaty of Berlin, the Ottoman Empire had lost considerable territory in Europe. The proportion of the Arabic-speaking population of the Empire had shot up. Sultan Abdülhamid was aware of this change in the demographic balance of Ottoman lands (Karal, 1983, 331), and his concern for the Arabs was so keen that at one time he thought of making Arabic the official language of the Ottoman Empire (Karal, 1983, 546 and Tahsin, 1931, 150–151). Nevertheless, the Emperor also wanted to underline the common cultural element which united Egypt, the Arab portions of the Empire and the Turkish-speaking populations (Karal, 1983, 545–547). He was aware that Islam was a cultural force and a source of Ottoman patriotism (Karal, 1983, 543–546). It could be exploited for the social and political mobilization of his subjects, and also "to create a feeling of hope" among them (Duguid, 1973, 140 quoting Ramsay, 1915–16, 408).

The many strands which appear in any undertaking by the sultan and his secretiveness increase the difficulties of isolating his pan-Islamic policy from his concern for Islam as a principle of solidarity for his subjects. Such a policy did exist and is not simply a reflection of his "superstitious" nature (Abu Manneh, 1979, 138 for a list of theories centered on superstition). Sir W. Ramsay, who trekked through the Meander Valley and adjoining regions in the 1880s and 1890, mentions on the authority of a "foreign consul" how in about 1882 the *delil*s, the men who were organizing the lists of pilgrims, began to be "people of a different class." "They were educated men with whom begging was a mere pretense, and who stirred up people to make a great effort for the regeneration of Mohammedan power" (Ramsay, 1896, 188). This he attributed to the sultan's policy. The international dimensions of that policy appeared in the emissaries he dispatched to Java,

Iran, Turkestan, China, India and Africa. Concurrently, the sultan arranged for delegations from distant lands to pay homage to him (Karal, 1956, 546–547). Both moves projected a new meaning onto the institutions of the caliphate, that of the protection of Muslims throughout the world.*

A second facet of pan-Islam involved the sultan's use of Muslim religious orders. In the nineteenth century, these had "anticipated the need for reform," rejecting "such practices as compromised the unity and transcendence of God" and stressing "a return to the simplicity of mythical, unadulterated Islam" (Trimingham, 1973, 104). Nineteenth century Sufi revivalism resulted in the creation of a number of new orders, redirected the energies of some of the most venerable and "was primarily directed towards and effective in missionary activities" in fringe areas of the Muslim world (Trimingham, 1973, 132). This development served the sultan in his own policy of fighting colonialism by working for the disaffection of the Muslim populations under colonial rule. We know that he used the *Halidi-Nakşibendi şeyh*s—as well as others—in the 1880s (Le Chatelier, 1910, 54–58; Gündüz, 1984, 304).

To give the institution of the caliphate a new gloss, and to underline the image of his leadership of all Muslims, the sultan needed a somewhat different policy, and here he had the assistance of the Arab *şeyh* Abul Hudā al-Sayyādī (1850–1909). Abul Hudā was from a family with roots in a town near Aleppo (Abu Manneh, 1979, 131). By 1875, he had already scored some success in a career in the Learned Institution (*Ibid.*, 134). His conservative leanings earned him the confidence of the sultan, who brought

---

*The sultan suspected that one of the persons intriguing to undermine his caliphate was the Khedive of Egypt (Hirsowicz, 1972, 303). Similar dangers originated in Arabia. From the very beginning of his reign the sultan had tried to honor and placate Arabia by placing the provinces of Mecca and Medina at the head of Ottoman provinces in government listings. In the late 1880s the sultan made a special effort to recruit Arab students from the Hijaz, Yemen and Tripolitania into the Military Academy (Ergin, 1939–1943, III, 973). In 1892, he established the "Tribes School" (*Aşiret Mektebi*) in Istanbul. This school was to recruit the children of prominent leaders in Arabia and to use the graduates to enhance feelings of attachment to the empire (Ergin, 1939–43, III, 980; Karal, 1962, 401). Later, children of Albanian and East Anatolian notables were brought in. The school was closed in 1907 following a food riot which seems to have been a preliminary to more concrete demands (Ergin, 1939–43, III, 973).

him to Istanbul as an "adviser" (*Ibid.*, 137). There, Abul Hudā set to work in propagating in towns and cities of Syria the *Rifai* (*Rifā'ī*) order to which he belonged. He was also asked to write and publish "religious and Sufi works" (*Ibid.*, 140).

Between 1880 and 1908 he fulfilled this obligation with gusto, writing no less than 212 books and brochures. Throughout, he repeated the main theme which he had broached in his first publication (A. Manneh, 1979, 141). This concept, which he sought to convey in the booklet was that:

> . . . absolute government was the primary system of government in Islam, contrary to the view that it had developed in the course of Islamic history. . . . By his will, God has created and regulated this world. He then sent prophets to lead mankind to Him, like shepherds to His subjects. . . . The greatest of these prophets, Muhammed, drew the hearts of the believers to God and laid down the foundations of unity on a stronger basis. . . .
>
> In time, . . . the Caliphate was transmitted to the Ottomans and reached Sultan Abdülhamid II. Already known for his virtue and devotion, the Sultan, after his ascendancy, showed religious zeal, upheld the Shari'a and worked for the protection of the *umma*. As demanded by their faith, Muslims ought to be obedient to Him. . . .
>
> Sufi shaikhs obliged their followers to bind their hearts in loyalty to the commander of the faithful and taught them to help him in words and deeds. . . . By stating these and many other commandments, Abul Huda wanted to convince his readers that unqualified obedience to the Caliph was a basic duty in Islam. . . . Indeed, for the sake of defending the *umma* and the land of Islam, Muslims ought not only to be submissive to the Caliph but also unite and bind their hearts to him. (*Ibid.*)

Butrus Abu Manneh has stated that the sultan's strategy was to create a pan-Islamic focus for the inhabitants of Syria and thereby defuse their incipient Syrian nationalism. This is a plausible thesis but one which acquires greater depth both in the general context of the sultan's conciliatory moves to the Arabs and also in the context of other Arab propagandists whom he patronized. Among these, an important personality was the son of the founder of the *Madanīya* (*Dārqawīyya*) order, Şeyh Muhammad Ibn Hamza Ẓāfir al-Madānī, of Misurata in Libya. The *Madanīya* was one link in the chain of orders ultimately traceable to the North African Aḥmad bin Idrīs (1760–1837). Idrīs had included in his teaching a new, "higher purpose," i.e., "the unity of the endeavour of Muslims united in the bonds of Islam" (Trimingham, 1973, 115 citing Idrīs' biographer Shams ad-dīn b. 'Abd al-Muta'āl). This aspect of Idrīs' work was resurrected in Şeyh Ẓāfir's *An Nur As-Satī* (*The Brilliant Light*, publ. Istanbul, 1884; Trimingham, 1973, 126, note 1).

> The Sultan allotted him a home near the Palace of Yildiz Kiosk and three Madanī *Tekkēs* were established in Istanbul. From these went out propaganda seeking to influence Shaikhs of various orders. Emissaries, protected through the imperial power, won recruits among Algerians employed by the French . . . but in Morocco its relationship with the Turkish government discredited it. In Barka it became linked with the Sanūsiyya . . . *Muqaddams* [A sectional leader in a Sufi order, Trimingham, 1973, 307] were also found in Egypt and the Hijaz. (Trimingham, 1973, 126)

Whether Abul Hudā was able to maintain his influence over the Sultan through "astrological and divinatory powers" (*Ibid.*, 127) or because of his influence over the *tarikat* is not known.

In 1892, the sultan added the Muslim reformist Cemaleddin Afgani to the pan-Islamic propagandists which he kept on tap. The sultan was aware that Cemaleddin had been associated with schemes to create an Arabic caliphate (Keddie, 1972, 374), but he seems to have thought of using him to elicit the co-operation of *Shi'ites* in schemes of Islamic union (Keddie, 1972, 380–381). However, the sultan found that Afgani had his own ambitious schemes which had embarrassing consequences for the external policy of the Ottoman Empire vis-a-vis Iran. Cemaleddin died in 1897, more or less disgraced, and watched by the sultan's police. His influence while in Istanbul may have touched a number of budding intellectuals such as the poet Mehmed Emin, who later combined a strong Islamic commitment with Turkish and populist nationalism.

Persons who congregated in Istanbul and discussed the revitalization of Islamic culture, primarily with an eye to its political consequences, were not only those invited by the sultan. One Islamic propagandist who, presumably, arrived in Istanbul without invitation (circa 1885) (ed. Gövsa, 14) was Abdürreşid İbrahim. Born in Siberia in 1853, he had studied in the *medreses* in Mecca and Medina and had also established contacts with Namık Kemal and Ahmed Vefik Paşa during a stay in Istanbul (*Ibid.*). The link with Vefik Paşa is important, in the sense that this Ottoman statesman was one of the first personalities in Turkey to try to find roots for Turks in their early Central Asian culture. Returning to Siberia after this interlude, Abdürreşid had established schools there on the model of what he had seen in Istanbul. He is stated to have convinced 100,000 Siberian Muslims to migrate to Istanbul (*Ibid.*). In 1893 he was elected *kadı* of Orenburg. At about the same time (?)(1895) he published in Istanbul a work entitled *Çulpan Yıldızı* (*The Morning Star*), "a violent diatribe against the Czarist regime and an inflamed appeal for the political and cultural rebirth of the Muslim world" (Benningsen and Quelquejay, 1964, 44 Note 1). He also published a number of attacks against the activities of Russian missionaries. Said Nursi was in touch with him in 1907–1908. During the Balkan War of 1912–1913 İbrahim published articles in Turkish newspapers in which he preached holy war. After 1908 he travelled throughout Asia to survey the state of Muslims in Asia. The result of his researches appeared in a two-volume work entitled *The World of Islam*.

In 1889, the new German Emperor William II made his first visit to Istanbul. This seems to have been the turning point in a new, pan-Islamic thrust. Pan-Islam was now required to support German diplomacy (Emin, 1930, 38). After a second visit to the Kaiser in 1898, the sultan embarked on the construction of a new railway line to Arabia, the Hicaz (Ḥijāz) Railroad, financed by donations of Muslims throughout the world. It was the most tangible form of his pan-Islamic policy. This was a means of securing access to the sacred places of pilgrimage in Arabia-Mecca and Medina (Landau, 1971, 19–20).

On a number of occasions the pan-Islamic policy of the sultan has been minimized. Some authors try to point out that the idea of a revived caliphate had been inspired by a British poet and Middle East "expert" Wilfrid Scaven Blunt (Berkes, 1964, 268). But even without foreign stimulation the attractiveness of such a policy seems self-evident (cf. Le Chatelier, 1910, 54 and Yalman, 1930, 180).

It was from Islam that the Muslim Ottomans could draw the emotional resonance that would mobilize both upper and lower classes. It was Islam that would provide a store of symbols which could compete with the national symbols of the Greeks or the Serbs. It might well be that when those educated in the *medrese* tried to write religious tracts for the common people, "they produced masterpieces of gibberish" that sounded like "magical incantations" (Berkes, 1964, 193), but it was this incantatory quality which gave these tracts the ability to re-contextualize a religion which was on the way to becoming a pale reflection of its golden image. Re-contextualization here refers to a reaction to the way in which the whole ness of Islam in traditional society had been transformed into something fragmented, driven out of the context of political and economic life, even as it survived in the religious-social context.

Islam as "culture" meant the culture of the Arabs, and the first decade of the reign of Sultan Abdülhamid was a time during which the intellectual virtues of the Arabs and the value of their classics were at a premium in the Ottoman capital. Some have attributed this to the sultan's conservatism, which no doubt was tangible. But the sultan's influence does not explain the heated debate beginning in 1882 that went on between the defenders of the ancients (Arabs) and the moderns (i.e., Ottoman Turks influenced by the civilization of the West).

On the one side figured Hacı İbrahim Efendi, a man who had established a reputation for modernizing the teaching of Arabic in Ottoman schools. On the other side were Ebüzziya Tevfik, a former Young Ottoman, and Said Bey, the son of Kemal Efendi, the reformer of religious schools (see above p. 110).

The defenders of the Arabic thesis, argued that it was not Turkish which constituted the root of Ottoman, the language used by the educated elite, but Arabic. This was also true with regard to grammar: "If Arabic rules are not observed, the language will be damaged. If none of the observed rules are kept, it will be necessary to extract from the language all the Arabic words, as well. If we do this we shall have to speak without a language" ("Tekmile", *Ibid.*, August 3rd, 1882; Kushner, 1977, 65).

Hacı İbrahim also made the connection between language and culture. Arabic was the core of "arabism" (*arabiyet*), a rooted, cultural heritage.

> From where did the Muslim faith and the Illustrious Law, which admittedly accompanies all moral virtues, come to us? From the Arabs. From which language did the religion of Islam and the Law of the Prophet emanate? From the Arabic language. Can one understand the Faith and the Law without knowing Arabic? No. One cannot. ("Ihtarat", *Tercüman-ı Hakikat*, July 26, 1882, Kushner, 1977, 67)

The Hacı İbrahim controversy was not an artificial creation by a conservative sultan but, on the contrary, part of a dialogue between Ottomans who were trying to find their roots. The sultan knew how to use this search for an identity, but there is no evidence that he had initiated it. Another person, who, at the very same time, was trying a similar experiment was the writer "Muallim" Naci.

Muallim Naci

In the 1870s Süleyman Hüsnü Paşa had prepared anthologies in which the great deeds of the earliest Turks would be underlined; and he used these in the Ottoman military schools to fire patriotism among the students. This development has been fairly well covered by recent research. It is seldom realized that a parallel attempt to interest students—future intellectuals—in the products of Eastern culture was also taking place in the 1880s. These pieces were the translations from Arabic and Persian of the Turkish litterateur "Muallim" Naci (Tansel, 1961, 161). Naci's writings give a conspicuous place to his belief in Islamic values. Some of his poems are based on events of Islamic history. He seems to have navigated a middle course between an understanding of the benefits of Western civilization and a deep belief in the authenticity of the message of the Prophet Muhammed. This enabled him to attack the bigotry of some of the Muslims he saw around him (Tansel, 1961, 168) and to berate others who refused to acknowledge the new conditions created by the technological advances of the West. Naci's epic poem *Musa bin-Eb'il Gazan yahut Hamiyyet,* published in 1881 related how an Andalusian Arab general had fought single-mindedly and without help to maintain the integrity of an Arab kingdom in Andalusia. One of the lessons that he attempted to get through to his readers was that the Arabs of Andalusia were once unified and could therefore resist foreign encroachments (Tansel, 1961, 169). At the same time, Andalusia was a country where science had progressed because skills were rewarded by the ruler. Because those in power had later forgotten their responsibilities and had plunged into dissipation, the protection accorded to men of science disappeared, and the state was thus weakened. At a time when the Arabs only kept Granada, Musa entertained thoughts of surrender. In Naci's poem, Musa, defeated in battle, commits suicide. This poem was an immediate success and was used in schools for the purpose for which it had been meant, namely the inculcation of a new inner commitment to the preservation of the empire (Tansel, 1961, 172).

In a number of works on religion, Naci tried to provide comments which would place a work such as the *Qur'ān* in perspective for those who did not know Arabic: an adumbration of one of Bediüzzaman's approaches (*I'caz-ı Kur'an,* Istanbul, 1883; Tansel, 1961, 176, note 1). In a book entitled *Hikem-i Rifâi,* he tried to provide an anthology of the sayings of the founder of the Rifâi (*Rifā'iyya*) order, Ahmad al-Rifā'i. The book by al-Rifā'i had already been seized upon as a fitting piece of propaganda for Sultan Abdülhamid's Islamic propaganda expert, Abul Hudā. Naci used Abul Hudā's work to prepare an anthology with a commentary (Tansel, 1961, 177).

What is interesting about this activity is the extent to which Naci is using the Islamic classics to make them available to a class of readers who presumably would not have had access to them in earlier times because they could not read the originals in Arabic. Now, the greater literacy of the *Tanzimat* school population allowed these works to be disseminated in a fashion that had not been attempted before in Islamic history. The stratum of "carriers" of the Islamic message was being widened to include persons who were not Islamic intellectuals but who could now act as middle range Islamic propagandists. The extent to which Naci's and Abul Hudā's activities were coordinated is not known, but some general agreement between them as to the new opportunities that were opened up by the new educational plant of the *Tanzimat* for the spread of Islamic culture must have existed.

The sultan, as well as many leading Ottoman intellectuals, had tried to use Islam as the basis for an ideology because all felt the need to counteract the centripetal forces of differentiation which were forcing Ottoman ethnic groups away from a center. In the sultan's plans, Islam was, once more, to assume this function. An Islamic ideology was also to remedy the increasing distance between cultural strata which were now in process of formation. This was a new phenomenon: the imperviousness of the new cultural strata—Westernized/traditional—was replacing a system where personalistic forces had been much stronger, strata more diffuse. But things did not work as the sultan proposed: the educated became increasingly differentiated from those still immersed in the traditional stream, and the mobilization of Ottoman Muslim masses around a new Islamic culture was an immense task which at all times exceeded his means. Two important developments added to the already existing rift in Ottoman society which was being reorganized around a Western cultural pole, the spread of Western modes of daily life among the officials and the influence of positivism among intellectuals.

The Ottoman Capital in the 1890s

When Said Nursi arrived in Istanbul in 1896, he was stepping into an urban setting which had changed considerably since the first years of the

Tanzimat. According to Arminius Vambery, a Hungarian orientalist with a life-long interest in the history of the Turks, these changes had been gathering momentum since the end of the Crimean War (1854–1856). Vambery who had closely followed the events of the reign of Sultan Abdülhamid, and had met with the sultan, portrayed the sharp contrast between the Turkey he had known in earlier times and the Turkey of the 1890s.

> Allow me to cite certain characteristic facts expressing the state of things which prevailed in those times and the general disposition of minds in that epoch. Despite an intimate and exclusive frequentation of Turkish society in those years, I had only come across a few Turks who, while on one hand learning the languages, the mores and the usages of the Occident, were also inspired by its energy, its perseverance and its activity, those fundamental qualities of cultivated persons in Europe. Even among the men who were leading the movement [of reform] and who were the least influenced by religious fanaticism, one could remark a strong dose of indolence, of apathy and indecision as well as a look veiled by fanaticism. (Vambery, 1898, 10–11)

It is probable that, despite the ethnocentric references which crop up in Vambery's pamphlet, the original impetus for its production had been the desire to encourage Ottoman officials. Throughout the pamphlet Vambery implied that the most crucial changes in the Ottoman Empire had occurred during the reign of Sultan Abdülhamid II. This emphasis was meant to refute the picture of the sultan as a mean despot which was building up in European public opinion. Vambery went on to describe a change which may be described as one of social consciousness:

> In my time even enlightened Turks, with the exception of a few higher functionaries influenced by European civilization, had only a very vague notion of the ideas of nationality and the fatherland. The historical past and the ancient Ottoman grandeur was present only in the minds of some, for the study of national history was completely neglected. Religious discussions and unimportant details of the life of Muhammad or of the first period of Islam had exercised a greater attraction on the minds than the history of the formation of the Ottoman Empire. (Vambery, 1898, 21)

What is remarkable about this description is that the subjects which Vambery described as preeminently interesting to Ottoman officials in the 1850s were the same subjects which, according to the founder of the Committee of Union and Progress, İbrahim Temo, were discussed among the more conservatively inclined provincial adolescents who were accepted to the Military Medical School preparatory section in the 1880s. We may say that one of the things that changed between 1800 and 1895 was the "problem-setting mode" of educated Ottomans while that of the provinces remained unchanged, despite superstructural changes.

In the early stages of the *Tanzimat*, the perception of historical reality was filtered through the historical-conceptual scheme of educated Ottomans of the time. This scheme was a Muslim Ottoman world-view and seems to have continued to function as the intellectual frame of reference in the Ottoman provinces long after the Ottoman capital had changed in this respect. No doubt Said Nursi's ability to achieve considerable resonance with his message in the provinces in the 1920s was still partly related to this lag.

The more intellectualistic arguments that Vambery adduced for the progress of the Ottoman Empire appeared together with more superficial arguments about the appearance of Turkish officers: "Instead of the officers of olden times, dirty and dressed negligently, one encounters today elegant soldiers with a well-groomed look." Superficially, the description of these sartorial characteristics appear to be marginal to Vambery's main argument about intellectual change. In fact, it points to an aspect of social change that was probably as important as that in the superstructure, namely the increasingly functional differentiation of Ottoman society during the nineteenth century. Thus, in the era covered by Vambery, the army was transformed from a "slovenly" band into the regimented, disciplined and docile instrument, led by a corps of officers whose specialized skills of command were magnified and transformed into a profession by Prussian manuals of soldiering. General von der Goltz, who was in charge of Ottoman military training after 1883, was to produce such a manual entitled *The Nation in Arms,* in which the officer was made into an exemplary figure leading by the force of his moral dedication symbolized by his impeccable gear. Von der Goltz was a prominent military thinker who "saw the military in its total relationship to the society in which it existed" (Griffiths, 1966, 58). For him the officer cadre made up a social class; its life-style had to be consciously manipulated and its boundaries defined to make it into a solidary, compact group. This manual was translated into Turkish in A.H. 1300 (1882–83), but its influence no doubt antedates the translations.

The intellectual atmosphere which prevailed in the Ottoman capital also appears to have been more lively than can be gathered by the existing, mostly negative, accounts of Sultan Abdülhamid's reign. This contention can certainly be supported up to the early 1890s. It is true that we cannot describe what was going on in Istanbul in the 1880s as a flowering of

Ottoman culture, but the intellectual experimentation which was taking place was remarkable and is attested by the rich publishing history which coincided with the first decade of the sultan's reign.

In those years Ottoman intellectuals had begun to cut loose their moorings to official circles and government bureaus which in the past had provided for their employment, sustenance and intellectual stimulation. With the increasing readership of newspapers and edifying articles in magazines, an audience had formed for the mass media. Intellectuals were assuming the characteristics of an intelligentsia, linked to the public by a new function shaped by the newspaper, that of weighing public policy. In the press and in the other publications of the time, however, two themes can be recaptured. One, already of long duration, was the malaise caused by a new species of over-Westernized Turk. The second theme, much more latent, was the increasing unconcern for religion, which, in its more definite or philosophical form, may be termed "positivism."

Les Précieux Ridicules

The *Tanzimat* statesmen and their cohorts had established in the upper spheres of officialdom in the capital a fair replica of the type of life which one could find in the great European capitals. Istanbul had been invaded, not only by imported cloth and by printing presses, but by cafés and dance halls. These new-fangled institutions were concentrated in Péra, the European quarter of the capital, where the Royal Prussian orchestra gave concerts, Sarah Bernhardt performed and where the Café Couronne had gathered pretty Austrian girls as *serveuses*. In Péra one could receive mail through the uncensored postal services of foreign powers; one could also buy books and newspapers which would have placed their purveyors in greater jeopardy on the Turkish side of the town across the Galata bridge.

By the 1880s there existed a Turkish clientèle, partly made up of young fops who originated in the upper class circles of the *Tanzimat*, and who catered exclusively to Péra's way of life. A satire of this superficial integration with Western civilization was embodied in one of the first important Turkish novels of the century, Recaizâde Ekrem's *Araba Sevdası* (*The Love of Carriages*). The hero of this novel, Bihruz Bey, is someone totally alienated from local Ottoman culture and disgusted by popular mores. Bihruz spends his father's wealth in acquiring the most elegant horse-drawn carriages. He has his suits made at the best Western tailor in Péra. He spends a few minutes in his government bureau every day but looks for adventures in the city parks the rest of the time. Meeting lower class Turks who are on an outing in the Park, and witnessing their strange oriental garb, he wonders whether "*le carnaval est arrivé*" (In French in the novel.). The change in orientation symbolized by Bihruz Bey was deeply offensive to traditional Ottoman society. At the most superficial level this new behavior was a denial of Ottoman-Islamic culture. But there were additional levels at which Ottoman culture was being subverted. Ottoman wealth had always been embedded in a social nexus which limited its effect. Great wealth was the apanage of officials in the traditional system but it was also—theoretically and often in fact—limited by its function which was also largely political. Wealth was used to generate prestige; it was used by officials for the upkeep of a personal staff of subaltern officials in a patrimonial system, and for the expenses generated by their office. If the sultan decided that they were not serving these political ends, the official's wealth was confiscated, a practice which stopped only in 1826. What was happening now was that economic transactions were acquiring an autonomy which was undermined by the old ideal of Ottoman economics subservient to political goals. Bihruz Bey and his mindless expenditures represented this erosion of an old ideal. At a time when the old Ottoman guild and craft system was crumbling, this subversion caused serious repercussions. But it is remarkable that the idea of uncontrolled economic activity never acquired widespread legitimacy in the Empire despite the greed which individual statesmen showed during the *Tanzimat* era and the fortunes which some of them were able to amass.

Positivism

The hard-headed attitude of the Ottoman statesmen in the years antedating the *Tanzimat* shows their willingness to enforce a species of *raison d'etat*. This political attitude accorded no special dispensation to the men of religion when the security of the state was at stake. It also brought with it a pragmatism which predisposed Ottoman statesmen to positivism. The philosophical underpinning of positivism, was of course, different from that underlying the views of Ottoman officials, but the pragmatism underlying western European science did provide a common ground for both. The practical benefits of industry, in the sense that modern industry served to make an industrially advanced state a forceful international factor, had not escaped the Young Ottomans. Science and industry were thus key words for Turkish modernizers, but the early nineteenth century Ottoman experience with industry had been bitter, and science seemed a way of mastering the power held by Western states which had more widespread applicability than industry.

A survey of the books published in Turkey in the first decade of the reign of Sultan Abdülhamid II reinforces the conclusion that measures taken for the modernization of the Ottoman Empire were also forcing a pattern of translations and publications which were focused on science. These appeared primarily as an adjunct to the new technologies that were being introduced into the empire. Thus we witness a rise in the number of books on the geography of Turkey and of the world. Manuals of mathematics with books on integral and differential calculus come into use. Handbooks for engineers, conversion tables for weights and measures, works on topography and geography surface. Part of the publications were the consequence of what appears to have been a partial adoption of the metric system in 1882 (*J.A.* 5th Ser., 13, 428–442).

Turkish literateurs of the time showed an interest in science which expressed itself in a wide range of translations from the West of popularizations of science. These became common in the 1890s (Tansel, 1946–51, 4–5).

The debate concerning materialism as a philosophy had begun somewhat earlier and was fuelled by the short, but productive, life of Beşir Fuad. Beşir Fuad was the editor of the first Turkish literary periodical to place a special emphasis on the development of science and the scientific world view.*

In 1886 Beşir Fuad published a book with the title of *Beşer* (*Humanity*). In his preface he stated that Herbert Spencer's classification of the sciences placed those aimed at the preservation of health at the head of the list, and he noted that the development of the arts was placed at the tail end of this list (Okay, n.d., 105). He implied that in the Ottoman civilization of

*The journal was entitled *Haver* and appeared for four issues in 1884. The extent to which the term science could be a cause for misunderstanding was well documented by one of the major disputes that erupted on the editorial board of the *Haver.* Western mathematico-physical sciences had been introduced into Turkey under the rubric of "*fen.*" This differentiated modern science from traditional religious sciences known as "*ilim.*" A member of the *'ulema* class apparently thought that these were the sciences on which the journal was to concentrate. He accepted to sit on the editorial board but later protested that the only science was the "science of *kelam*", i.e., the science of dogmatics (Okay, n.d., 49–51) and resigned from his post.

his time the contrary held true. The book consisted of a popularization of the advances scored in physiology and seems to have been strongly influenced by Claude Bernard's *Introduction a l'Étude de la Médecine Expérimentale.* Other contributions of Beşir Fuad were also in physiology. One of his most interesting works on the physiology of the brain may have been inspired by Büchner's *Kraft und Stoff* (Okay, n.d., 112, note 28). A number of Fuad's articles were translations of pieces having appeared in popular magazines such as *La Science pour Tous* and *Die Natur* (Okay, n.d., 117). His literary-interests were focused on Zola, who, for him, represented the literary equivalent of the scientific attitude. Zola was, indeed, trying to apply to the analysis of society some of the approaches that Claude Bernard had used for physiology (Okay, n.d., 150). The cumulative cultural change experienced by Ottomans was having an effect on their religion. Thus the Turkish novelist Halit Ziya [Uşaklıgil], who lived in the more cosmopolitan setting of İzmir, was already disgusted at the time of his adolescence by the ignorance displayed by *imam* in their sermons (Uşaklıgil, 196, 229).

The relatively open nature of Turkish intellectual activities in the 1880s can be seen in that Ahmed Mithat Efendi, while publishing contributions by the advocate of Islamic classicism, İbrahim Efendi, also gave a sympathetic hearing to Beşir Fuad. Ahmed Mithat Efendi himself now tried his hand at "naturalism" (Okay, n.d., 230). His son-in-law "Muallim" Naci, whose contributions to the re-Islamization of Ottoman culture we have surveyed, joined in these activities, taking up the translation of Emile Zola's *Therèse Raquin.* Thus, experimentation in the best sense of the word seems to have been the hallmark of Turkish intellectual life in these times. But the relatively unsophisticated attempt to catch up—and make everyone else catch up—with Western thought ground to a halt in the mid-1890s. Turkish literateurs now adopted the tactic of taking the premises of Western scientific thought for granted without making too much fuss about them.*

---

*The change may have been due to the tightened censorship which was implemented after 1895 and to the blow by Ottoman censorship which stopped the periodical *Mektep* the author of an article on Indian (?) Pantheism had been taken to task after a denunciation that he was spreading materialism. An alternative explanation would be that the psychological positivism of Paul Bourget, and his analyses of Western pessimism which replaced Turkish scientism were more apposite to the mood of the Turkish intelligentsia at the time. The sultan's shadow was lengthening and the entire cast of Turkish life was becoming more oppressive.

Distantiation

In the aftermath of the new censorship of the 1890s symbolism was adopted by a new generation of Turkish literateurs. This generation was also increasingly alienated from the "*carnaval*" and had a tendency to distance itself from popular culture. Distantiation was a relatively new development in Turkish intellectual life; it was also the mark of the new generation's attitude towards religion. But this was only one aspect of their alienation-from the general cast of traditional Ottoman culture. In that culture, refinement and sophistication had been outstanding, but on the other hand, an aspect of modern Western European bourgeois culture which was in the process of formation had not yet taken hold. In Europe both legislation and city planning were gradually turning the city into a place where the upper classes were physically isolated from the lower. This was one way of separating "vagabonds" and "criminals" from the productive strate of society (Sennett, 1973). In the Ottoman Empire, this Victorian trend to a real differentiation had not been so clear. The world of baggy pantaloons which Bihruz Bey found so distasteful had previously been part of the world in which the upper classes were immersed even though their life conditions were different. The officials were in touch with the world of shadow play and people's romances. This was a grand guignolesque world whose representation of sexual acts on the scene placed prudish Victorian onlookers in a state of shock. The new generation of the 1890s emphatically distanced themselves from these populistic features of traditional culture. In literature this appeared in the disappearance of the device whereby the narrator would take the reader aside to explain what was afoot. Ahmed Mithat Efendi had used this method constantly, but it was soon to be considered jejune by the generation that took over from him.

To understand the causes and the effects of this distancing of the educated from the masses we have to look at the work of Goody and Watt (1968, 57) and the parallel findings of Sennet. Goody and Watt point out that the advent of literate culture enables a person to avoid culture in a way that would not be possible before extensive literacy was obtained. Preliterate communication being principally through forcibly shared symbols and rituals, the individual is immersed in contact with his immediate group through these channels. The symbolic system of literacy changes all this by enabling the symbol-user to keep in touch with society *without* being in constant, personal, face-to-face contact with the community. Sennet (1973) has shown that nineteenth century culture, and especially the culture of its new cities, led to types of ecological concentration that increased this isolation effect. A similar effect may be postulated for Istanbul, where the number of publications inspired by Western literature suddenly shows a steep rise in the 1870s, and where the build-up of the new quarters away from the "rabble" was taking place at the same time. Thus, communications developments were taking the literate elite of the Ottomans away from the people, but once again, through the characteristics carried by a new patterning of communications rather than by the specific ideas of the West.

Preciosity, positivism and distantiation all came to a head in 1896 when Hüseyin Cahid Yalçin, yet to be one of the leading journalists of Turkey, turned his wrath on Arab culture and flatly declared that Ottomans had no need for it. A number of *'ulema* rose up in alarm at these "lucubrations" and the decadence they underlined. The original article and the protests together produced a *cause célèbre*. The most violent protest was that of the future *şeyhülislâm* Mustafa Sabri Efendi, who had to go into exile after the Republic was proclaimed in Turkey in 1923 (Berkes, 1978).

Already, beginning with the 1860s, a type of apologetic literature had emerged, rushing to the defense of Islam as a superior culture to which the parlous condition of Islamic states could not be attributed. Ahmed Mithat Efendi, who could not quite make up his mind as to where he stood in relation to the European dispute regarding the conflict between religion and science, had, nevertheless, bravely taken up the defense of Islam shortly thereafter. Neither was this a completely unambiguous stand, since he collated his defense to a translation of Draper's *History of the Conflict between Religion and Science*. The literary production was paralleled by a much more fundamental reassessment of Islam which found its source in the contributions of Cemaleddin Afgani, the premier Muslim reformist of the nineteenth century. Cemaleddin had clashed head on with the Ottoman *'ulema* when he had claimed that prophethood was an "art" in the Ottoman capital in 1869. These deistic inclinations were forgotten when, later in the century, he started an attack against materialism. Two more strands in his thinking were to have an influence after his death in Istanbul in 1897. One was the idea that the revitalization of Islam would only be achieved through the revitalization of Islamic states and the recapture of their strength on the international scene. The second, which Professor Fazlur Rahman has pinpointed, was a new humanism, an interest in man as man. Cemaleddin was so sure of the superiority of Islam that he believed that Europe would, in the long run, embrace Islam in the place of Christianity, an idea which recurs in Said Nursi. Afgani's influence was perpetuated through the reformist program of his disciple, Muḥammad 'Abdū, whose life was centered on the idea of the unity of God and the conviction that reform meant foremost the reinstilling of the conception of God as the unique and sole master of the universe (Hourani, 1962; Kerr, 1966). Muslims had to study the *Qur'ān* and immerse themselves in its idiom to recapture this primal element in Islamic faith. Again, an echo of Muḥammad 'Abdū's idea of an immersion in the *Qur'ān* as well as his attempt to reach the masses reappears in the teachings of Said Nursi. A third person in this well-known triumvirate of Islamic reform was Rashīd Riḍā, in whom Muḥammad 'Abdū's stress on the unicity of God took the form of a strict puritanism and an attack on Sufism. To a limited extent we also find echoes of these ideas in Said Nursi, but in him the formalistic rejection of Sufism is contradicted by a revaluation of the mystical world view.

The more profound problems of philosophy which cut across the ideas of the three major reformers of Islam, one which they never faced as a formal proposition of metaphysics, was the basic disjunction between the world view of the Enlightenment and that of Islamic thinkers. As Hamilton Gibb has pointed out, two important changes occurred in the philosophical stance of Europe during the eighteenth century which transformed Christian theology. One of these was the idea that God was not simply a transcendent Being, "quite distinct from the world which He had created," but that He was immanent either in the conceptual apparatus of humans or in the more general sense in nature. The second was the belief that the ultimate sanction of religion was not to be given in the hereafter but that religious values were to be shaped inside the world (Gibb, 1945, 41). In the long run, orthodox Muslim reformers who were well grounded in religious studies could not readily agree to these ideas: they spotlighted the transcendence of God. Said's ideas also constitute an answer to these formal problems. Mysticism as an attitude of wonderment at God's creation, as a way of integrating oneself with the harmony prevailing in God's creation set a *mood* which deflected Islamic resistance to philosophical speculation on immanentism. Similarly, the idea of the phenomenal world as God's reflection allowed him to bring in what can only be described as a deistic picture of the workings of nature.

Said Nursi was able to work on this intellectual inheritance because of the explosion of writing, comment and discussion which followed upon the Young Turk Revolution of 1908. The Young Turk era was also one in which the materialistic inclinations of some Young Turk intellectuals surfaced and, conversely, some Turkish Muslim super-conservatives began to voice their skepticism about the achievements of Muslim reformers. A number of themes appear in this setting which have to be pinpointed insofar as they establish a background for Said Nursi's views.

The Young Turk Revolution ushered in a decade of intellectual controversy among intellectuals in Turkey during which a number of positions crystallized, the survival of which was carried into Said Nursi's project to abandon politics and devote himself to the Muslim education of a rural clientele. The confrontation of "religious" and "idealistic" views of life with "materialistic" visions played a particularly important role in these developments of the Young Turk era.

Between 1908 and 1918 materialism appeared under two main guises. One was a somewhat crude materialism of Büchner, the second a form of deism. The Young Turks were sympathetic to this second form because it allowed them to praise Islam as the most excellent and advanced of all religions while engaging in positivistic reforms of society. Among the latter the reform of the marriage and family laws of 1917 was the most conspicuous (Bouvat, 1921).

Büchner came to the fore primarily in the ideas of Baha Tevfik (1881–1916), a journalist who, with his brother Fikri, started a series of publishing ventures to popularize the ideas of the leading Western exponents of materialism. Among these one may count the *Library of Scientific and Philosophical Progress* (Bolay, 1967, 25), the *Journal of Philosophy* (1911) and the periodical *Intelligence* (1912). Baha Tevfik impartially attacked all persons he considered charlatans, religious reactionaries or nationalist ideologists. He translated Büchner's *Kraft und Stoff,** Ernst Haeckel, Fouillé's *History of Philosophy* and wrote *Sensibility and the New Morality* and *Nietzsche.* He is the first person to have leveled a sustained attack against the separation of sexes in Turkey because he considered it to undermine normal family relations.

Baha Tevfik was the prime target of conservative Muslims, but neither did they spare the deist Celal Nuri, whom they considered to be a sly hypocrite trying to introduce materialistic conceptions under the guise of a defense of Islam. What Celal Nuri was trying to do in his work entitled *The History of the Future (Tarih-i Istikbal)* was to propagate the idea that Islamic tenets amounted to an acceptance of the laws of nature. He should

---

*which already was clandestinely circulated among students in the 1890s and against which a refutation had already been written in those years (Adıvar, 1944, II, 56, note 2)..

have known better since the similar ideas propagated by the Indian Sayyid Aḥmad Khan had already caused considerable scandal in the preceding century. Celal Nuri was faced by a two-pronged attack in which on one hand figured Şehbenderzâde Ahmet Hilmi speaking for orthodox Islam and on the other İsmail Fenni (Ertuğrul) voicing the synthesis of mysticism and orthodoxy. The important difference between these two writers was that while Hilmi had only negative arguments with which he tried to destroy Büchner and Haeckel's theses, İsmail Fenni offered his readers a model of integration with the cosmos modelled on the theosophy of Ibn al-'Arābī. This adumbrated a view of the universe that we find in some of Said Nursi's ideas. We have already seen how Said Nursi was drawn into this controversy.

Of a more radical cast was the reformism of the Russian Musa Carullah Bigi, the person who had commended Said Nursi for his defense of freedom. Musa Carullah took to task all of traditional Islamic learning and especially the scholasticism of *kalām* thinking. He was therefore roundly attacked by the more conservative thinkers among whom appears Mustafa Sabri, the man who had rallied Muslims for an attack on literary decadents. Bediüzzaman considered both to have taken extreme positions. He believed Mustafa Sabri to have a slight edge over Musa Carullah, but was repelled by Mustafa Sabri's denigration of Ibn al-'Arabī (*Lem'alar,* 259).

In the years 1908–1918, intellectual circles in Istanbul eagerly took up the discussion of Islam's place in Ottoman society. A somewhat unexpected aspect of the following debates was the coolness with which many prominent Turkish-speaking Ottoman *'ulema* met the reformist current which had been brought to maturation in the Muslim world during the late nineteenth and early twentieth centuries by such outstanding personalities as the Egyptian *âlim* Muḥammad 'Abdū. The opponents of reformist Islam voiced their ideas in the *Beyan ül-Hak* and were led by Mustafa Sabri Efendi, who was to become *şeyhülislâm* in the year 1919–1922 after the flight of the Young Turk triumvirate. These circles were particularly disturbed by the proposal to re-open "the gate of interpretation" (*içtihad*) to Islam and to bypass the precedents established by the classical commentators of Islam. For the truly conservative as well as for the masses it represented an extreme rationalization of Islam or, alternatively, a destruction of the accommodation which Islam had reached with localistic practices. For the *'ulema* it meant an undermining of the traditional legalistic apparatus. Since orthodox interpretation of religious law flowed from the commentaries of the founders of the Islamic schools of law, incursion into freer hermeneutics meant to part company with those schools. Those who engaged in these practices were accused of being "without school" (*mezhepsiz*), an attack that implied that one was feckless and irresponsible. This accusation is one which still has weight in Turkey today.

Forward-looking *'ulema* and laymen, by contrast, expressed their views in the periodical *Sırat-ı Mustakim* (later *Sebil ür-Reşad*) and did take sides with 'Abdu's school, the *Salafīya*. One of the leaders of this group was the poet Mehmed Akif, whose epic *Safahat* had aspects of a program of socio-religious reform. Included in the ranks were learned Muslims such as Mardinizâde Ebülülâ, Bereketzâde İsmail Hakkı, "Manastırlı" İsmail Hakkı and M. Şemsettin. The latter, who was later to take the family name of Günaltay, played an unusual role in the history of Turkish Islam in the twentieth century and deserves more than cursory attention. In 1914 his *Zulmetten Nura (From Darkness to Light)* set a program for the retrieval from current Ottoman Islam of what—in the light of the then received Western ideology—could be considered the most progressive aspect of Islam. In 1928, after the proclamation of the Republic, he emerges once more as a figure in an Istanbul university commission formed to modernize Islamic ritual and the setting of the mosque. In the commission's proposal, ritual was to be made "clean" and "orderly," the language of worship was to become Turkish, ritual was to be shaped so as to offer an "aesthetic appeal," and the service was to be led by persons who understood the "social content" of the *Qur'ān* (Jäschke, 1972, 39–41). Günaltay later took part in the politics of the single party of the Turkish Republic, the CHP, and emerged as prime minister in 1949. Some of the liberalizing moves that the CHP took with regard to its strict secularism bear his imprint.

Ziya Gökalp, the ideologue of the Young Turks shows many similarities with Günaltay in his stand towards religion but with a starker sociologism due to the influence of Durkheim. He wanted Islam to be made understandable to Turkish-speaking worshippers. He saw religion as the foundation of a national "collective conscience" but at the same time as an item of personal ethic. Prayers were to be in Turkish and the "Turkification" of ritual was to him a means of anchoring the religious commitment of the rural population. His inspiration had partly mystic-sufi origins, and a major theme in his work was the replacement of the fear of damnation and the promise of the rewards of paradise with an internalized ethic.

Conservative and progressive Ottomans seem to have shared the conviction that Anatolian Islam, both as it appeared in the Sufi lodge or *tekke* and the *medrese,* was suffused with superstition, although different reasons were proferred for this state of affairs and different solutions were proposed.

Young Turk religious reforms proceeded in a stream parallel to "progressive" thought. Among these one may count (Jäschke, 1972, 70) the reorganization of the program of instruction of the *medrese*, the training school for *kadı*s (*medreset ul-kuzat*), the school for preachers (*medreset ül-vaizin*), the school for the training of administrators of pious foundations, and the new statutes on the administration of the *medrese*. Educational requisites of a higher type were now mandatory for preachers, the Council on Muslim Judicial Rulings (*Hey'et-i İftaiye*) was required to take into consideration all schools of Muslim law in reaching a decision, the duties of *müftü*s were delineated, and family law was rationalized in 1917 (Jäschke, 1972, 55 and 70 f.). The reform of the Islamic institutions continued after the flight of the Young Turk leaders with the establishment of an Islamic Academy (*Dar ül-Hikmet il-İslamiye*) (March 5, 1918; Jäschke, 1972, 56). Said Nursi was, as we saw, appointed to this academy upon his return from Russia. Among his colleagues figured Mehmed Akif and "İzmirli" İsmail Hakkı. Said seems to have suffered his breakdown at this time, and this prevented him from participating in the work of the academy.

The goals of the academy as they appear in its program show parallels to the modernizing aims of the Young Turks. The academy was to propagate Islamic principles through the preparation of sermons, catechisms, manuals for *medrese*s, and the publication of classics of Islam required for the teaching of theology. However, the decisions of the academy seem to show a much more simplistic, moralistic tone than the aims implied (Albayrak, 1973).

One cannot but be impressed when one covers the history of these years by a common theme which is the attempt to draw a personal ethic out of the fund of Islamic mysticism. This trend, popularized by Şehbenderzâde Ahmed Hilmi in his novel *Amâk-ı Hayâl* (1910), continued during the Republic, and one of its most prominent contributors, now working as a private person, was "İzmirli" İsmail Hakkı. A man much less in the limelight in the 1920s and 1930s was the sociologist and Istanbul University Professor Hilmi Ziya Ülken. Today he can be counted among the persons who throughout the 1940s and 1950s carried the torch of a social ethic drawn out of Islamic mysticism (Özberki, Master's Thesis, Boğaziçi). Üken's immersion into Marxism in the 1930s only serves to underline the continuity of his early and late thought with respect to the potential of Sufi ethics.

Said Nursi's reliance on the undiluted message of the *Qur'ān*, the fact that he addressed himself to the rural population, and his use of a Sufi resonance to try to devise a social ethic may have been influenced by the preceding background. However, in a striking departure from this setting, he shunned the obviously Durkheimian scaffolding that appeared in the ideas of some of the religiously influential thinkers of the years 1908–1918, and which one can even find in the program of the *Dar ül-Hikmet il-İslamiye.* We now get a better understanding of the transformation that was involved when the "old" Said shed his persona to become the "new" Said. The new Said was taking leave from the intellectualization of religion to grasp the bedrock of the "mysterium tremendum." For him, faith now overtook religion as "reasonable," although the latter still occupied an important place in his teachings.

Chapter IV

Matrix and Meaning

A: Nurculuk and the Outer World

To analyze the convolutions and describe the components of a movement as complex as *Nurculuk* necessarily involves a degree of artificiality and simplification. Nevertheless, a preliminary distinction which brings some order into the picture consists of separating the forces that shaped the external mechanisms printing the social tracks onto which the movement could be switched from the satisfaction of "inner needs" of its disciples. I shall try to outline these external forces in this section while describing mechanisms related to "inner needs" in the next.

The most remote of the external determinants, those that operated as long-term trends, are part of a world-historical development to which a number of labels may be attached. Whether these labels highlight the spread of an "Atlantic" cluster of cultures, or the formation of a system of world-economy, or the increasingly hegemonic position of the European state system, or even the penetration of colonialism and imperialism in the Middle East, they refer basically to the same phenomenon of a communications revolution which increased the interconnections between the less developed and more developed parts of the world. For the Ottoman Empire this process would be congruent with structural changes that followed upon the *Tanzimat*. I have attempted to show how forces which fall under this heading operated in the Bitlis area in the 1870s in my introductory chapter. I took up the structural transformations of the Ottoman Empire in Ch. III. But world-historical structural changes also changed the dynamics of Islam as a system of social relations. Ottoman Islam was also drawn into this process and the outcome affected the readiness of the rural masses to listen to the message of the *Risale-i Nur*. Among these developments we may count the gradual inclusion of larger sections of the population into the social communication network and, among processes once removed from this world trend, the expanded scope of *tarikat* activity in the Muslim world and the survival of religious networks in Turkey during the Republican era. As a world-historical development, these may be subsumed under the rubric of the "mobilization of the periphery."

Religion and the Expansion of Communication

By the end of the nineteenth century a much larger part of the population of Istanbul had been drawn into new configurations of social life than was the case even in the middle years of the *Tanzimat*, but the provinces, too, were becoming less isolated. The way in which Said Nursi could receive information about the ideas of Muḥammad 'Abdū from students passing through the province Mardin gives us an inkling of the consequences of the global communications change for its inhabitants. An accurate description of these communications links cannot but take into account the fact that they already were quite developed in the Islamic world at a much earlier date; also, that Mardin was on one of the trade routes which had been used for centuries to link various parts of the Islamic world.

With the decline of commerce in the East the economic dimension of inter-Islamic communications had shrunk, but its religious function had survived.

Ahmed gives us a striking description of its importance in the 19th century:

> Islamic societies are notorious in requiring a holistic framework of analysis due to their homologous structural arrangements and in the universality of their politico-religious symbolism which are maintained . . . with contiguous Islamic communities and persistent contact, in particular, with Mecca and Medina. These latter cities act both as Islamic source points for socio-religious activities and as disseminating points for revivalistic-reformist ideas and movements. Conceptually, this locational factor gives the Islamic world a physical orientation around which to order its existence and from which to derive its spiritual inspiration. Universal and easily identified Islamic symbols are carried into and exist in most remote Muslim societies: numerous identical words and verbs, common socio-religious festivals and certain normative values. Various groups, both formal and informal, keep the channels of communication open without the Islamic world: hajjis, pilgrims, missionaries, scholars, migrants and traders. These channels sometimes block up or fall into disuse but have generally remained functional. It is this channel, for example, that provided news of a Turkish victory over the Greeks in Europe in the late 1890s and stirred enthusiasm among the Pathans in the North West frontier of India against the British. (Ahmed, 1980, 85)

It is a homologous segment of this communications network, shaped at the local level, which provided the basic facilities for the spread of Said Nursi's ideas.

The Revival of Sufi Orders

Recent scholarship has chronicled the revival of Sufi orders during the nineteenth century. It has also described their shift to a more worldly stance in which figure socio-political mobilization and the politicization of Sufi *pirs* (Trimingham, 1973; Metcalf, 1982, 8). The spread of *Nakşibendi müceddidism* was, in fact, part of this larger revival which was to transform the Islamic world. The manner in which Sultan Abdülhamid II engineered his own policy of proto-nationalist propaganda carried through the Sufi orders was another eddy in the same stream (Abu Manneh, 1979). In Rumelia too, developments occurred which, emerging from a different sultan, nevertheless paralleled those initiated by Mevlana Halid in the East. Here, a more latitudinarian current, that of the *Melami* acquired a new vitality during the nineteenth century. In earlier centuries in the Ottoman Empire the *Melami* had at times acquired notoriety as religious groups suspect of some form of threat to the state. The revival of the order, however, underscored the same pietistic characteristics which appeared in the *müceddidi Nakşibendi*. The substance of this quite novel proselytizing in the Balkans may be described as an attempt to re-awaken the Islamic community of believers (Gölpınarlı, 1931). When the boundaries of the Ottoman Empire shrank, in the aftermath of the Balkan War, some *Melami*s emigrated to what remained of the territory of the Empire. Although they are considered to have fueled conservative currents among the young Turks, no mention is made of the name of the order concerned. At least one account of those times mentions that it was "dervishes" who were partly to blame for disrupting the relations between Muslims and Greeks in Western Anatolia (Sotiriu, 1980, 78). The underground revival of Islamic orders in the Ottoman Empire in the 19th century, therefore, seems to have been widespread and to have taken in the Balkans as well as Eastern Anatolia and possibly even Western Anatolia. Although we have few details of the way the movement affected İsparta—Said Nursi's designated place of exile—we know that the provinces provided fertile ground for its persistence.

Ottoman provinces witnessed the decline of the Ottoman Empire through a number of contrasts which developed during the nineteenth century. There was, at first, the rise of non-Muslim minorities on a new tide of privileges. The presence of foreign consuls to which great deference had to be accorded was new and it rankled. Towards the end of the nineteenth century Greeks started a slow take-over of the distribution of foodstuffs and of essential implements for the rural populations in western Turkey. Retreat on all these fronts produced an apathy which must have been enhanced by the ravages of continued wars on the population. Provincial Turks who saw themselves as Ottomans and Muslims perceived all of this as a decline of Islam. Sir William Ramsay states that, already in the 1880s, a ray of hope had emerged in Western Anatolia as a result of the support by Abdülhamid of Muslim activism (Ramsay, 1915–16, 407–408). Yet in the 1920s a widespread anomie was all that could be seen in Anatolia by foreign observers. This was partly the consequence of intra-communal squabbles involving non-Muslim minorities (1908–1915) and the destruction wrought by the Greek invasion of 1919. Said Nursi emerged at a time when the exchange of population between Turkey and Greece had created a new demographic picture and had left many economic slots unmanned in western Turkey.

Young Turkey, the Provinces and Religion

By the beginning of the 20th century the cultural gap between the Westernized, often agnostic or atheistic intellectual and the lower classes had created a feeling of popular suspicion against secularist modernizers. This feeling became widespread at the time of Young Turk rule: many pious Muslims considered them to be men of no religion (*dinsiz*). Since the Young Turks, influenced by a positivism of sorts, directed their efforts to the spread of educational opportunities, the improvement of agriculture and the elimination of the influence of local notables who were exploiting the peasants, this reaction is understandable. Part of it was due to the defensive reaction of the religious establishment. Part of it has to be attributed to the Young Turks' rather devious and purely formal attempt to use religious sentiment. In order to win support for their reformist program, they organized their own Islamic propaganda for internal as well as external consumption, but had little use for the religiosity of the small town or the village. Here, life was still centered on the common participation in Friday prayers, the observance of Muslim feasts and the observance of Muslim ritual. Not the least of these influences was the way in which the aesthetic appeal of religion worked as a focal point to create a general climate of sacrality as distinguished from the varying strength of piety among individual townsmen. An Ottoman intellectual who later opted for Marxism remembered that religion had affected him in this particular mode in his childhood (circa 1900):

> In our city, that is to say in Edirne, religion, more than a fear or mystery was like an ordering of the world. From the top of every hill in the city, mosques rose, each with its own characteristic and every one lovelier than the other. The city owed so much of its ornamentation to these that when one lived in their shadow it was impossible for anyone to escape being influenced by the meaning of these minarets and domes, each one of the products of the skills of a greater master builder than the other. (Aydemir, 1967, 31)

But while the sober Islam of the craftsman in Ottoman cities remained unshaken, this did not mean that the situation which confronted Islam had not changed even in the rural and the small town setting. Both towns and villages were being propelled into new situations if only because of the greater penetration of government into areas where its influence had been much more indirect in the past. The population of the Ottoman Empire which had not had much contact with its center was now increasingly in touch with it due to the new administrative system, the modest but increasing expansion of the road network, the important projects of railroad construction and the spread of a national market from the west toward Central Anatolia.

İsparta: 1926

When the Turkish government exiled Said Nursi to İsparta it unwittingly provided him with a most suitable base for proselytizing. İsparta was a Western version of Bitlis with many differences but with a number of striking similarities.

İsparta was in an isolated, mountainous region which, in Ottoman times, specialized in the production of men of religion. The many *medreses* and *tekkes* scattered throughout the province were the institutional base of this specialization. But the province differed from the Eastern regions of Anatolia in that the network of Islamic education was much looser, less pervasive. Said Nursi's work was to fill in these interstices. A certain division of labor characteristic of the province also prevailed. In the center of the province and in the peripheral districts functioned a number of religious "colleges" (*medrese*). In towns, and especially in the main center craftsmen specialized in leatherware and rug weaving. The villages produced cereals, raisins and opium. In 1892, Cuinet's figures showed a net favorable balance of trade for the province of 35,000 T.L. Trade was controlled by Armenians and Greeks. Figures for 1885 and 1914 (Shaw) indicate that the Muslim population of the central sub-province of İsparta (Merkez Kaza) which was 43,000 (rounded figures) in 1885 grew to 46,000 in 1914. By contrast the

Greek population of the same administrative unit grew from 4,000 (rounded figures) to 6,000. We cannot follow this growth within the limits of İsparta township, but Cuinet's figures mention a Muslim population of 13,000 and a Greek population of 7,000 in what one surmises are figures for the township. The notorious unreliability of 19th century statistics do not allow any speculation on this score except that the growth of the Greek population in the township must have followed that recorded for the central sub-province of İsparta (Cuinet, 1890, I, 846–852; "İsparta," 3504–3655).

In the late nineteenth century educational networks comprised about 200 *Qur'ānic* primary schools serving a population of about the same number of villages. *Tarikat* were also ubiquitous: *Mevlevi*s and *Nakşibendi*s prevailed. A tomb of 'Abd al-Qādir does not seem to have referred to the illustrious founder of the *Kadiri* order but to a namesake. The religious life of the masses in the province was centered on visits to tombs of prominent *âlims* who had originated in the province and who had acquired the status of holy men. About 30 to 40 *medreses* continued to provide religious training in the 1870s.

Developments during the nineteenth century disturbed what seems to have been a stable, symbiotic arrangement with Muslims concentrating on their religious institutions while Greeks, Muslim immigrants and a much smaller number of Armenians controlled business. The *Tanzimat,* with its opening up of new trade and other channels was the source of these changes. The final achievement of the late *Tanzimat* (or of the years of the reign of Sultan Abdülhamid II, 1876–1909) was the establishment of one middle school (*rüşdiye*) in each sub-provincial center and the founding of a lycée in the provincial center. The already-existing specialization of İsparta in education may have been the reason for which a girls' teacher training school was established already in 1875. (Accounts of the educational development of Republican times point out that it was the ubiquity of the *medrese* which facilitated the spread of the secular "laic" education of the newly founded Republic.) But the *medrese* network itself expanded considerably in the late nineteenth century. Educational statistics for 1903 mention a total of 60 *medrese,* twenty more than in 1877. As difficult as it is to give credence to the sultan's statistics, some remarkable increase in the number of *medrese* students must have occurred (statistics show an increase of more than 100%). The change is plausible in the light of a number of structural changes in the province. One of these was the general demographic increase. Again, we note that the population of the province as a whole had doubled during the reign of Sultan Abdülhamid. A source of this increase was refugees from the Balkans who were settled in the province following the war of 1877–78 with Russia. A source of expansion of the *medrese* population may have been the rise in the rate of unemployment following the influx of refugees, i.e., of young men who could find nothing better to do than to fill the *medrese*. There exist verses by a local poet which lampoon these students and the lowering of religious learning which this dilution had caused. Changes in the demographic picture had already occurred in 1877 when Circassians from the Caucasus were settled in the province. This was repeated after the Balkan wars of 1913, refugees being settled this time in the sub-province of Keçiborlu. On the other hand, the growth of the Muslim educational network may have been part of governmental policy. One aspect of the policies of the *Tanzimat* was the expansion of educational facilities which would set up new methods of instruction: the *rüşdiye* was the institution which exemplified this change. Often, however, the *rüşdiye* was too expensive to staff. Ahmed Şerif in his voyage through Anatolia found such a *rüşdiye* in an undeveloped part of İsparta: the building had been constructed, but there were no benches or teachers (A. Şerif, 1909). Under these circumstances it must have been a temptation for the architects of the *Tanzimat* to either expand or to close their eyes to the expansion of the *medrese* network, which demanded neither new teachers nor pay for them, since the teacher of the *medrese* was primarily supported by the local population. At any rate, *Tanzimat* administrative rulings show continued support of the government for *medreses* (interview with Mehmet Genç, November, 1984). The special conditions of Sultan Abdülhamid's reign only emphasized such an end. The local Greek population had been creating modern schools in İsparta, and their educational establishment was flourishing. Here, again, we have some difficulty with statistics, but regardless of which way these are interpreted the Greek rate of scholarization—in middle schools—is clearly much higher than that of Muslims. This was also true of Armenians. In a sense, then, the local Greek population provided the same demonstration effect that the missionaries had shown in Bitlis.

The upward trend of the Greek population of the province is closely linked with the expansion of the coastal economy. The latter was now connected with new roads and railway links to the hinterland of which İsparta was a part. The province showed an important agricultural potential. The trade in opium was so profitable that in the early 19th century the state had made it a state monopoly, but there were too many leaks in the system, and the state eventually abandoned the field. Another source of income for

İsparta was the distilling of rose oil, the technology of which had been brought by the Balkan immigrants of 1878. After 1890 the state encouraged the weaving of proper carpets, thus replacing the local production of *kilims* by more valuable rugs. The government also established a school for rug weaving in İsparta in 1891. In all cases, however, the value added to the products of İsparta was siphoned off to Aegean ports and to the clearing house town of Aydın. It was because they understood the opportunities opened up by the sale of this produce of İsparta that Greeks, already established in the province, had flocked in much larger numbers to the hinterland during the late nineteenth century.

This trend was reversed at the end of W.W.I.: Greeks began to emigrate from the area even before the official exchange of populations of 1924 between Greece and Turkey. There must have been severe strains which developed between Greeks and Muslims antedating the Greek-Turkish confrontation in the 1920s. Both movements together emptied positions in the structure of the business community which Turks now began to fill: Turks stepped into occupations as middlemen and traders that they never had filled before. Another political development of benefit to the Muslim population was that during the Turkish War of Independence of 1919–22 the province was providentially drawn into politics and emerged with a shining image vis-a-vis the Ankara government. The background of this political coup was that during the war of independence İsparta was in the region occupied by Italians. The *müftü* of İsparta organized a guerrilla unit against the Italians which he called The Iron Regiment. One cannot but see in this terminology the influence of Turkish nationalist rhetoric of the Young Turk era. The Italians, however, were gentle in their response and kept out of trouble. The local resistance forces were primarily involved in the incarceration of the representative of the sultan, whom they refused to turn over to Istanbul. After the establishment of the Republic, the *müftü* of İsparta and a number of other notables took their seat in Parliament. İsparta notables thus became allies of the Republican People's Party, the single party of the Republic. That they were rewarded is clear from the ease with which the industrialization of the province followed the founding of the new regime. A yarn factory was established in 1924–26, and this was followed by the founding of the Şarkikaraağaç Bank (1927). But while the notables were becoming increasingly city-oriented, the rural population was losing the organic link it had established with the *'ulema* since the doctors of Islamic law had been disestablished by the Republican government on March 3, 1924. The *'ulema* had lived in their midst even in the most remote districts. A society which was primarily kept together by cultural relations with a parallel symbiotic economic structure was being shaken; a new social entity, established on the basis of market transactions and close relations between the notables and government, was rising. A rural-urban cleavage developed which had a cultural, rather than strictly economic, character. Said Nursi owed some of his support to the persons who were disoriented by this fundamental change in the pattern of social relations.

Secularization

Following the inception of the Republic, the new regime undertook momentous steps towards secularization. On March 3rd, 1924 the caliphate was abolished. So were the Ministry of Religious Affairs and that of the Pious Foundations, as were all religious schools (*medrese*). The training of men of religion was placed under the auspices of the government and suffered a sharp decline. In 1926 the Swiss Civil Code was adopted (Toprak, 1981, 54 f.). This was followed by an educational ideology which, in primary schools, impugned the *'ulema* for the decline of the Ottoman Empire. In the new schools they were described as ignorant and reactionary fanatics who had exploited the Turkish people. The uneasy conjunction of this image with that of a Turk as a Muslim attentive to his religious duties still persists in the present-day school program.*

There were a number of reasons for which this secularizing stance unhinged the provincial population of Anatolia. The mere description of this transformation from a setting in which Islam had occupied a central place to a secular "laic" society gives us an inkling of the radical change which was achieved in a short time. Nevertheless, the type of disruption caused by the change only emerges when one brings up the details of this slice of Turkish social history. In İsparta—as in Bitlis—the *'ulema* had not only been men of religion, they had formed a net of lower order social leaders; they had been rural beacons linking the culture of the masses to the "great" culture of the cities. All of these blows to the religio-social structure of İsparta had resulted in a situation in which traditional symbols were clung to with the tenacity of those who felt they are about to lose their "map" of the world. However, this new clientele required to know more about this map than their ancestors would have.

---

*This was written in 1984. The extent to which Islamization has progressed since can be followed in that the sentence is no longer as true as it was in 1984.

In Barla, Said Nursi gathered around him a clientele both different and more numerous than the persons who had gravitated to him in earlier times. His early followers had consisted primarily of his students at the Horhor Medrese in Bitlis and also of intellectual peers who appreciated his learning. Now the intellectuals with whom he had discussed the future of Islam in Turkey were replaced by peasants, craftsmen, small traders and their sons, who were beginning to attend the lower grades of the Republican educational establishment. This cohort was led by men who had been trained in *medreses* and whose social origins are best described as provincial middle and lower-middle class. Among them figured a minor notable and *imam* of the village of Barla, where Bediüzzaman was in enforced residence, Said Nursi's personal servant, a trader, the son of an officer with a long residence in Damascus bearing the sobriquet of *hafız* (*Qur'ān* reciter), a primary school teacher, a man who had risen to the rank of sergeant during his military service, the *imam* of the village of Bedre, a barber, three men of modest background whose professions could not be ascertained, and the son of a lower ranking religious functionary (*hoca*) (Şahiner, 1978 and 1986, II, 101–120).

First Followers

A number of letters addressed to Said Nursi by some of his followers at the time when he was exiled in Barla provide us with clues concerning the appeal of his message. Since these letters are written by followers with a background of *medrese* studies (in one case a military academy background), they are not necessarily representative of the value which his message had for his illiterate followers, but they do make up a set of responses that were important in the formative stages of the movement.

The most articulate of his followers (in relation to the number of printed letters) turns out to be Hulusi Yahyagil, whose biography I give below in Chap. V. An officer with the rank of captain at the time he first met Said, Hulusi was obviously a person who was highly responsive to religious "music." For him, Said Nursi's primary contribution resided in information concerning theological issues which provided him with clues that, apparently, enabled him to solve theological puzzles which he had been unable to unravel on his own. Hulusi seems to have been primarily interested in the mystical-theosophical tradition, but he also appeared to be seeking a satisfactory picture of the cosmos (*Sikke-i Tasdik-i Gaybî*, 1960, 43, 49–51, 52, 84, 91, 95, 104). For another follower, the *imam* of the village of Bedre, Said Nursi's contribution was his ability to overcome the *imam*'s own pessimism: he felt that Said's writings were a "balm" at a time of confusion (*Ibid.*, 36, 43, 56). The *imam* was also grateful for information about Islam that was unobtainable in other sources (*Ibid.*, 35). For the *hafız* "Little" Ali of the village of İslamköy, Bediüzzaman provided an answer to the question "Where do we come from and where are we going?" (*Ibid.*, 36, 70). To him it was a way of nullifying the effects of the "dead end of philosophy."

A common element in all these comments is dissatisfaction with the available information on religion. Disciples are interested in having a better understanding of the elements of Islam; they are trying to elaborate a more internally consistent picture of their religion. They have inquiring minds and even "Little" Ali has something to say about "philosophy," i.e., the speculations of Western secular thinkers.

One person to whom Said Nursi gave particular attention was an ex-officer, Re'fet by name, with whom he had an extensive correspondence. He appears to have been delighted by Said's combat against what Re'fet described as "becoming beggars of Europe for science and enlightenment" when the *Qur'ān* could be used for these ends. An important aspect of the style of these letters and of Said's own pronouncements is that they freely use such concepts as electricity, motor, factory in the context of the revitalization of religion. The teachings of Said are described in one instance as "the electric bulbs of the Nur factory." One of the earliest messengers of the group is still known as *"Santral"* (telephone exchange) Sabri. Here again, the impact of the mechanization of the ambient world seems to have been effective in as isolated a region as Isparta. These questions about religion were generated by the *Nurcu*'s confrontation with a new body of knowledge acquired by chance or through the channels which made some of the "modernization" of the center trickle into the countryside. One level of their religious understanding which was affected was the issue of Islam in the world at large.

The Republic had started a secular attack on the idea of an Islamic community which had been the ultimate legitimating symbol of society in the Ottoman Empire. This aspect of Muslim "collective representations" was denied a role in Republican Turkey. The Kemalist system replaced them with the secular ideology of the Republic, with a new creation myth which sought the roots of modern Turkey in the achievements of the Turks of Central Asia, and a new social propellant, namely the idea that the future of Turkey consisted in the elaboration of a modern society taking its cues from Western solidarism and positivism. The socially less-favored Muslims of the provinces also had greater need than before for a legitimating canopy since they had begun to be drawn into a more complex system of national communications where they were seeking their place. In the views of this early clientèle of *Nurculuk*, Islamic discourse was a beacon that provided a solution for such a search.

Networks

The criss-crossing network of the many Sufi orders which had a hold in Anatolia set the stage for the operation of more restricted, smaller communications systems which operated according to similar principles of network formation; one of those crystallized around the person of Said Nursi. The basic matrix for this replication was the *Halidi* establishment in eastern Turkey and the notables of the Bitlis region who had more or less solid links with the *Halidi*. Said Nursi had been a lecturer at the Horhor Medrese at the time of his exile and, therefore, kept this connection alive with a number of his students in the years that followed his departure from Bitlis. A number of his *Halidi* friends who taught in other *medreses* also kept in touch with him. Religious leaders and tribal chiefs who had been part of the group which left Bitlis to establish obligatory residence in various parts of Turkey in 1925 also kept their contacts. This was done either through correspondence or by the intermediary of persons travelling from East to West who brought him greetings and information. It was through this network that the news was spread that Said had turned over a leaf in his life and that he was producing some new commentaries on the *Qur'ān*. A survey of persons who figured among a large group of sympathizers (Şahiner ed., 1978) shows that many of these came from the middling stratum of Turkish provincial towns and that among them contact with Said was established through personal connections more than by an exposure to his theories. Letters which were written to Said by his first disciples show that the movement was organized in the vicinity of Barla by a "staff" composed of men of religion of lower rank or laymen knowledgeable about religion, and that they communicated with persons of a similar background spreading the message further afield (*Barla Lahikası, passim*).

Networks and Politics

The involvement of the *Nur* movement in Turkish politics has often been a theme which has been invoked to attack it. That such an involvement exists today cannot be denied. One instance would be the support which the *Nurcu* gave the Demokrat Party in the 1950s and the Turkish clerical party, the MSP, in the elections of 1973. The movement then switched its support to the Justice Party. Said Nursi's own relation to politics shows a more complex pattern, which explains the involvement of Turkish religious groups in the political process better than does a simple tally of support for political parties.

Said Nursi's first career is an instance of an intermeshing of personal, ideological and political concerns. His second career, that of a teacher of the truths of Islam, showed what may be called a long-range political purpose, which was the revitalization of Islam as a world force, but he did eventually add shorter term political goals to this purpose temporarily. The appearance of the Demokrat Party as a hegemonic political party in the 1950s set a new field for the influence of religion in politics. As we already saw, Said took advantage of this setting to get one of his followers who had been elected representative from İsparta in 1954, Dr. Tahsin Tola, to lift the interdiction against the printing of the *Risale-i Nur.*

The Demokrat Party, however, did not let its guard down in its attitude towards the *Nur* movement. It did not allow Said Nursi to enter Ankara when, towards the end of his life, his followers attempted a show of strength by inviting him to visit the capital (1959). Thereafter he was also forbidden to move from his place of residence. Even though he was on the move again, shortly after this interdiction, the attitude of the authorities toward the measures to be taken to restrict the scope of his burial ceremonies shows that they were apprehensive of political repercussions related to his image even after his death.

During the Demokrat era (1950–1960) a number of notables from the eastern provinces of Turkey were elected to the Turkish parliament. Of necessity, the membership of this group overlapped with those of *tarikat* formations. Sometimes this was so because tribal leaders (who were part of the local notability) were also religious leaders, or because these representatives had relatives among religious leaders, or because they had attended religious training. Links with Said Nursi emerged from such propinquity. An example would be the relation between Said Nursi and the local notable, Kinyas Kartal. Kartal was elected to Parliament in the 1960s as a representative of the Van province. In his attestations for Said Nursi, Kartal relates that when in 1925 the notables of the Bitlis-Van area, a mix of tribal leaders (Kartal's role as a "tribal" leader is one he assumed after his migration from Russia, where he was an officer in the Czarist Army) and religious personalities (*Son Şahitler,* II, 16 f.) were arrested, was also taken into the net. The group included Said Nursi; they were shepherded together to western Turkey, although Kartal was sent to enforced residence to another town. A similar picture emerges from the statements of Giyaseddin Emre, independent representative from Muş in 1954, elected on the Demokrat Party ticket in 1957 and arrested after the military intervention of 1960 (*Ibid.*, 49 f.). Emre took upon himself to speak for Said Nursi on a number of occasions during his political tenure.

All of these strands show that the interweaving of family ties, notable status, *tarikat* membership, religious education and bonds of friendship made up a network which was both instrumental in recruitment to *Nurculuk* and, also, legitimized Said's message. This network found opportunities to perpetuate itself on the national scale as a result of the more intense social mobilization of Turkey after 1950. Following the death of Bediüzzaman, its ideological focus shifted from his person to that of his writings. In a sense, then, the step taken by Said Nursi in the 1920s, adumbrated by the steps in his maturation and the transition from the teachings of a charismatic leader to theses expounded in print (the *Risale-i Nur*)—was a correct assessment of the potential presented by the new field of action for religion initiated by changes of social structure during the twentieth century.

The support of the *tarikat*-notable network of Eastern Turkey was paralleled by a similar but different network which operated within the general area of İsparta-Eskişehir-Afyon in the western provinces of Turkey. Here, local political influence appears to have been much less an elite process than it was in Eastern Turkey and showed a much more populistic tinge. In İsparta, religious leaders also wielded considerable social prestige, but there were no notables with power comparable to that of tribal leaders. Of the first twelve disciples of Said Nursi almost all are from the western region and are characterized by this populistic syndrome. Their social origins are varied; some of them of a truly rustic cast, others obviously with wider connections. At least six of them had family or more direct ties to the religious establishment and religious institutions (*Ibid.*, 101–120).

The lines of force which drew persons to Said overlap and work cumulatively, but I shall try to underline one of the dimensions more markedly in each of the case histories I examine in the next section.

B: The "Inner" World

One of the puzzling features of Said Nursi's writings, which emerges from the corpus known as the *Risale-i Nur*, is its helter-skelter, relatively unsystematic structure. A section of these collected sermons such as *Lem'alar* (*Flashes of Light*), for instance, covers the following subjects in its first few hundred pages: Jonah, the meaning of his tribulations; the affliction of Job (*Ibid.*, 19f.); an interpretation of the *Qur'ānic* verse of Man's attachment to the transitory as summarized in a *Nakşibendi* axiom, commentary on a verse of the *Qur'ān* concerning the leadership of the Muslim community (Fazlur Rahman, 1979, 170); an interpretation of *Sūra* 48 ("Victory") on the moral strength instilled by Islam even in times when this religion appears to have lost its moral authority; God's way of warning humans; following the path of the Prophet Muhammad at a time when unauthorized innovations (*bid'at*) are rife; an answer to Re'fet Bey's two questions concerning God's control of one's deserts (*rizk*) and the seven layers of heaven and earth. The list goes on with such questions as: How is it that partisans of the devil are able to score successes in this world?; Teachers of religion state that the earth stands on a steer and a fish, but geography shows that the earth is suspended in space (there is neither steer nor fish). What is the truth of this matter?; What is the mystery of the expression "In the name of God, the Compassionate, the Merciful?"; Why didn't the predictions of such clerics as Çaprazzâde Abdullah Efendi, who, during the preceding month of Ramazan predicted that the Muslim community would experience important reversals of bad fortune, materialize?; Explanation of the causes of Said Nursi's "Crisis of Conscience" of 1921.

To unravel these utterances we have to fit into the shoes of those to whom they were addressed, and this involves a reconstruction of the entire mental map of Bediüzzaman's followers.

The external developments which promoted the spread of *Nurculuk* provide us with a pattern of tracks which shaped the opportunities and delineated the boundaries of the movement. This is a feature in the growth of *Nurculuk* which one has relatively little difficulty in tracing. To recapture the inner spring that animated the *Nurcu*s is more arduous, because these ideas present a number of interpenetrating facets.

In the most general sense, Bediüzzaman was making use of an existing Islamic "idiom" to establish resonance among a clientele whose day-to-day life was integrated into this set of meanings. We may start with the resonance created by a concept which reappears frequently in Said Nursi's homiletics, that of the Islamic community or *umma* (See Gibb, 1963, *passim;* Hodgson, I, 173–74; Watt, 1960).

Hodgson gives a cogent description of this structure:

> Muslims share their experience in a total society, comprehending (in principle) the whole of human life, the Ummah, built upon standards derived from

> the prophetic vision; comprising a homogeneous brotherhood, bearing a common witness brought to mind daily in the salat worship and impressively reaffirmed en masse each year at Mecca. (Hodgson, 1974, II, 338)

The *umma* was a conception which was used by Muslims to apprehend the central realities of Islam. In the Muslim theological frame, its definition and conditions of emergence as well as the promise of its perpetuation were contained in the *Qur'ānic* injunction to Muslims to "Propagate the Good and arrest Evil" (Hodgson, I, 387). The attempt to follow this injunction took a variety of forms during the centuries that followed the Prophet's mission. One which comes to mind is the construction of canonical frames for a Muslim society as was the case among the 10th century Muslim conservatives known as the "*Ahl al-Ḥadīth*" (persons who lived by the example of the Prophet Muhammad). Sometimes the dedication to "arrest" evil appeared as a reaffirmation of the Muslim ruler's obligation to enforce Islamic values. A concrete example of this in the Ottoman Empire was the puritanical movement of the times of Sultan Murad IV, which opposed social practices such as smoking tobacco and innovations in Muslim ritual. Birgi, the home of Kadı Birgevî, the cleric who was the inspiration for this movement was, like İsparta, a mountain fastness of Orthodoxy. In the 20th century the Muslim brothers show a third version of the same type of grouping (Mitchell, 1969).

A characteristic feature of the *umma* is the license the community of believers arrogates to itself in taking a critical stand towards the authority of officials. The recent Iranian revolution has been built on this potential for contestation which all Islamic societies hold. In Iran, the potential was exploited to the full, but the study of Islamic revitalization movements in the contemporary world shows that this was no isolated instance. In Muslim societies modernization has been accompanied by a reactivation of contestation legitimized by the theory of the community's rights—and obligations.

All of these aspects of the action of the *umma* in its actual settings do not give us more than a derived "macro" image of its nature. A means of getting closer to its social morphology would be to disentangle the repertoire of social relations which the *umma* brings with it. By repertoire I mean a series of vocables, values, concepts, material implements, life strategies, social positions and spaces, myths, sacralized locations and time scales. One may get a deeper insight into the *umma* not by analyzing these elements in their isolation but by seeing them as a constellation with changing *interrelations*. This is what Foucault calls a "discourse" (Foucault, 1977). I believe this to be—among others—a convenient approach to the analysis of the action frame of the *Nurcus*.

Said Nursi was re-establishing himself inside this discourse, and he assumed a directing role in its re-emergence when he shifted his stand from that of the old to that of the "new" Said. He was now using a lever which was that of Muslim "civil society" to achieve political ends, i.e., the mobilization of Muslim Turks as Muslims. While Said used components of this discourse (i.e., the *position* of an *âlim* [a learned cleric], the *figure* of a Saint, the *tradition* which opposed pious Muslims to "Pharaoh," the *style* of the mystics, etc.), he also transformed it. The transformational possibilities he brought to each were centered on three "second order' (i.e., more abstract) features of this discourse. These were a conceptualization of social relations as personalistic, a folk cosmology with imagistic moorings, and an allusive, obscure, highly metaphorical rhetoric.

A Personalistic View of Society

For those who have inherited the Western European conceptualization of social relations, "society" exists. It exists as a pulsating, integrated, supra-individual being which has "needs," gives "orders" or requires "sacrifices." In Adam Müller's pithy summary it is: "Ein grosses, energisches, unendlich bewegtes und lebendiges Ganzes." This, of course, is an artifact which is no older than the modern nation-state from which it takes its pedigree. We see society as a totality which has priority over individual wishes. This totality is conceived as integrating a number of second-level components. The latter are abstract entities which operate in pursuit of their own "needs" and which can be understood without reference to the persons of whom they are composed. Among these so-called sub-systems figure The Family, Labor and Social Class or Strata, The Educational System or The Government. A somewhat different picture of society was held by Ottomans and especially by the Muslim Ottoman living on the margin of the political elite of officials. It is this view of the world that we also find in Said Nursi. It portrays society as made up of constituents such as "fathers and mothers," "our ruler" or "rulers." It mentions the Master and his Pupils, master craftsmen and hard working artisans. The linkages between these figures are pictured as consisting of "filial piety," "keeping one's engagements," "the sacredness of an oath," "establishing bonds of friendship," "fitting into the neighborhood," and "trying to establish a respectable status as a member of a (partly) religious community."

All of these concepts may be described as personalistic. I have already pointed out that this stand is not a defense of individualism. The concepts depend on a view of society as composed of "real" persons interlinked with bonds which acquire their meaning from the human element subsuming them. Roy Mottahedeh's *Loyalty and Leadership in an Islamic Society* has shown to what large extent such personalistic links were involved in shoring up the political institutions of the Buyids, a 10th century Muslim dynasty. The European feudal parallel immediately comes to mind.

In the Ottoman Empire, with its extensive crystallization of institutions, the situation differed from that of the Buyids. Ottoman statesmen did have a conception of society as made up of a state and also of orders (*erkân*), and their stance in the affairs of state was shaped by this model. Another way of describing this characteristic would be to point out that Ottoman public law (*örf-ü sultanî*) was more highly developed than that of earlier Muslim empires. Conversely, in the Ottoman Empire, the civil sector of society, that part of society which operated outside officialdom, may have been more deeply suffused by the *şeriat*. The latter operated as an approximate equivalent of private law. Also, the world of *şeriat*, that of the private individual as framed by Islamic society, was, of necessity, a personalistic world since the message of the Prophet Muhammad, the *Qur'ān*, was a message to men and not to society. In Hamid Enayat's pithy summary: "The Qur'an recognizes man (*insān*) irrespective of his political beliefs and political standing but has no word for " 'citizen' " (Enayat, 1982, 127).

In empires preceding the Ottoman, men of religion, doctors of Islamic law, i.e., the upholders of the *şeriat* were often the representatives of the people vis-a-vis the class of officials. The Ottomans settled the problem this posed for the center by making state officials of the most prestigious section of the *'ulema*, but they could not modify the populistic formulation of politics which took its strength from the *şeriat*.

In an ideal-typical Islamic society the efficacy of personalistic relations which underlie the exercise of *şer'i* civil rights arises from the fact that personalism constitutes a system of social relations in its own right. This system cuts across the system of public law: on it depend, in large part, the strategies that will lose or gain status, and the cohesive forces that keep society together. In such a society oral performances are a greater test of one's worthiness as a repository of knowledge than the production of research papers. Personalistic relations and performances of speech are neatly imbricated in the system.

In town life personalistic strategies and forces are highlighted by the quarter (*mahalle*) of the town, a basic unit of social life. As has been pointed out in the case of Morocco:

> Ideally, the households of a quarter are considered to be bound together by multiple personal ties and common interests. These complex ties are said to symbolize *qaraba*, a key concept which, literally, means "closeness". As used by urban and rural Moroccans, *qaraba* carries contextual meanings which range imperceptibly from asserted and recognized ties of kinship to participation in factional alliances, ties of patronage and clientship and common bonds developed out of residential propinquity. (Eickelman, 1976, 96)

Seem as a system of social relations, the personalistic element explains some aspects of the religious strategy of Said Nursi, i.e., his special emphasis on changing man's inner world as the touchstone of a revitalized Islam. Here again, two forces worked concurrently: the mobilized self was one of the requirements that had been brought about by the modernization of the social structure, but the best way to implement the mobilization was to anchor it in persons by making faith something that was cultivated by truly autonomous individuals. Islam as an ideological canopy would provide the external impetus to mobilization, Islam internalized would provide the internal thrust coming from individuals. The importance of this internalization followed logically from the personalistic system, for where there are no holistic conceptions of society to work with—other than "Islam"—then the end one pursues is not to change society as a whole but the individual and his "heart." It is this set of opportunities for the mobilization of the heart that Said Nursi seems to have had in mind when he shifted from politics to the conversion of individuals.

Another characteristic of the personalistic universe of Islam is that *ibadet* (*'ibāda*) (worship of God) undertaken by an individual creates lines of force which set him on a precise course, individually and socially. Said Nursi would have agreed (had he been cognizant of Weber) that *ibadet* rationalizes life by framing it in a set of moral constraints which switch all persons who worship simultaneously in the same direction. Said repeatedly points to this aspect of worship. He mentions, for instance, that when one person says "God is great" he has to realize that he is only one of thousands who at that moment, i.e., at the time of prayer, are repeating the same words. In a number of passages we are reminded of al-Ghazālī's ideas that faith in and by itself generates a power of which the Faithful themselves are unaware.

In Islamic society, the elaboration of identity according to Islamic rules is not only an internal process; the same process has an outward dimension which links the personalistic system with social interaction. The self-image elaborated in the silence of one's internal struggles has to be tested against the conceptions that others hold of oneself. This is true of all societies, but it acquires an added importance in the society I have tried to describe to the extent that the internalized pieces of the culture are much more frequently tested in outward actions or statements (Eickelman, 1976, 132–214). This is the field where the self-image works or fails to work, i.e., does or does not produce the expected social outcomes. In a personalistic setting the solidity of an institution is dependent on the reciprocal process of the subject's being able to withstand constant questioning. One of the consequences of this institutionalized strategy is that social status also acquires provisionality. Here the questioning mood is set by the communities dispensation to make the Good prevail and combat Evil. The unstable equilibrium which follows from testing builds one of the strongest bulwarks of the Muslim conception of social equality.

> God's will legitimates the present—and ephemeral—distribution of social honor as a God-given state of affairs. The ranking of individuals in relation to one another is never taken for granted but is constantly empirically tested. Provisionality is the very essence of the cosmos. Consequently, attention is focused upon assessing exact differentials of wealth, success, power and social honor among particular men as a prelude to effective, specific social action. . . . (Eickelman, 1976, 126)

We can now understand how, in Said Nursi's writings, "children," and the "aged," both functions of the concept of *insan* (man) are two basic analytical categories used by him to conceptualize social relations (*Mektubat*, 394). Said Nursi was making use of folk conceptions in which *insan* was more important than *erkân* (orders). The latter, the concept of orders of society, the bureaucrat's way of describing social relations. Said Nursi's personalistic classification appears also in the thought of other modern Islamic fundamentalists such as Mawdudi, in whose scheme of social reform orphans make up a similar fundamental category (Enayat, 1982, 109). This system, where the person is at the center of economic and social relations, differs radically from one in which mechanical social processes have taken over. An example would be the contrast between the Muslim system of economics in which, ideally, personal welfare is the unit *against* which the efficiency of the market is measured and the liberal economists' market system, where it is the ***efficiency of the market*** which is the main point of interest.

In the same vein, in Said Nursi's writings, social security is conceptualized as a function of the elaboration and support of strong family ties: the feeling of responsibility of the young for the old takes the place of social insurance (*Mektubat,* 240). *Zekât* (obligatory almsgiving) emerges as a contribution to equity, social order and stability.

There exists an undeniable, potentially authoritarian element in these patterns of relations which emerges most clearly in the one-sided obligation of children to obey their parents and for parents to obey God. A contemporary *Nurcu* woman now a "guest-worker" in Germany complained that it was because she recognized this one-sided obligation that despite the fact that her horizons had broadened in Germany and she had gradually acquired a new confidence in herself and autonomy towards her husband she did not object to his sending 200–300 DM from her own earnings back to the village to her husband's parents (Schiffauer, 1924, 493). But the relation is authoritarian only for those who perceive it as such. In the case of Said Nursi's followers, the positive aspects of obligation towards parents *when placed within the total system of Islamic relations* appears to be greater than the burdens it generates.

Personalism in the sense in which we see it used by Said Nursi has a number of further connotations. Since Adam was the first man to be taught the name of Allah, which embraces all of his other names (theophanies), the concept "descendants of Adam" is the conceptual unit through which society should be apprehended. A speculation of Bediüzzaman which is related to this trend of thought is his assertion that one should remember that one of the Names of God (through which the phenomenal works is activated) is *Farid,* or "The Individual" (BSN, 271). Thus even individuality has as its referent, the divine and not the person's make-up or characteristics.

Notice that "personalism" as a conceptual template is not a psychologism but rather a non-psychological explanation. The characters in the plot presented by Bediüzzaman are functions of their place in the family circle. Their actions are seen as explained by the position they occupy; it is this position or status which produces the dynamic of social action. The focus is not on the subject but on the predicate. It is this view of society as a set of positions informed by *Qur'ānic* requirements that builds the image of society. Society, then, is not directly explainable by the *Qur'ān* but more correctly by the positional set derived from *Qur'ān* injunctions. The reproduction of the system in a new setting now becomes easy for the Muslim ideologue in the sense that it is these positions which have to be reproduced, and that he can easily reassemble them in the correct order since they are limited in number.

Personalism and Ethics

Of all the themes he presented in the *Risale-i Nur,* Said Nursi was most adamant about the necessity to revitalize Islamic ethics. Sometimes this emphasis had pragmatic overtones, as when he described religion as a balm to the wound suffered by individuals. More often it was a theme which underlined the harmony that one would achieve by remaining in tune with the frame of the universe as taught by Islam.

Nevertheless, for Said Nursi the *Qur'ān* is primarily a means of placing restraints on the dangerous appetites of man. As he put it:

> The aims of the *Qur'ān* are to provide a barrier against the appetites of man (*hevesat-ı nefsaniye*) thus encouraging him to engage in higher pursuits, giving satisfaction to his higher aspirations and directing him towards the achievements of human perfection. (Mürsel, 1976, 1975 citing Bediüzzaman, *Sözler,* 138–139)

His fundamental fear is that the *me* will take over in a Muslim's life. This, according to him, has been promoted by contemporary materialism. Another of his fears is that of the disintegration of society. These two thoughts are closely interlinked: in fact, the salvation of the Islamic nation lies in one's keeping immersed in the network of relations between relatives and believers (Mürsel, 1976, 174, citing Bediüzzaman, *Şualar,* 355) and the ethical concerns that are generated in such a setting. This view is projected onto Said's ideas concerning society and the nation:

> One's country too is a house, and the fatherland is the house of a natural family. If the belief in the hereafter rules in these large houses, an immediate consequence is the inception of the development of sincere respect, serious compassion, affection and helpfulness which do not depend on material rewards; guileless service, sociability and generosity without hypocrisy, and virtue and greatness without pride and the flowering of human qualities (*meziyet*). It says to children: "There is a paradise: abandon sloth." It says to young men: "Hell exists, stop your drunkenness." It says to the tyrant: "There is a reckoning with utmost suffering; you shall be struck," and forces him to bow his head to justice. It says to the old: "There is a most exalted, divine and continuous happiness greater than any which you may have lost,

> and a fresh, permanent youth which awaits you; try to gain these," and it changes his tears to laughter. (Mürsel, 1976, 168, citing, Bediüzzaman, *Şualar,* 262)

Thus Bediüzzaman's world of ethical commands proceeds from the family and the community—the basic components of society according to Said Nursi—to the state. It is for the family and the community that the state is created rather than vice versa. We can understand, in this light, how the rival, "godless" theory of an autonomous state, created to bring happiness to society, would have been considered a liberating influence for secular radicals such as the young Turks. It is in this respect that the view of the state of Turkish bureaucrats, developed during the *Tanzimat* and emerging with a new dimension in the ideas of the Young Turks, may be seen as a liberation from the shackles of community life.

The conceptual constellation of women, family, community, and man as a prisoner of his appetites which anchor this type of ethic agrees with observations about Islamic societies in other parts of the world. The absence of a real boundary between the private and the public—in the sense that the *şeriat* claims to control the public realm—provides the clue to this ethic. In a number of instances Bediüzzaman states that the real foundation of the moral incompatibility between Islam and modern, Western (materialistic) civilization is that the former takes persons as basic units of social life while the latter is based on concepts such as the nation (Şahiner, 1979, 200–201).

One of the most interesting aspects of the personalistic view of life is the way in which it centers history on the formative years of Islam. The latter is explained in function of the primordial role of Islamic *Urzeit* and its mythical figures. The role of the unusually gifted *person,* and *elect* of God, thus finds one more conceptual crag onto which it fastens.

Underlying the entire personalistic scheme is the assumption that the search for truth also should be conducted in a personalistic mode, in the sense that it is prophets, and,. after them, saints—persons who have been selected by God for special dispensation of his grace—who are the intermediates between God as the creating principle and the world he has created (Bediüzzaman, *Mektubat,* 74). Saints are the repositories of truth. Here again the success of Bediüzzaman was due to his ambiguous stand regarding the role of the Saint (*pir* or *veli*) which he adopted but also transformed.

Bediüzzaman's stress on the personalistic element provided the rural population which flocked to him with a map of social relations that Kemalism had neglected. Kemalist ideology was long on views concerning the virtues of Turks, the benefit of secular republicanism for personality expansion, and the contribution of universal education to progress. It was short on methods that would enable individuals to tackle issues arising in the family circle. It did not answer queries relating to the authority of the father, or as to what the new place of women in society would be *after* republican secularization and the adoption of the Swiss Civil Code in anything approaching the detail of the most commonplace Islamic "catechism" with rural diffusion. Neither did Kemalists have a view of rituals that would give meaning to life-stations such as birth, adolescence, marriage and death. Anyone who has had the occasion to witness the groping attempts of brides, bridegrooms and their families to infuse some color and warmth into the bleak process of Turkish civil marriages will know what I mean. The superficiality and lack of organic linkages with society, of Kemalism—which was successful in many other ways, as we have seen—appeared in such lacunae. Said Nursi's teachings filled this gap by providing such a map of family norms, in particular the respect to be shown to the father and to elders.

In addition, the traditional Islamic idiom of personal and social values was the social foundation which could be used as a springboard, in the search for a more meaningful universe going *beyond* the family.

In his discourse about society, Said Nursi does not see himself as a subject who states propositions about an external entity, society, without taking into account his personal involvement in it; for him society is not an "It" but an "I." Two quotations will make my point clearer. The first is Cooley's definition of the primary group:

> By primary group, I mean those characterized by intimate, face-to-face association and cooperation. The result of intimate association, psychologically, is a certain fusion of individualities in a common whole, so that one's very self, for many purposes at least, is the common life and purpose of the group. (Goody, 1977, 157 quoting Cooley, *Social Organization*, 1909, 23)

A second source gives us a description of what knowledge meant for the Ancient Greeks. For them:

> knowledge was not something . . . acquired as a possession but something in which they participated, allowing themselves to be directed and even possessed by their knowledge. In this way the Greeks achieved an approach to truth that went beyond the limitation of modern subject-object thinking rooted in subjectively certain knowledge. (Palmer, 1969, 165)

Said Nursi's attitude towards society, as well as his conception of knowledge, could not be better described.

What I mean by an "I" is also better understood in relation to what we know about the contrast between oral and scriptural cultures. Ong describes this difference as follows:

> In the absence of elaborate analytical categories that depend on writing to structure knowledge at a distance from lived experience, oral cultures must conceptualize and verbalize all their knowledge with more or less close references to the human lifeworld, assimilating the alien, objective world to the more immediate, familiar interaction of human beings. (Ong, 1982, 42)

I would propose that—although very closely linked to a culture of writing—the culture fund which Said Nursi taps is one where there are still survivals of orality. Furthermore, that this appears as a tension between those aspects of his style that are highly abstract and refer to the divine and aspects that are highly personalistic and apply to day-to-day social relations. There remains something of an understanding of society taken from an oral culture in his message.

A summary of findings concerning the sociological imagination of Said Nursi would emphasize one main point: Bediüzzaman does not have a holistic understanding of society: he sees society as made up of persons. But here we have to emphasize another feature which runs counter to this first finding: these persons are not real but "virtual" persons. They are defined not as individuals but as positions or roles that those persons would fill. The "Good Society" is one where this pyramid of roles—derived from the *Qur'ān*—is constituted. If we take "discourse" in a restricted sense to mean the instrumentality enabling a person to speak about society, we can see how the elimination from the social vocabulary of the names of these roles, as was done by Republican Turkey,—that is, an incomplete conceptual set—may lead to the inability of a person to form propositions about society, to speak out about it intelligently. The ensuing frustration was assuaged by the discovery that such a discourse was one of the facilities offered by Said Nursi.

Innovation

Even though Said consistently used a personalistic classification for concerns which we would classify as social, he also brings some modifications into this classification. New terms begin to appear in his writings which are taken out of the Ottoman reformist officials' or Ottoman intellectuals' vocabulary. Such is the concept of *hayat-ı içtimaiye-i beşeriye,* a notion which is used as a synonym for "civilization" (*Emirdağ Lahikası,* 178).

A similar term is that of *hayat-ı içtimaiye* (*Mektubat,* 69) or "social life," which sometimes takes the form of *hayat-ı beşeriye-i Islâmiye,* (the social life of Islam). However, on this occasion too, the description of the functions of an official is characteristically traditional. The official (*memur*) has two duties to perform in society: to keep dangerous characters at bay (*muzır eşhas*) and to help persons who are useful (*nafi*). The imprint of truly Islamic views concerning the boundaries of society also appears in Bediüzzaman's criticism of Turkish nationalism and his support for inter-Islamic solidarity (*Mektubat,* 298).

Said Nursi lived at a time when antithetical ideas of progress were clashing in Europe. There was, on the one hand, the residue of the idea of progress as it had been proclaimed by the Enlightenment philosophers. But there was also the late 19th century discouragement with Western civilization and denial of its assessment of human potential for good. Nevertheless, there seems to have been a diffuse sense in which the optimism of the earlier period prevailed and affected even persons such as Said Nursi. While there is no conclusive proof of this venue into his ideas about morality, and even though the medium that he used to crystallize these ideas was that of Muslim mysticism, we discern in his preaching a softening of the orthodox Sunni stress on the torments of Hell which are promised to sinners. There is, conversely, a new stress on the benevolence of God and on *şefkat* (affection) as the bond that links God and the believer.

In the most general sense, Said Nursi is aware that his time, the time of modernity, bears a special mark. He sees the three concepts which characterize these times as *malikiyet* (private property), *serbestiyyet* (freedom), and the growth of science. The era preceding the era of freedom is that of economic exploitation (*ecirlik devri*) (*Sözler,* 661), which Said Nursi describes as follows:

> The rich, which constitute the elite, have made the poor and the lower classes (*avam*) into servants in exchange for a wage. That is the owners of capital have employed those who only dispose of their labor (*ehl-i sây*) and workers for a small wage. In this stage exploitation has increased to such a degree that while a capital owner sits in his palace and earns a million a day through the banks, a poor worker labors in the mines underground for a pittance. This condition created so much hatred and rage that the lower classes rebelled against the upper.

These thoughts were presumably inspired by the two years that Said Nursi spent in Russian camps just before the Russian Revolution. In one instance, Bediüzzaman states that Islam constitutes an alternative to communism (Mürsel, 1976, note 13, citing *Rumuz,* 23). There is, then, a sense in which Said Nursi appropriates the notion of historical progress. And, in another light, the poor can only be influenced by forces that affect their "heart" (*Mektubat*, 416). Conscious of the extent to which "bolshevism and socialism" were becoming powerful forces (*Mektubat*, 41) he considered nationalism *passé* and Islam a current which would show renewed freshness. Another liberating addition to Said Nursi's repertoire was the idea, already alluded to in Ch. III, of the rationality of Muslim ethics. The thesis that religion could not any more be simply declarative (one of Said's oft-repeated statements) but had to rely on convincing arguments (which, incidentally does not mean the arguments of philosophy) was, no doubt, an aspect of his shrewd understanding of the process of modernization as it grew in Turkey after 1908. A German anthropologist has recently confirmed this insight. Werner Schiffauer, whom we have already quoted, gives us an extremely interesting description of the process by which the rationale of an ethico-religious command in an urban (German) *Nurcu* frame leading to a negotiating stance replaces the rigidity these values carry in the Turkish rural setting. What Said Nursi spotlighted in a time dimension, i.e., against the background of modernization, Schiffauer studies spatially, i.e., during the move of a woman from her village to Berlin. In Berlin the woman takes up house-cleaning work while her husband is unemployed. She joins the *Nurcu* at first because she has to defend herself against the "other"—the Germans—and has to set a frame of identity for herself. But once in the group she becomes intellectually and ethically much more mobile than she was in the village. The symbolically charged performances of daily life which are inflexible and obligatory in the narrow frame of village life (e.g., covering one's head with a shawl) acquire more play in the perspective of the *meaning* which is now considered to underlie the act itself. This meaning opens up new options for use of this performance. Meaning becomes the deeper legitimizer of religious value (Schiffauer, 1984).

Folk Conceptions Mobilized

Modern Islamic fundamentalist reformers have exerted themselves to conjure out of Islam what they consider to be unwarranted, superstitious accretions upon its "pristine state." They point out that it was this extraneous, irrelevant layer of superstitious beliefs which caused the stagnation of Islamic civilization. Accretions resulted in the Muslims' forfeiting their role as vanguards of civilization and progress (Kerr, 1966, 106, 108). This, of course, indicates that Muslim reformers accepted some of the accusations against Islam that were elaborated in nineteenth century Europe. It also shows that an existing Islamic suspicion of the theological sapience of the masses fitted in nicely with the thesis that Islam was backward, since the reformers stated that such idolatrous practices had fastened primarily on folk Islam. The reformers' efforts were therefore in part directed to stamping out folk Islam.

For purposes of mass mobilizations that was a mistake. The extent of this error, which with time was to beget dire consequences for the strategy of the elite reformers, has been elegantly analyzed by the late 'Abd al-Ḥamīd el-Zein, whose analysis cannot be improved upon (el-Zein, 1977, 246):

> . . . the authority claimed by theological Islam is contested by the recognition that in any given cultural system, a folk theology may be found which rivals formal theology in its degree of abstraction, systematization and cosmological implication. It is even possible to argue that this folk Islam constitutes the real Islam and that the traditions of the *Ulema* developed historically out of already established principles of the spiritual reality entwined with the life of the Islamic community. In fact these opposing theologies are complementary. Because each form both defines and necessitates the other, the problem of determining a real as opposed to an ideological Islam becomes an illusion.
>
> On the most general level of abstraction, folk theology involves reflection on principles of ultimate reality, nature, God, man and history which are formally expressed in traditional literature, folk tales, heroic stories, proverbs and poetry. For instance, in the tale of *Seif bin dhi Yazan,* the reality of the world according to Islamic principles and the existence of the Prophet was known before the actual historical birth of Mohammed and his articulation of that doctrine. Therefore, in the folk conception, counter to the view of historians and Islamicists, direct reflection upon the order of the world, rather than the actual statements of the Prophet and Quran, lead the mind to the origin of that order.
>
> The order of both the natural and human world rests (*sic.*) upon a hierarchical principle which arranges each thing or person continually in an ascending order: fire to water, the segments of a tribe to the tribal section, to the tribe as a whole. . . . At the end this order arrives at the World of Spirituality which both creates and maintains these connections. . . . The entire world becomes an open text where God reveals his language and his will. The Quran, too, is read and interpreted within this paradigm.
>
> Ideally, the human mind must admit to itself this natural logic. However, because man deviates from this destiny by imposing false and alien con-

> cepts upon the world, mind and nature are not initially in correspondence. The role of the Prophet and the saints is to bring these two dimensions together. . . . History in this paradigm never refers to the ever-changing creation of new meanings in human life but to the struggle to recapture and immobilize an eternal experience.
>
> While nature is continuous and ordered, history remains discontinuous and chaotic. In folk theology the remembrance of the Prophet, the actions of the saints, and all rituals attempt to transform the discontinuities of history into the natural order by processes of ritual repetition which stops the passage of time. . . .
>
> While in the folk tradition the order of nature and the Quran were regarded as metaphors, the strict and formal theological interpretations gave complete authority to the sacred book to define the order of the world. (el-Zein, 1977, 246–247)

Part of what el-Zein considered to be "folk Islam" in fact is of Neo-Platonic origin and figures more in the theosophy of the mystic orders than in folk Islam. But, in the case of Turkey, it is true that the folk conception may be seen as a direct reflection upon the order of the world. Thus an interpretation of the *Qur'ān* which linked it to the order of the world, that of Said Nursi, found an eager audience for reasons that went back to features of folk Islam as well as for reasons linked to modernization and the spread of communications.

To look at Said Nursi's ideas in the perspective of Orthodox Muslim theology therefore yields a relatively poor harvest. Works critical of Said Nursi written by modern academic Islamists such as those of Armaner and Kutluay miss the point entirely when they parade these theories as strange and confused. It is much more rewarding to see Said as using both the *Qur'ān* and residues of Anatolian mysticism as a transformational medium which allow him to engage in a number of simultaneous operations, establish contact with popular religion, draw followers of the folk variety of Islam in the direction of a belief focused on the unicity of God, shift the dead weight of traditional Islamic orthodoxy and join the stream of an understanding of the laws of nature as it appears in modern Western European thought.

In fact, this activist use of mysticism has other parallels in the history of reformist Islam. The description by Trimingham of the use of mysticism by the 18th century *tarikat* activists would be quite apposite in our case:

> Their ways maintained established liturgical and ethical sufism, having little in their method and training that old Sufis would have regarded as mystical.

> This is shown by their practice, lack of guidance of neophytes and rejection of esoteric teaching, and by such aspects as the kind of material drawn from classical Sufism, especially the prophetic tradition, which they incorporated into their manuals to justify every statement. (Trimingham, 1973, 107)

Mytho-poetic Integration

Even though Said was educated in the tradition of the mystic orders, he assumed an antagonistic stance towards them because he believed that re-instilling faith in the hearts of Muslims was more important than subtle arguments about the ways in which the divine showed itself. Nevertheless, his understanding and especially his interpretation of the *Qur'ān* is marked by the mystic's style. This appears, in particular, in his interest in the metaphorical *sura*s of the *Qur'ān* and in his elaborate disquisition on the "secrets" that may be unravelled through a *Qur'ānic* hermeneutic. It is on these metaphorical *sura*s that he fastens in his own commentaries, and it is this approach which allows him to find meanings and directives in the *Qur'ān* which, according to him, have relevance for all times. Another, more utilitarian, justification that he uses in support of his language is that allusive and metaphorical rhetoric has a direct impact upon people's hearts which classical theology cannot match. Possibly these are the two sides of the same coin: the quality of the *Qur'ān* that confers hermeneutic freedom on the exegete is the same which appeals to the heart of the believer.

Style and Symbol

The modern historian Vico was one of the first thinkers to point out that the dynamic of human behavior has greater affinities with poetry than with mathematics. Said Nursi's appeals have a charm which derives from an intuitive understanding of this quality. By his use of the idiom of mysticism, Said Nursi avoided the trap into which fundamentalists such as Muḥammad 'Abdū had fallen, namely to close the "emotional outlet afforded by Sufi mysticism" (Gibb, 1945, 75).

The Anatolian population to which he addressed himself, on the other hand, had for long been living in a twilight zone where poetry, religion and mythology blended easily. This was partly the consequence of the trickling down to lower classes of the theosophy of Muhyiddīn ibn al-'Arabī. In fact, Said Nursi believed this theoretician of Muslim mysticism to be in error. He pointed out that the latter's theosophy (*philosophia divinalis—hikmet-i ilâhiye*) had the effect of nullifying the necessary distinction between the duties due to the creator and man's nature as a reflection of the creator among many believers who took him as a spiritual guide.

Conversations with contemporary *Nurcu*s confirm the feeling that the incantatory style of Said Nursi still plays an important part in attracting a clientele to the order. The magnetic effect of Said's arch, convoluted style and the import of what often amounts simply to ungrammatical phrases is difficult to understand for persons who come from the state-subsidized orthodox Muslim elite establishment, i.e., the Faculty of Divinity at Ankara. Be this as it may, the allusive, and superficially obscure, style of the sage, has had an undeniable power in winning over disciples. This power may have derived from an irreducible core which can best be understood in our attraction to magic realism in literature (Jameson, 1986). As for Bediüzzaman's style, it can be traced to two different sources. For one, Said Nursi's mother tongue was Kurdish. He became fluent in Turkish only after the age of twenty. His second language was Arabic, the traces of which can be seen in his rich arabicized vocabulary which gives a special ring to his Turkish phrases; there is even something evocative of the *Qur'ān* in his rhetoric.

The manner favored by the mystics which he studied in his youth is no doubt another source of obscurity. Persons like Ibn al-'Arabī were relatively clear when they tried to explain how their doctrines stood in relation to those of the Islamic philosophers but were almost incomprehensible when they explained their own thought. This hermetic quality also appears in Said's works. However, it was not only the tradition to which the leader was heir that shaped this hermetism: the clients were also ready for it. Two elements in the intellectual background of his clientele seem to have been involved here. First, Anatolia—as I have already alluded—was a land where the theosophical speculations of the mystics were transmitted to the masses by learned Ottoman Muslims. A much wider appeal was that of the ineffable meaning which mysticism was considered to conceal. The power of Bediüzzaman over lower-class followers has to be understood at this second level. What we are dealing with in the majority of his works is a comment on the mystery (*icaz*; *i'jāz*) of the *Qur'ān* and now we enter an area where Said does not any more pursue proof which figures so prominently in some of his statements. Here, symbols and metaphors appear much more charged with indescribable meaning than in the discursive-learned tradition. For the less educated this aspect of the *Risale-i Nur* was no doubt apprehended as quasi-magic.

Two examples from the *Risale-i Nur* will illustrate the imagistic fund which Bediüzzaman was revitalizing:

> Know, aberrant and confused Said that to be able to achieve the revealed knowledge of spiritual truth and look and see the flourishes in the verses of the *Qur'ān* with its armor of proofs it is necessary that you . . . refrain from extending your hand to seize a light that shines upon you. . . . I have observed that the witnesses and proofs of spiritual truth are three in number:
>
> Some are like water, they can be seen and felt but cannot be seized. In this part it is necessary to dismiss thought and plunge into it. . . . The second part is like rain. It is felt but cannot be seen or held. Turn against its forgiving breeze with your face, your mouth, your soul. . . . The third part: it is like light. It is seen but cannot be felt or held. Therefore turn yourself towards it with the eye of your soul. . . . (*Mesnevi-i Nuriye, 153*)
>
> The higher recipients of knowledge have preceded us in faith and confirmation not by knowledge and conceptualization but by two modes which are much more exalted and valuable than these. One is to study the book of the universe and to look at objective knowledge such as is found in sources like the *Ayet-i Kübra*, the *Hizb ün-Nuriye* and the *Hülasat ül-Hülasa*. The other and the strongest is to peruse the map of human verities which emanates so purely from conscience and feeling that it may be characterized as equal to the Real [*Haqq al-Yaqīn*,—"The vision of the Reality of Absolute Truth" (Schimmel, 1975, 176)] which belongs partly to the phenomenal world and is also an index to human pride and to its nature and thus rises up to the state of a belief free of all doubt and perplexity. . . . (*Emirdağ Lahikası*, 143)

Muslim Idiom and Self

Recent studies of societies in change have once more underlined the relations between the dynamics of identity formation and religion. Comte and Saint Simon (taking their cue from de Maistre and de Bonald) both have a niche in the ancestry of contemporary thinkers who emphasize the important function that religion should continue to assume during modernization. Comte (who had in mind the disestablishment of the Catholic Church in France) believed that the secularization of society by the French Revolution had deprived French society of the cement that bound it together. He thus voiced a thoroughly "Durkheimian" opinion. But another level at which religion is drawn into our study of modernization is the impoverishment of the traditional means available for individuals in building their selfhood and identity. In Brittain's words: "There is no longer an institutional source from which individuals can draw their values and locate their identity" (Brittain, 1977, 45).

This occurs at a time when the expansion of social horizons caused by urbanization and the change in social communication patterns requires many persons who are moving from the village into the city (or who are exposed to the new problems of the city in the village) to use their religious affiliation as a mooring for their identity. Mattison Minnes, in an article on the Muslims of Tamilnadu in India shows that in the circumscribed life of the village, Islam is taken as a "given" of everyday life both by the Muslim and the Hindu population of the villages: neither of these groups feels the need to underline their religious affiliation. In the city, where life-styles are more fluid, where tradition is not part of everyday life as in the village, Muslims begin to wear Islam as a "badge" and become dependent upon religion for a definition of their identity (Minnes, 1975).

The specific mechanisms through which individuals draw their identity from religious symbolism seems to be confirmed by the studies of child psychology of Melanie Klein, but also by a host of social scientists with differing approaches. The superb study of the Freudian anthropologist Morris Carstairs in a community of high-caste Hindus is one example (Carstairs, 1961, *passim*).

Whether mystical seekers of the old, traditional type who rallied to Bediüzzaman because of their quest for a grail, or sons of peasants who were receiving a secular primary school education in the Republican educational system, all his clients were deprived of a resource which operated at a deep individual level: they were not entirely cut off from the symbolic apparatus of Islam, but they could only use these resources with stealth. Because Islamic cues which directed this process had not been disturbed in the family by 20th century secularization, the picture of the moral universe which capped these family values was of necessity also left as a relatively undisturbed residue. This residue clashed with the positivistic world view promoted by Kemalism and thus Bediüzzaman had fertile ground on which to sow his ideas concerning the total involvement of the individual in Islam as a solution for the tensions generated in the individual.

For one of the more interesting hypotheses concerning the way in which this process worked we have to go to C. G. Jung. In Jung's view the self is not only maintained in one's encounter with others; there is a subconscious level of the building of the self which is related to the use of symbolism, and among this symbolism, religious symbolism figures most prominently.

In Jung's work this appears as the idea of an "organizing center active in the psyche" (Frey-Rohn, 1974, 68). This organizing activity takes place through a stock of archetypal images (*Ibid.*, 285). Men's ideas about God are part of this stock of archetypes which humans use for the purposes of "individuation" or to discover their "self" to become a separate entity or whole (Hillman, 1974, 66). In this view the formation of the self is a conscious as well as sub-conscious process. The archetypes which are evoked during this process have a "distinctly numinous quality" (*Ibid.*, 282). In a sense, then, archetypes prefigure the idea of God as well as providing man with a base for developing his identity as well as a self. The internal mechanisms which Jung called "archetypes as such" are parallel to the culturally determined conceptions that we have of deities. The archetypal images provided by culture trigger the internal mechanism of archetype activation which eventually leads to the discovery of the fullness of the self.

For Jung, therefore, religion is an internal process, one which relates to finding the fullness of the self through the intermediary of archetypes which are supra-cultural but at the same time recur in recognizable form in each culture. But at the same time, when individuals share a common myth, the projection of this shared God-image into the focus of the religious community, such as the church in Christianity, makes the stuff of a religious collectivity (Edinger, 1973, 65). What Jung tells us, then, is that the symbols of a culture are organic products which cannot be discounted at will. To the extent that the Turkish rural world was cut off from its mythopoetic moorings by Republican secularization, it experienced the loss not only of the moral directives contained in the discursive arguments of Islamic ethics but also of the dynamic element allowing man to come to terms with his self. The traditional symbolism understood as a means of coming to grips with one's life prospects was an important aspect of Said's charisma. For many Turks—of lower or upper class—religion as a mystery had provided an open door for the solution of a number of problems of individual adjustment that the orthodox scripturalists of the city had ruled out as irrelevant to religion. Not only did mysticism, Sufism, allow full scope to man's intuitive spiritual senses, but it allowed the psychological mechanisms linked to this intuition—mechanisms which were linked to a transformation of the self—to come into operation. To understand the mechanism that Bediüzzaman's preaching activated we have to see that ethics do not consist only of moral commands but also provide means of integrating a person into "an environment felt as a cosmos" (Hodgson, 1974, I, 362).

A fund of charged symbolism is, of course, most useful in trying to materialize a project such as the one which Said had set himself. But we have to look at a second dimension of morality and ethics to understand both his project and the readiness of some to take it up. Marshall Hodgson has spoken of this dimension as follows:

> Exploring the meaning that given symbols can bear seems a major part of any comprehensive attempt to make sense of one's self and the universe. For when one tries to present ultimate cosmic and moral insights, one is at the limit of conceptual discourse; that is, at the point where the terms in which logical sequences issue, are strictly speaking, indeterminate (e.g. the finiteness or infinity of the universe, the causal determinacy of all sequences at once, the value of any calculation). Here, logical deductions produce antinomies. Hence one must speak, if at all, in symbolic images that evoke emergent associations rather than fixed propositions, and this is done most richly in what are called mythopoetic forms, adumbrating truths about life that every hearer can grasp at his own level of understanding. (Hodgson, 1974, I, 224)

At a time when the world was being progressively de-mythologized and bureaucratized, these mytho-poetic forms were also being chased out of modern Turkey. They consequently assumed the value of scarcity in the inner world of Turkish Muslims.

A methodological point which is of key interest for an understanding of the way in which Said Nursi's idiom worked is that morality as command depends on discursive resources whereas morality as means of finding an integration with the cosmos is dependent just as much on semiotic resources, i.e., on the resonance created in the individuals by these symbols. Said Nursi's discourse contained resources of both types. This is where he had a superiority over the more orthodox Islamic reformists.

The threshold of communications which Turkey had reached during Said Nursi's life has also to be taken into account at this point. Said Nursi had decided, somewhat reluctantly—as I point out on a number of occasions—that he was not going to establish a *tarikat*. What he was interested in was the perpetuation of the message which he offered to his followers. The printed word, i.e., Said's *Risale,* thus took over from the traditional pattern of a charismatic leader selecting another charismatic leader to succeed him. Since the *Risale-i Nur* was to carry this charisma, his followers and their successors, using his book as a guide, were to work for themselves instead of concentrating on the Master. In other words, they were thrown upon their own resources. This internalization was, once more, a shift in the direction of setting for persons an inward world of morality and ethics, albeit within the frame set by the *Qur'ān* and its interpretation by Said Nursi.

Of central importance for us is that:

1. the discourse which Said was using now increasingly was directed to the use of a mobilized rural population.
2. that these constituted a specific repertoire; that Said was making a special use of the "discourse," and that he was *transforming* the totality represented by the relation between *pir* and *mürid,* leader and disciple while saving the idiom in which it was embedded.

In Said Nursi's message a beginning is made in shifting the central role of the leader to the message itself, thus establishing a new form of integration into Islam. A much more universalistic mode of integration is thus opened up to followers. The process of transference to a *pir* is modified and shifted onto the symbol of the unicity of God and, on the other hand, onto the *Risale-i Nur.* Together with this is offered a new set of symbols which are those of nature. Here figure, and are underlined, the vegetable and animal universe. Said Nursi constantly mentions trees, plants, flowers, bees, birds and insects as witnesses to the act of creation. Notwithstanding all of Said Nursi's protests against materialism, there is therefore a shift of emphasis from the *pir* to a more abstract deity on the one hand, and a focusing of attention on the biological universe on the other.

CHAPTER V

The Saint and his Followers

IN THE RURAL settings in which he acquired his largest group of followers, Said Nursi was considered a Muslim saint, a person to whom extraordinary powers are attributed, but one whose saintliness was not acquired by an act of canonization. In Islam, sainthood is an attribute of the religious prestige which persons build up in their community during their lifetime. Thus sainthood is a somewhat different matter than it is in Christianity. Muslim "sainthood" involves a whole set of distinguishing characteristics which I shall try to cover below. Once this Islamic framework has been described, the more properly sociological problems to be resolved concern the way in which a saint was able to act as a magnetic pole in relation to his disciples. This involves questions relating to the quality of leadership, to collective representations, to charisma, social networks and the psychological needs of persons who were drawn to the saint.

Said as a Holy Man

For the *Nakşibendi*, sainthood is the "pivot of all spiritual realization" (Chodkiewicz, 1986, 23). It is this numinous content which made *Nakşibendi şeyhs* charismatic organizers of the masses. Mevlana Halid had added one item of his own thought which gave even greater spiritual power to *şeyhs*: namely, that in his case, the link which brought master and pupil together would survive his demise. Bediüzzaman's counsels to disassociate oneself from such personal bonds must therefore be seen as a significant departure from his predecessor's practice. It was only after the age of forty—in the image of the Prophet Muḥammad—that Said Nursi began to acquire a large number of followers who may be described as disciples. From that point onward (1926) his attraction and prestige were not only dependent on his learning or on the unusual figure he cut among the *'ulema,* but on his quality as a holy man. It was after his exile and enforced residence in western Turkey that such charisma as was attributed to a living saint was added to his prestige as a recognized teacher of religion. Said writes about his exile in an isolated hamlet in the lake region of Western Anatolia, Barla, as having been a veritable bounty for the demarcation of this religiously purer vocation and for his return to the true faith. By this he meant that he had been taken out of the hurly-burly of political life from which he had—possibly half-heartedly—tried to escape on a number of occasions.

Sainthood

The study of Islamic sainthood relies on investigations which have focused on the Maghreb, Africa, India and Indonesia, but neither our knowledge of *marabouts* nor the fund of information on Indian Islam apply to the Ottoman sphere. Here, Islamic sainthood requires a special problematique which no one has yet elaborated. Once more, the greater institutionalization of religion in the Ottoman Empire, as compared to other areas of Islamicate culture, is the datum which demands that one place Ottoman sainthood and the conception Ottomans held of it in a special compartment. While popular saints were revered locally, the central religious establishment (*ilmiyye* in Turkish) saw sainthood as the product of a disciplined vocation, and this discipline was located in the rules of the *tarikat.*

The close links Ottoman *tarikat* had with the Ottoman state induced the leaders of these fraternities to carefully weigh their power options as local leaders and keep the countervailing power of the state in mind at all times. Since with few exceptions intellectual creativity in the *tarikat* was of a high level, this quality elicited a certain deference among the bureaucracy, many of whose members had multiple *tarikat* affiliations. Ottoman *tarikat* bore the imprint of these contradictory statuses.

All of this was reflected in Said Nursi's assessment of religious orders. The contentiousness he adopted in his relations with his Halidi teachers was eventually replaced by a relative aloofness, which one may follow in his judgements concerning five areas directly related to the issue of sainthood in the Ottoman Empire. These were the proper role of the *tarikat,* the value of Sufism for a Muslim, the rightful place of a *veli,* or elect of God, the interpretation to be given to the idea that a *mahdi* or millenarian figure would rise up in times of trouble to save Islam, and finally, the correct standconcerning Ibn al-'Arabī's idea of the unity of being (*vahdet-i vücûd*).

In the Ottoman Empire *tarikat* played a major role as purveyors of local social services, as centers where the authority of lodge elders was used to sort out various local problems and also as educational facilities as well as channels between the rural population and the government. Sufism, the search for a direct link with the divine, was an aspect of supernumerary religious acts and was regulated by internal *tarikat* codes. Intellectualistic forms of Sufism based on meditation were held in great respect, while the more ostentatious ascetic practices were considered crudely populistic. Since many of the *tarikat* lodges disposed of vast resources (Farughi, 1984), they were also kept under strict surveillance by the government. Conversely, their influence extended to Istanbul, where various *'ulema* defended their corporate interest (Gibb and Bowen, 1957). It is this last feature which distinguishes the majority of Ottoman *tarikat* from their equivalent in other parts of the Muslim world. Faced with the controls imposed by an array of sophisticated clerics who also showed a suspicious and skeptical mind, a local popular saint did not elicit official deference unless he had a well–established reputation. He was nevertheless a person who wielded considerable influence in his locality.

The issue of how to recognize a *veli* was subtly different since the position of such a recipient of divine illumination was well–established in Islam. In the Sufi tradition of Islam, religion was not only a revelation but also a mystery (Trimingham, 1973, 133). Some men could acquire esoteric knowledge by a method of "spiritual progression" (*Ibid.*, 135) achieved through the intercession of a chain of elect masters, or by direct inspiration from God. Some men, however, had special gifts which gave them an unmediated mystical understanding of life without intercession or ascetic discipline (*Ibid.*, 140). Here again, two types appeared, those chosen by God from eternity and those who received his favor in the immediate present.

Two theories converged in this understanding of the ways in which esoteric knowledge could be gained. One was the doctrine of *an-Nūr al-Muḥammadī* or the idea of the Muhammadan light. This was the "image of God in its primary entity, the divine consciousness, the pre-creation light from which everything was created. . . . The world is a manifestation of that Light; it became incarnate in Adam, the prophets and the *Aqṭāb* (sing. *Quṭb*, 'Axis'), each of whom is *al-Insān al-Kāmil* (The Perfect Man)" (*Ibid.*, 161).

The second theosophical theory explained the nature of the *Quṭb:* "The need for the direct knowledge of the Word of God brings *al-Ḥaqīqat al-Muḥammadiyya,* the Logos, in every epoch to take on the form of one known as *Quṭb zamānihi* (the Axis of his age), who manifests himself only to a few chosen mystics" (*Ibid.,* 163). This theory was a major contribution of Ibn al-'Arābī (1165–1240), the mystic whose influence on Anatolian folk Islam I have described as pervasive. In fact, the order of ideas in this set could be reversed, for the theory of "light" was evolved to provide a "philosophical basis for the practical devotion to saints and prophets" (*Ibid.,* 161). In the ages succeeding the elaboration of this theory, the conception was vulgarized, and all types of holy man began to claim the status of *quṭb.* In Anatolia, local saints or *veli*s were revered in many places: villages, towns or cities. Threatened at the time of its foundation and also later by a series of popular movements led by charismatic leaders, the Ottoman state kept a strict surveillance on would-be *quṭb*s and *veli*s.

The *mahdi* or *sahib zuhur* was a figure who was much talked of among the populace but whose conditions of emergence was interpreted with utmost caution by the *'ulema.*

Vahdet-i Vucûd was the esoteric doctrine propounded by Ibn al-'Arabī. Many of the most sophisticated pious believers held these pantheistic beliefs (Fazlur Rahman, 1979, 145), but without advertising them since this doctrine of the Unity of Being had often served as a target for the attack of puritanical *'ulema.*

From Saíd Nursi's answers given to queries which were posed to him between 1925 and 1950 we understand that all these issues were still in the forefront of the minds of his supporters in the İsparta-Afyon region. There are three levels at which Said Nursi's encounter with sainthood may be analyzed. The first is the statements regarding sainthood we find in his writings. There are often answers to questions posed by his clientèle. A second is the ambiguous attitude or the issue he adopted during his lifetime. A third level takes in the perceptions of his followers as to his own merits as a *veli.*

Tarikat and Tasavvuf

For Said Nursi the "purpose and end" of *tarikat* are gnosis (*mârifet*) and also to pursue an understanding of religious varieties (*inkişaf-i hakaik-i imâniye*). It is a means of underscoring the superiority of *Qur'ānic* truth "through a voyage undertaken with the gait of the heart, due to and afforded the protection of revelation. A voyage appealing to the senses but embarked upon bare [i.e., stripped of worldly attachments] and endowing the traveller with a partial gift of ultimate perception." "*Tarikat* is, under the name of *tasavvuf*, (*taṣawwuf*) a mystery offered to humans and a step in the maturity of mankind" (*Mektubat*, 415).

God has made man's heart part of the cosmic "machine" (*Mektubat*, 416), and the most important task that can be given to the heart is to direct it to repeat the names of God (*Zikr-i ilâhi*), thereby gaining a means of communicating with the divinity. Persons who are affiliated to a *tarikat* have an easier time keeping their faith intact when faced by the intimidation of the Godless (*Mektubat*, 417). For those who live isolated "in mountains or riverbeds," or, for the aged, *tarikat* is a means of showing that the "savage" material world which they face can still hold a "smile" for them. *Tarikat* are also a resource that enables Muslims to close ranks when faced by the "politics of Christianity" (*Mektubat*, 417).

The Veli and the Mahdi

The quality which descends upon a *veli* is a "proof of the prophetic mission." It is also a proof of revelation, a mystery on the road to a full understanding of Islam and a resource for the development of Islam (*Islamiyet sırrıyla bir maden-i terakkiyat; Mektubat*, 416). The vocation of a *veli* is both very easy and very problematical, very short and very long, very precious and very dangerous. Persons who feel inspired often take this to be a sign of having been chosen as a *veli*. In many cases they are simply deluded. Bediüzzaman adds that he had seen many people who thought of themselves as *mahdi* but simply deceived themselves and did great harm to Islam. Like the orthodox *'ulema* Bediüzzaman was cautious about the validity of "uniquely privileged mystical knowledge" (Fazlur Rahman, 1979, 161).

Vahdet-i Vücûd

To Bediüzzaman, those who believe in this theory are threatened by the danger of appraising the phenomenal world as the projected shadow of the divine essence, which to them becomes the sole reality. They thus radically undermine one's relation to wordly matters. But faith cannot be built on shadows and demands that the world be taken as real. Followers of this extreme stance can only cause the weakening of Islam.

To the extent that both *şeyh* and *veli* were expected to intercede for them with divine powers for wordly concerns or to perform miracles, the average, unsophisticated Muslim would have difficulty discriminating between these two roles. But at this point Said was adamant: he refused to be drawn into the role of miracle-maker.

To those who expected him to show his miraculous powers, he offered an amusing parable. "One day," he related, "a man took his son to a jeweller's shop. He intended to buy him some beautiful jewel. But the son was very young. Upon entering the shop he noticed multi-coloured balloons hanging from the ceiling. When his father asked him what he would like, the son pointed to the balloons and not to a single valuable object." "I," he would add, "am not a balloon peddler."

Both for Sirhindi and for Said Nursi the problem of conciliating the unicity of God with the status of *quṭb* created a delicate problem of logical consistency. Sirhindi has fought pantheism and had come up on the side of the image of a single, all-powerful God. But at the same time he did not supress completely the idea of an "axis" and of his own special spiritual gifts, powers and authoritativeness as a religion leader (Friedman, 1971, *passim*). Said Nursi, too, thought of Sirhindi as a *quṭb*. With some hesitation, as can be seen in some passages of the *Risale-i Nur,* he wondered whether he himself had not been chosen by God for such a role and looked at the signs which would show this election. Thus we know that he accepted as a gift a coat worn by Mevlana Halid in view of the conviction that he was his spiritual successor (BSN, 1976, 287). He also took for granted the concept of *velayet* (*wilāya*; Trimingham, 1973, 134; *Lem'alar,* 22), i.e., the *status* of a God-chosen elect. But there are many other passages in this writings where he rejects the idea that he possesses extraordinary powers and defines his role as simply that of a teacher of religion. The gist of his teaching, with its emphasis on the unicity of God and his suspicion of persons who took upon themselves the attributes of saints, stresses a transcendent power which, indeed, is a characteristic of his work as a whole. For him, true faith mattered more than the persons who had pretensions of filling the role of *quṭb*. On another occasion, he speaks of a *quṭb* as living in Mecca the way one would speak of any contemporary religious official, stating that the judgment of the *quṭb* on how to deal with a particularly heinous Turkish secularizing politician (İsmet İnönü?) had been wrong, and his own judgement had been right. But in the last instance, it seems justifiable to think that Said Nursi came to the conclusion that the creative power of God was a more universalistic theological umbrella under which to work for the unification of Muslims than the congery of saints who each had a prestige limited to a province or, at most, a country. There were few saints whose resonance carried across Islam.

Following are a number of illustrations of the way in which the various strands which are found in *Nurculuk* drew disciples around Said. The life of Abdülkadir Badilli, taken from a volume of attestation of his disciples concerning the influence of the Master on their life, provides a good example of the way in which traditional social networks continued to operate during the Republic, giving substance to Said Nursi's influence.

Abdülkadir Badilli

Badilli was from a transhuman Eastern tribe. His family was that of the tribal chiefs. His father and his brother are described as having been drawn to *tarikat*. His childhood was thus markedly influenced by what Badilli calls "the attempt to live, to some extent, by the precepts of *tarikat*, which, in our childhood, we had learned to be the only means of salvation" (Şahiner ed., 1977, 294). He continues, "There existed in me, just as in all of us, a desire to find a *mürşid-i kâmil* (perfect guide)."

He had heard his uncles mention the incident of Said Nursi's exile many times, a recollection to which his uncles added their praise of Said. Greater details about Bediüzzaman's life were provided by Tahsin Efendi, a man who acted as tax collector for the village, who was also from Eastern Anatolia and who had met with Said during the latter's enforced stay in Kastamonu (1936–1943). In 1953 Badilli's father returned from a trip to Urfa. He brought the news that some of the disciples of Bediüzzaman known as the *Nur* "students" had established themselves in Urfa.

Badilli had been given a Muslim education in the village. This consisted of a knowledge of Arabic characters which enabled him to read the *Qur'ān*. There were no government schools in the vicinity, but his father thought this was an advantage since it kept the children from going to town and being subverted by what he described as movies and song. He encouraged his children to familiarize themselves with the rural setting and particularly to ride and hunt.

One day, again, his father went to Urfa and met with two *Nur* students. He talked to them of his son and asked them to take over his son's education, as Abdülkadir's mother had died. He also gave a petition to the governor, a man described as "leaning towards the Demokrat Party." This probably meant that this governor was sympathetic to the liberalization of the strict policy of secularism which had prevailed in Turkey until 1950. The petition demanded that the surveillance of the students by the police should be terminated since the *Risale-i Nur,* the compendium of writings by Said, was a positive influence for Turkish society.

The junior Badilli went to Urfa, found these two disciples, and demanded to be admitted to the order by Said Nursi. He was informed that Said Nursi was no *şeyh* and that to join the group one had to study Bediüzzaman's books. Abdülkadir states that he could not believe that such a famous religious figure would not "provide one with the way" (*tarikat vermek*). He was not convinced by the arguments of Said's disciples, suspected he had been tricked, and demanded to see Said Nursi. He was then informed that if he copied the full length of a brochure of Said Nursi's writings he would acquire the right to see the leader. He took the brochure with him and returned three days later, triumphant, having copies of the entire text in Arabic script. He was then allowed to make his way to İsparta and gain access to Said Nursi. Said gave him a warm welcome and Abdülkadir thereafter returned to Urfa. He sold his hunting gun and his gear and began to work on Said Nursi's writings for two years together with a group of initiates in Urfa. On his mother's death he had inherited forty sheep, and he decided that he would devote the proceeds of these to buy a reproducing machine so as to spread the word of Said Nursi. He set out on the road to Istanbul to buy the machine. He visited his spiritual guide both on the first lap of his trip and on the return.

An interesting insight into the way finances were transacted in the sect appears at this juncture. The *Nur* sect was primarily financed by the sale of the brochures of Said Nursi. Said himself did not accept money offerings of gifts. Old style offerings in kind were thus effectively blocked. When Abdülkadir arrived in Barla on his return trip, he remembered that one of the important sermons of Said Nursi which had inspired particular reverence in him had been printed in one of the ephemeral journals that the group published from time to time. However, the journal had been seized by the prosecutor's office some years before, and Said was keeping what he had been able to recover, following the dismissal of the charges against this publication, in his own room. Abdülkadir asked whether he could have a copy of one of the periodicals. Said answered that these copies were extremely precious since they had been engaged in a fight for the faith (*gazidirler*). They were worth one hundred lira each—a very large sum at the time. "I shall give you one for ten liras," Said said. Receiving the money, he then handed it to one of his attendants. This scene seems quite characteristic of the shrewdness with which the sale of the *Risale-i Nur* was made to support the movement, although Said himself with his meagre diet, unfurnished room and frayed shirt cannot by any means be considered a recipient of any largesse.

In the case of Abdülkadir Badilli, we have patterns of affiliation which may be considered to be a continuation of a mode of membership in a religious group that had not changed for centuries, although Badilli's search did not have the obsessive quality which we see in the next subject.

Hulusi Yahyagil

Hulusi Yahyagil was born in 1895, in an area of Turkey west of Bitlis (Elazığ, Elaziz or Mamuret ül-Aziz as it has been known at various times). His father was that peculiar product of the *Tanzimat* which was known as an officer from the ranks (*alaylı*), one of the *bêtes noires* of the Young Turks and of progressives in general. Officers promoted from the ranks were made officers without having completed their regular studies in the military academy, either because they had some quality which made them good leaders in the field or because they carried some authority outside the army which was needed for the army. In this case, Yahyagil's father must have been made an officer because he was a member of a locally prominent family of notables (Şahiner ed., 1978, 35). Hulusi also chose a military career and did enroll in the Military Academy, but was unable to complete his studies because of the onset of the First World War. He was sent to the front, saw considerable action, and came back to complete his studies in the Military Academy. He was later engaged in the repression of the Kurdish rebellion of 1938, and we understand from his correspondence with Said that this was an unusually painful duty for him. But even though he was a loyal soldier, Hulusi seems to have been a "marginal" in two respects. For one, the army did not mean for him the total involvement in a new war machine which it was for many career officers. Second, the relatively minor reward for his services in the army may have resulted from the fact that he was still not trusted because he came from a region of Turkey where rebellion was endemic. His eventual retirement with the rank of colonel points in that direction. Possibly, it was this marginal status which did not allow Hulusi to immerse himself in the behemoth of military organization and power but rather led him to seek the meaning of Islamic mysteries.

There is something compulsive about Yahyagil's attempt to decipher the mysteries of Islamic lore which points to a deep-seated drive, an attempt to find the means of solving a basic conundrum which, one suspects, is related to a basic aspect of identity or of the self. In 1916, with bullets flying around him on the Turkish eastern front, Hulusi was trying to find the authorship of a mystical poem. The poem was concerned with the author's desire to be brought in to the presence of God—even if it be in the way in which Kitmir, the dog of the Seven Sleepers of Ephesus, had been brought into the presence of God through His infinite mercifulness. Hulusi found only one person interested in discussing the poem with him: the son-in-law of Şeyh Riza Talabani, the head of a *Kadiri tekke* and the scion of a prominent family with hereditary charisma. Two items emerge from this account: Hulusi's friends and acquaintances were persons who were also interested in religion; second, Hulusi was embarked on a voyage of exploration, most probably a voyage of self-exploration.

In 1928 Hulusi was posted in Eğridir, a small provincial town near the place of exile of Said Nursi. One of his friends was a local man of religion, a person considered as simple-minded, who bore the sobriquet of Mustafa the Madman. Mustafa showed Hulusi a copy of Said Nursi's sermons known as *The Little Words* and told him that he would find in Said the answer to his search.

For anyone who has read Ottoman provincial religious history, the group which thereupon set out to find Said gives one a strong impression of the re-enactment of many similar expeditions to find a holy man. Here they were, a small party on horseback, Hulusi, by then a captain in the army, "Mad" Mustafa, flanked by another Mustafa, "Yellow Knife" by name, and "Dread" Hüseyin, a veritable cross-section of middle class Turkish provincial life on a trek across the mountains. The party found Said, Hulusi had a long conversation with him, and then they departed.

Hulusi established a relation with Said Nursi which was built on a stream of letters in which Hulusi would ask Said Nursi to enlighten him on problems of Islamic culture or religion. Through Hulusi too, Said Nursi kept his contacts with local sages in the eastern regions such as Mehmed Lütfi of Pasinler, Erzurum, and a *halifa* of Mehmed Küfrevi, the latter a sect leader who had given Said his last lesson as a student (Şahiner ed., 1978, 55). But while there is no doubt that these exchanges were set in a traditional mode, they contained a new element. This appears quite clearly in the reception which Hulusi received from Said: at their first meeting Said stated quite categorically that the party had come to the wrong place if they were looking for a *şeyh*. He added that he was no *şeyh* but an *imam* (leader of the community), adding, "Like Gazali or Sirhindi" (Şahiner ed., 1977, 85).

Hulusi later affirmed that it was, indeed, in Said Nursi's books that one should look for the message and not in the man. Although whenever he was able to do so, he attended the meetings of the sect—which consisted in reading an excerpt from Said's writings and proposing suitable commentaries—what he saw in these writings was the same ineffable quality he had sought in the saint (*Ibid.*, 86).

This concentrated spirituality which pervades the career of a military man is an aspect of the attraction of many persons to Said which has to be tackled to unravel the foundation of his charismatic appeal. For it is quite clear that charisma here has the meaning of an answer to a problem—often shared by many others—which originates within the psyche of the person subject to the charismatic influence. To understand the institutionalization of Said's sect, the issue of internal force-propelling persons like Hulusi has to be broached.

In the case of Hulusi and that of Abdülkadir Badilli, the quest was one for a leader. This was partly a matter of following established procedures or harkening to clues which in the Turkish setting were as plain as those plotting the lines of a spiritual itinerary in the Medieval West. But the road leading to the Sufi master or even to the Orthodox *medrese* teacher was more restricted. In seems to have consisted of a duplication of the relations established between father and son. It thus prepared the field for both the acceptance of religious symbols and their anchoring of the self. How this constricted process of self-definition worked in its details is another matter which cannot but be the subject of speculation. It is an area of empirical research which must develop before the phenomenon of affiliation to mystical orders is further clarified.

The same juxtaposition of external constraints, i.e., social networks, and cultural resources for the solution of internal problems, appears in the case of Mustafa Sungur, who became one of the closest companions of Said Nursi. Here, in addition, we have an ideological, cognitive dimension. In this case we observe a link between the internal and the external dimension of religion: we feel that what is being worked out is the ability to find one's inner, unchanging self through clarifying the function of a cognitive frame, in this case, particularly concerned with time.

Mustafa Sungur

Mustafa Sungur was born in 1929 in Eflani in the Black Sea region to a family of modest peasants. This is how he describes his first contact with the *Nur* group:

> The first time I came into contact with the *Risale-i Nur* I had been handed a set of the *Ayet-i Kubra* [Reprinted in *Şualar* n.d. n.p. 88]. This was a brochure of twenty type-written pages. In the summer of 1946 I was seated in a barber's chair and was reading these lines for the first time. The lines which I was reading were striking thunderbolts in me. The emanations which emerged from these lines went right to the core of my soul. (Şahiner, 1977, 368)

The *Ayet-i Kubra* was one of the *Flashes of Light* which Said's followers had been propagating, and its introductory paragraph read as follows:

> Whenever a visitor arrives in our country and opens his eyes his sees the following sight: a most generous feast table and a most artfully prepared exhibit hall and a most impressive army headquarters and field for drill and an itinerary on which appear amazing sights which encourage one to go further and a place of study full of meaning and philosophical sustenance. When he begins to wonder about the owner of these beautiful guesthouses he sees, first, the beautiful writing of light which proclaims to him that they have the answer to his search. He then looks and sees that there is an appearance of the divinity which makes hundreds of thousands of heavenly objects one thousand times larger than our earth. Some of them go seventy times faster than a cannon-ball held up without the help of any props and gyrate incredibly fast and harmoniously without having to oil this mechanism which constantly lights innumerable lamps and directs boundlessly large masses without a single grating noise or irregularity and who, just as he makes the sun and the moon attend to its duties without any rebellion, makes these masses attend to their duties . . . and within the activity of this divinity, a magical emanation of true planning, administering, regulating, purifying and assigning duties. (*Şualar,* 88)

The progression here is from a perception of the harmony of nature to a search for the author of this harmony, and it was this progression which presumably was so satisfying to Mustafa Sungur. Mustafa Sungur continues:

> That same year, for the second time and in the same month I listened to a lecture on faith from a notebook where the text was written in Arabic characters. I had this text read and re-read to me several times. I later found that this was the text of the *Twenty-Third Word.*

The *Twenty-Third Word* was a sermon on faith which began as follows:

> Man reaches the highest perfection through faith, and he thereby acquires a value which makes him worthy of Paradise. And, conversely, steeped in the darkness of unbelief he descends to lower depths and becomes fit for Hell. For

> faith enables man to link man to his exalted creator. Faith is a joining, and, thereafter, man assumes a value in virtue of divine arts and the embossing of the divine names on men. Unbelief severs this link and this severing causes the divine artfulness to be disguised. Its value, thereafter amounts simply to the value of its material component. As to matter, since it is bound to be ephemeral and transitory and is of the nature of temporary, animal life, it is totally worthless. (*Emirdağ Lâhikası*, 289)

Mustafa Sungur thereafter got hold of a few more of the brochures of Said Nursi. He states that it was as if he were breathing them "like air, drinking them like water."

> . . . for indeed, I had achieved the true light of faith. This was to bring me new and fresh life. The passage I had listened to was a comment on the *Qur'ānic* verse about the believers emerging from darkness into light. The truth of the verse, the lesson in the brochure and my internal state fitted together exactly. It was as if a boundless universe which had been stretching from earliest time to eternity was being revived for me, as if, as a consequence of these sermons, I was finding a happiness which derived from the feeling that a boundless cosmos stretched from the beginning of time into infinity. I later understood that this was a manifestation of the light of faith.

This passage is one which shows how the inner state of a follower, rather than his network affiliation, could become a propelling force that made followers join Said Nursi. It also shows that the metaphysical speculations of Said Nursi and the demands of the newly emerging educated group in Turkey would in some cases meet at mid-point. Mustafa Sungur was the son of peasant parents. It was from persons with such a socio-economic status that students for the so-called village institutes which Mustafa was attending in 1946 were recruited. The schools were developed in the 1940s to train enlightened village teachers at the primary level who would also become village leaders. The programme of the schools was strictly secular, coeducational and emphasized group and community control by the students themselves. It tried to bring the students into contact with Western culture, literature, music and even social thought. At the same time the schools attempted to underline the practical tasks that would face a village teacher, such as advising peasants as to how best to till their land and marshall supplies for the village. The architects of this type of education were later to be accused of establishing a Trojan horse that would create the conditions necessary for the spreading of socialism and communism in rural areas. For some, the village institutes were dens of iniquity because they showed the influence of Marxism; for others, because the students were exposed to the teachings of Freud.

In the Black Sea region where he had originated, Mustafa Sungur was exposed to a type of strict puritanical Islam characteristic of this region. It is quite clear that despite the teachings of his own village institute, Mustafa did not have a clue that would enable him to build a complete cosmological system, however elementary. Sungur's insistence on the recapture of time and space through the medium of the sermons is particularly instructive. It was because he had finally been provided with a time scale that he felt so elated. His adolescent status probably had some relation to this perceived need for bearings, but it was the metaphysical content of the *Nur* teaching which made his re-integration into an acceptable time scale possible: this time scale was that of sacred time. This is not an isolated instance of educated persons finding that their need for a time scale was not being met by schools. Much of Turkish modernization during the nineteenth century had produced consequences which undermined the traditional sense of time. Part of this was an outcome of what Daniel Halevy (1948) calls the "acceleration of history." Part of it appeared in the change of the pace of life as regulated by religious rituals. But in the provincial town setting, the effect of this change was seen in the more shattering denial of the entire structure of Muslim time.

Ahmet Haşim, the Turkish poet who established his name in the second decade of the twentieth century, observed the following about the "acceleration" of time in Turkey at the beginning of the twentieth century:

> In olden times, just as we had a way of life, of thinking, of dressing which we could call our own, just as we possessed a sense of the beautiful which took its liveliness from religion, race and tradition, so too, we had control over our own "hours" and "days" which were in tune with this type of life. The beginning of the Muslim day was set by the glowing of sunrise and the end of the evening's last rays. The hands of the old, innocent watches which were protected by their strong metallic casings would amble past their enameled numerals in a way more or less connected with the pace of the sun, and, in a gait that was reminiscent of the tired feet of insects, would inform their owners of the time with the precision of approximation. Time was an endless garden and the hours therein were flowers whose colors were reflected from the sun and who inclined sometimes to the right and sometimes to the left. Before we became accustomed to foreign hours we did not know, in these climes, the twenty-four hour "day," black at both edges with the blackness of night, its back painted with various contrasting colors, with red, yellow or

> dark blue pigments, stretching like a large dragon from one midnight to the other. We had an easy, light, day of twelve hours which began and ended with light, an easily-lived day. Times which had been times of happiness for Muslims were measured in such "days." The Muslims recorded events which instilled pride and honor in them with such days. It is true that according to astronomical computations this hour was a false and primitive hour. But this hour was the sacred hour of remembrance. The acceptance of the Frankish hour in our customs and transactions and the fading away of the Alaturka hour into the mosques, ritual time-reckoning offices, and tombs was not without its momentous consequences on our view of the world. (Ahmed Haşim, 1969, 102–105)

The void in the structure of time which Mustafa Sungur felt was one which was, at the most general level of analysis, caused by changes brought about by the Republic when it instituted obligatorily the Gregorian calendar and time-keeping in 1928. It is not only that the time which was ushered in by the change as a different type of time but, as Ahmet Haşim points out, the metaphorical content of time had been lost. For Sungur and for many others from a similar background this was probably one of the important unheralded consequences of the secularizing moves of the Turkish Republic which had been proceeding since the early 1920s. What I mean here by metaphorical time is the image of time which an individual holds.

Just as biblical imagery provided the basic framework "for imaginative thought in America up until quite recent times" (Bellah, 1975, 12), so too it was on the metaphors of the *Qur'ān* that Muslims depended and still depend for imaginative creation, for self-placement and self-realization. For Sungur, it is at this point that the cultural process had been shattered, the metaphor of Muslim time had been erased. But the loss of the analytical, dynamic mechanism centered on the formation of the self that the metaphor controlled. Through the discovery of sacred time Mustafa Sungur had been able to place himself outside calendar time and recover a feeling of equilibrium at a personal level which the banning of sacred time by the Republic had precluded. Another element which Mustafa Sungur recovered with his integration into sacred time was a sense of history. In sacred time he was at the center of an eschatological process whose language was familiar to him. The time dimension of the Republic, on the other hand, was alien. The Republican severing of a cue which had enabled Sungur's predecessors to build their own time dimension had occurred at the very time when the ideologizing of Islam, which I described in a previous chapter, had made such an historical perspective necessary for the building of collective identity. Here we reach another boundary of the self, namely, the new Turks' conception of history.

History as an unfolding of secular stages was lost for the Turkish Republic because the only idea of history that emerged from its schools was that of youth on the march, building the future of Turkey. This image had replaced the Islamic metaphor of "the life of the single, indivisible entity, mankind" made possible by "God's contemplation, through all time of the human race made one and indivisible through God's creation of Adam" (Nisbet, 1970, 64). Although my quotation here is one which describes the Augustinian theory of history, it is close in its essentials to the Islamic feeling for history.

Mircea Eliade has said all that is relevant about time as "the most important fact in discovering man's relationship to the sacred" (cited by Shippee, 1974, 99, note 79). Mustafa Sungur's involvement is just one of the examples that justifies Eliade's view.

Abdullah Yeğin

In the case of Abdullah Yeğin, another follower of Said Nursi, we have an example of social mobility within the *Nur* sect which seems to set a fairly general pattern for the background of the leaders of this group.

One of the cities into which Said Nursi was sent into enforced exile after his stint in Barla was Kastamonu, a provincial capital and a center of Islamic conservatism, learning and anti-reformist currents. Bediüzzaman remained in Kastamonu between 1936 and 1942. It is here that he met Abdullah Yeğin, one of his most important future lieutenants.

In 1940–41 Abdullah Yeğin was in the second grade of "middle school." He learned that the owner of the house Said Nursi was renting as well as other men spoke of Said in flattering terms. He was thereby moved to find more about him. One of his schoolmates knew the sage and had gone to see him a number of times. They then arranged to visit him together. Said gave them a sympathetic reception and talked to them about the beauty of faith, about death and resurrection. Yeğin states that Said Nursi took up issues which were by no means esoteric but themes which the boys were already familiar with, such as the unicity of God, the limits of man's freedom and the danger of the times through which they were living. After this conversation some of Yeğin's anti-religious attitudes, which he attributes to the teachings of schoolmasters, disappeared. He was driven to ask the teacher to talk about the creator, a subject which, naturally, had never been broached in class. Said continued to lecture to the young boys and took them on nature hikes in which passages from the *Risale-i Nur* would be read when they paused. The school got wind of the student's forays and expelled them temporarily from school. The police stepped in and the government prosecutor interrogated the boys. When they stated that they had sought religious instruction, the prosecutor retorted that they could just as well have gone to the official in charge of religious affairs, the provincial *müftü*. Yeğin's own comment is, "I answered I did not know the *müftü*." This answer was not simply a means of getting the interrogators to relent: it pointed to the difference between a citizen's access to officials and to religious networks, a difference which had existed for centuries. Among the adolescents, no one in his right mind would have tried to gain access to the *müftü*, for the student stood outside the interaction of officials: students figured among "non-persons." Here again, the Republic was in error in thinking that adolescents in Kastamonu were, like Western adolescents, only adolescents, i.e., in the traditional Western understanding isolated from the stream of day-to-day adult concerns. In fact, the category of helpers which Said Nursi recruited from such young men made up a staff which was later to keep with him through thick and thin.

Mehmet Emin Birinci

One of the most complete accounts we have of a process of affiliation with the *Nur* movement is that of Mehmet Emin Birinci, again a young man of extremely modest background.

Birinci states that his association goes back to the year 1947. Birinci was in the last grade of primary school. This was a time of economic hardship for all. Birinci states that *Qur'āns* had to be hidden from the sight of tax collectors because they could be sold for villagers' debts to the state. In Birinci's village the inhabitants had banded together to pay for the village *imam* to provide religious teaching for the village children. Every year two men who were relatives of Birinci went to the Kızılırmak estuary as migrant workers to make up part of their cash income. In 1948 they returned to the village with a new attitude: they had become pious Muslims as a result of entering a *tarikat*. The next year they left once again for the estuary and found out that a holy man by the name of Bediüzzaman was living in the vicinity of Afyon. The news created considerable turmoil in the men who set out to acquire Said Nursi's writings before they returned to the village. The books were expensive, and they could not find the money needed to buy them. With the help of friends they were able to collect 33 lira. The books were ordered, and Sefer Usta, the village cobbler, brought them to the village in his sack. The sack was opened, and everyone tried to read the texts which were in Arabic characters. One of them read to Birinci the text of the *Fifth Ray.* Birinci states that this was exactly the type of message for which he was looking.

The enthusiasm of the newly-formed circle spread: Birinci read the brochure and talked of them to his friends. A number of villagers then decided to buy a subscription to the periodical which the *Nur* community was publishing. The periodicals arrived with an unanticipated bonus: the text of Bediüzzaman's defense in court. The general subject of conversation in the village now began to center on the *Nurcu* and their activities. Links were forged between the village and the *Nurcus* of the towns of Bafra and İnebolu in the vicinity and also with *Nurcus* in Istanbul. Birinci failed in the eighth grade, possibly because he was spending too much time with the *Nur* movement. He decided to drop out of school for a year. This gave him the opportunity to go to Samsun and to witness the trial of Mustafa Sungur, whom he visited in jail.

In 1952 Birinci tried to enter the Naval School but was rejected for reasons of health. He took up a job as a clerk in an hotel. Soon thereafter Bediüzzaman had to appear in court in Istanbul. Birinci witnessed the proceedings of the court and tried to contact Bediüzzaman without success. He ran a number of small errands for persons around Said, hoping to gain access to the leader. He could not contain himself any more and one day "stormed" Bediüzzaman's hotel room. Said Nursi, hearing of his repeated attempts, promised that Birinci would be included in his train. Birinci, elated by this meeting, eventually left his hotel job and, relying only on his savings, began to live in a sort of commune which was devoted to the study of the works of the Master.

Birinci now returned to his village. His uncle, who was unusually bold in his propagandizing activities, was being persecuted by the authorities. When acquitted, he went around the village with a sack of books on his back—the writings of Said—proclaiming to all who could hear: "These are the instruments which I used to blast the foundations of the State." Eventually Birinci was able to get a post as a village teacher. He was also prosecuted for religious activity but was acquitted. Returning to Istanbul in 1953, he found that his former commune had been dispersed. While he was trying to recreate it, a stove-maker who had just bought a house let the young man use it as a center for the new commune. The stove-maker was also drawn into proselytizing activities.

In 1957, when the *Risale-i Nur* began to be printed in Latin characters, Birinci was in Ankara helping with the work. By then, one of the *Nur* students, Dr. Tahsin Tola, who was also the editor of his works, had been elected to Parliament. The first batch of books to come off the press was sent to Istanbul under his protective eye. Birinci was arrested shortly thereafter. He was released and continued to work in the printing activities of the *Nurcu*.

The Person and Religious Resources

The preceding examples of venue into the *Nur* "sect" have no statistical validity. They, nevertheless, seem to capture processes which are different to study with statistical techniques because of the many variables they contain and because of the way in which they constitute part of a flexible set of strategies. Religious dogma and institution stand outside this process as resources which individuals use. It would seem as if a particular quandary affecting a person or a collectivity results in the more intensive use of one of these resources. Religious resources are thereby focused onto one specific area and this brings out the characteristics of that religion as it is practized at a particular time and place. But external structural constraints such as the increased need for a new view of history also, and simultaneously, affect religion. This variable is independent to the extent that it is the outcome of a process which takes place at the societal and world level, a process over which the individual does not have much control. Religious involvement, then, consists of relatively disconnected elements; nevertheless, all of them have to be taken into account if the total process is to be understood.

One process that the individual may control if he uses traditional religious symbols as part of his cultural baggage is to orient his life strategies with elements of his traditional religious, moral and intellectual equipment. With that relation established, external reality can be put into an Islamic framework.

Up to this point my description of Said Nursi's influence has centered on the processes which attracted a clientele through the relevance of his teachings to this set of persons in their quality as individuals. These were problems concerned with the elaboration of the self, issues related to the shaping of an identity. One gets a somewhat different view of things when one looks at these individuals as units in a group which formed around the sage. What strikes one immediately, in this perspective, is that the group so formed originally included no women. Even though *Nurcu* groups of women now function in a segregated, parallel stream to the activities of men, there were no women who actively contributed to the movement for a number of years. This purely male undertaking replicates a form of Middle East group formation which one also finds in the shaping of sects, military groups and literary *cenacles*.

The study of the group dynamic of *Nurculuk*, especially at the time of its formation, when such elements can be relatively easily isolated, shows what we may describe as a libidinal element which keeps the group together. Said Nursi's brittleness in his relations with his followers and his deep suspiciousness of some of those followers are reverse aspects of the cohesive power of these group relations. As I mentioned earlier, "depersonalization," the passage to a society of "blocks" and the idea of society as made up of such blocks was not an easy intellectual-cognitive watershed for Ottomans to negotiate. However, the establishment of the particular type of mechanistic-narcissistic group bond I have just described does in fact require a personalistic society. If group agglutination functioned in the traditional society on the basis of such bonding, if this was a basic resource of the society at large, then the emergence of a society of blocks must have been deeply frustrating for at least a section of rural society. It may well be that the deepest stimulant of Said Nursi's followers in clustering around him were the lines of force drawn by the implicitly learned strategies for social action in groups which the instructional modernization of the late Ottoman Empire and the Republic had displaced. The loss of such an instrumentality for clustering—underscored by the personalistic aspect of society and the segregation of sexes—may have been a form of social relations that could simply not be driven out of society. Here, once more, we have a development transforming libidinal foundations of social relations which is reminiscent of the same trend in Victorian England and in 19th century Europe. The general cast of social change as it occurred in Western Europe during modernization thus seems, once more, to be reflected in Ottoman society.

Chapter VI

The Machinery of Nature

THROUGHOUT SAID NURSI'S writings one encounters evidence of the impact of Western scientific advances. These passages are not isolated instances of an admiration for the magic quality of Western technology but, rather, well thought-out portions of a general view regarding the importance of science in the modern world. The following statement is characteristic of these musings:

> No doubt, mankind will, in the future, turn to science and technology. It shall take its strength from science. Sovereignty and force will pass into the hands of science. . . . (*Sözler*, 330)

At times, Said Nursi's approach to science shows the imprint of what may be termed pre-positivistic conceptualizations. This appears, for instance, in his classification of rhetoric as the most brilliant of sciences. But this view, supported by his contention that rhetoric is stated to achieve its greatest effect and popularity in our time, is most probably the product of a perceptive assessment of the power of mass media in modern society. After all, Said Nursi lived through the era of the Republic in Turkey, at the time when communications were opening up and its effect was being widely felt as a novel input into politics and social life in that country.

In the majority of cases, Said's views of science are best summarized by the quotation given above. On one occasion during his exile in Kastamonu students of the local lycée visited him and asked how they could elicit the most favorable setting for the worship of God. In answer, he advised them to concentrate on their studies of science. Undoubtedly, this emphasis was due to his conviction that the development of Western European science had caused Western civilization to outstrip Islamic civilization (Mürsel, 566 citing *Divan-ı Harb-i Örfî,* 62). Indeed, during the nineteenth century, science had been one of the major areas on which the defensive and apologetic attitude of Muslims had been focused.

In the Ottoman Empire, the history of this confrontation had become part and parcel of intellectual history. On the occasion of Ernest Renan's quasi-racist remark regarding the inability of the Arabs to think scientifically (1883), Namık Kemal, the Young Ottoman with the best worked-out political ideology, had produced a well-known rebuttal. Kemal based his riposte on the scientific productivity of the Arabs, thus being drawn into an argument which was basically irrelevant for the Ottomans as a whole. But this stance was characteristic of many Ottomans and Muslims to which Westerners trumpeted the congenital inability of Orientals to produce science. In India, an early conciliatory response to Western scientific hubris, that of Sayyid Ahmad Khan, had run into a frontal attack by the Muslim reformist thinker Cemaleddin Afgani. Ahmad Khan had proposed that Islam be understood as a religion which incorporated the modern view of the system of nature. This was branded by Afgani as blasphemous materialism.

Afgani's negative reaction contained a shrewd assessment of the force of Islam as idiom, as an interconnected set of propositions which owed their impact to their ability to create a separate world of meanings and affective commitment. But he too argued against Renan that there was nothing that inherently prevented Muslims from understanding science. The men of the *Tanzimat,* their opponents the Young Ottomans, and even Sultan Abdülhamid II were all of one mind regarding the urgency of establishing control over science by the Ottomans. Both the Young Ottomans and the sultan, however, appeared confident that the values of Islam and those of Western science could be merged in a new synthesis.

By broaching the problem of the place of modern science in Islamic societies, Said showed that he had an understanding of the relation between science and the power of the states who had harnessed science to their own purposes. Japan, a name that was often invoked by the Young Turks, constituted the model of his inspiration in this respect: science could be adopted without changing traditional culture. However, Bediüzzaman attacked the problem of the legitimation of science at a more fundamental level than the Young Turks had. The Young Turks had started with an intellectual revolution at the elite level and had tried to impose a vague form of positivism together with their various ideologies. Their support of religion was also part of this stance, in that they believed it underpinned social order and equilibrium. Bediüzzaman set out to create a native feeling for science at a much more fundamental level: he attempted to draw it out of religious symbols. Although he possibly did not realize it, this was a process to which modern science owed part of its origins. In early Renaissance Europe the symbolic resources of mysticism had operated as a springboard to secular scientific thought, and Said Nursi was following the same course. The extent to which a modification of the traditional Islamic message was consciously pursued is not quite clear, but that Said realized he was heralding many new *emphases* of Islam cannot be doubted.

The difficulties that would have to be faced by a Muslim who did not proceed from a tradition which contained mytho-poetic elements have been described by Sayyid Husayn Nasr:

> It is true that modern sciences have borrowed many techniques and ideas from the ancient and medieval sciences, but the point of view in the two cases is completely different. The Muslim sciences breathed in a universe in which God was everywhere. They were based upon certainty and searched after the principle of unity in things which is reached through synthesis and integration. The modern sciences, on the contrary, live in a world in which God is nowhere or, even if there, He is ignored as far as the sciences are concerned. They are based on doubt and having turned their back on the unifying principles of things seek to analyse and divide the contents of nature in an even greater degree moving towards multiplicity and away from unity. That is why studying them causes a dislocation with respect to the Islamic tradition for the majority of Muslim students. Unfortunately, not everyone is able to see the heavens as both the Pedestal of God's Throne and incandescent matter whirling through space. Therefore, the curriculum of the schools and universities in the Muslim countries, by teaching the various modern European arts and sciences which are for the most part alien to the Islamic perspective, has, to a large degree, injected an element of secularism into the mind of a fairly sizeable segment of Islamic society. (Nasr, 1961, 124–25)

To practice "Western" science as Said Nursi encouraged it meant to start from certain basic premises about a system of nature. Here any Muslim was faced with difficulties, for he had to link the system of nature to an act of creation and to the Creator himself.

In the writings of the orthodox Muslim theologians, God appeared both as tremendously powerful and, at the same time, distant. There was therefore no means of integrating God's ubiquity with Newton's system of nature. But for the mystics this linking was much easier, for God was not only everywhere, He was everywhere as a material reflection of his essence.

In Europe a relatively workable transition had been effected between religious and secular thought in the years preceding the high tide of Enlightenment. For one, the medieval metaphysical belief in the idea that a basic "but unseen harmony underlies the apparent discord of the world" (Anchor, 1967, 11) was easily translated into the Enlightenment idea of the regularity of the physical laws of nature. The bridge between religious and secular ideas had been provided not only by deism but by thinkers like Leibnitz. The many subtle graduations of enlightened secular thought also allowed for an eventual infiltration of the findings of physical science into the thought of Christian theologians. In Turkey there was no such intellectual bridge and, of necessity, it was the creative powers of the divinity which had to be underlined in making modern ideas of science fit with religious belief. Said Nursi used this idea to a large extent in legitimizing the conceptions of laws of nature which operated as the extension of God's design. Here he could work on the affective popular resonance of the idea of the pre-eternal light of God out of which came the clay of Adam and the body of the Prophet (Schimmel, 123f: here 126), and he could simultaneously rely on the mystic's symbols, which he was overtly fighting all the time.

In the context of the ongoing modernization of Turkey, the process that highlighted the importance of science were not simply those of a confrontation with the West. Other question marks emerged from the very penetration of science into Ottoman culture during the 20th century. Muslims who, in the 1930s, asked the questions reported in Said's *Flashes of Light* ("Is the earth supported on the horns of a steer?") were sincerely concerned with the lack of congruence between the cosmology which appeared in popular treatises on religion dating to the 16th century and the explanations provided by modern science. It was up to Muslim thinkers to find a conciliation between these diverging understandings of the cosmos. To the extent that Said Nursi was able to propagate his ideas, this was due, in some measure, to his ability to show that there were no incompatibilities between the *Qur'ān* and modern science. Part of the shift was effected in the somewhat superficial spirit of the so-called "scientific" interpretation of the *Qur'ān*: bacteria were "proved" to have been adumbrated by *Qur'ānic suras* (Jansen, 1974, 44), but part of Said Nursi's transition had deeper philosophical moorings.

A passage in Said Nursi's *Letters* (*Mektubat*, 187) in which he explains the relation between the *Qur'ān* and the created world shows that he sees the *Qur'ān* as fulfilling two functions. First, the *Qur'ān* does mention the phenomenal world but gives only uncomplicated images of it which are understandable to all (*suret-i basitane-i zahirane*). The *Qur'ān* glosses over our sophisticated phenomenologically grounded knowledge of the world because its primary function is to draw the believer's perception towards the Creator and not to the created. In a sense, then, the created is virgin territory yet to be explored. But there was more to Said's approach than this. By framing the system of nature in a mytho-poetic setting, in the way Muslim mysticism made it possible, by stressing the creative power of God, Said was able to create the feeling that the contents of the *Qur'ān* opened up a view of a universe in movement and that this could be used to build a new image of the cosmos. Through affective resonances which fastened on the evocative power of the style of the *Qur'ān,* such a new resource was made available to persons who, in the past, would have been passive participants in the "miracle" of the *Qur'ān* (*E.I.*[2], III, 1018–1020). Said's theses, expressed in the heavily arabicized style of the theosophers, was not so much an *explanation* of the system of nature as a call to consider the potential for creativeness that God had infused into the world. He was explaining the *Qur'ān* in Turkish but without impoverishing its affective hold. In addition, he was providing his followers with a means of activating their view of the universe. This element worked in tandem with his demands for greater religious activism on the part of Muslims.

To recognize that science had become a social pursuit, one that was important for the strengthening of Muslim society, was not tantamount to presenting a theological justification for this shift of focus. For, indeed, the new emphasis on nature did constitute a shift of emphasis as compared to the earlier, overwhelming importance of the relations between Man and his Maker. A passage from the *Risale-i Nur,* one of the many in the same vein, provides a model of this transition, from the relation between God and man to the relation between Man and "things," i.e., physical objects or biological processes.

> Then shall anyone who has done an atom's weight of good and anyone who has done an atom's weight of evil, see it (*Qur'ān,* 99, 7–8). If you want proof of this truth of the Wise Qur'ān look at the pages of the universe that are written on the pattern of the Perspicuous Book: and you will see in its many aspects the supreme manifestation of the Name of the Preserver and the sample of a sublime truth of this noble verse. For example take a handful of seeds of varied plants, which serve as little cases for many different kinds of plants, flowers, and trees, and bury and scatter them in the darkness of the soil which is nothing more than a simple inanimate substance. Then pour on that soil some water that has no discriminating faculty and goes wherever you

> pour it. And come back the next spring—at a time when the annual resurrection takes place, when the angel of thunder calls upon the rain—like the angel who blows the trumpet of resurrection—and those seeds receive the joyful tidings of recreation. Behold how those seeds buried under the ground in utmost mutual resemblance and confusion of arrangement will faultlessly obey the command of revival coming from the Wise Creator and will come to life under the manifestation of the name of the Preserver. Truly, in such fashion do they obey the command of their Creator. . . . Because you see that those little seeds resembling each other become distinct and differentiated. (Bediüzzaman, *Lem'alar,* 1974, 51–52)

There are many passages in the *Risale-i Nur* in which the regularities of nature *(nizam-intizam)* are described at length as proof of the work of a Creator.

In short, a justification was needed for the new emphasis on matter which went counter to the focus of traditional teaching as it appeared in popular catechisms highlighting theological and moral rather than cosmological concerns. It is difficult to state outright that Said Nursi came forth with a fully formulated theory about nature, but that he was using a number of cues found in the mystical tradition is clear. Even though the reconstruction of the way he used these cues turns out to be more systematic than what Said intended, the fact that a latent frame underlies his system of nature cannot be questioned. The following attempts to trace this frame.

Said Nursi had set himself against mysticism because he believed that it deflected Muslims from taking up the specific duties that were prescribed for them in the *Qur'ān*. For him, faith, "the heart," was essential in the Muslim's commitment. But this faith had to be an active faith, informed and guided by the specific injunctions of the *Qur'ān*. The wide latitude allowed by the teachings of the mystics did not produce the mobilized Muslim he wanted to create. In this objection to mysticism, Bediüzzaman was dead center in the orthodox scripturalist and fundamentalist tradition, as exemplified, for instance by the Muslim fundamentalist Ibn Taimiyya (1263–1328), who attacked the mystic's doctrine that "He who witnessed the Will of God feels no longer bound by the command of God" (Fazlur Rahman, 1979, 113).

Often Bediüzzaman, too, dismisses Ibn al-'Arabī's influence as harmful for the modern Muslim: *vahdet-i vücud* may promote materialism (among the unenlightened masses) and monstrous pride among others. Yet, his arguments are replete with echoes from this very man. We know through his use of the technical vocabulary of the mystics (*rububiyet, hüvviyet, enaniyet, âlem-i şahadet, âlem-i misal*) that his intellectual apparatus carries the trace of Ibn al-'Arābī's influence. He, therefore, must also have known the cosmological models that derived from the latter, either through Ibn al-'Arābī's own writings, or more plausibly through the work of his commentators. As we proceed we shall see that indeed he relies on the Muslim sage's arguments. These very sophisticated speculations provided him with the means of taking a first step towards an accommodation with the Newtonian model of the universe. Said had better resources at his disposal for such a task than the more orthodox, anti-Sufi Turkish thinkers of his time. Islamic philosophers also had an elaborate cosmology (Nasr, 1978), but the mystics were ahead of even the philosophers insofar as *semiotic* resources were concerned, i.e., where it became necessary to draw on the image of the cosmos. Said does not seem to have pursued this source of inspriation consciously, but in the end, his elegiac descriptions of the miracle of the "book of nature" derive from such a background.

One may think of Ibn al-'Arabī's influence on Said as a triggering effect, an idea which fits well with what Marshall Hodgson has to say of the effects of mysticism on Muslim thought:

> We have come to realize that the speculation of Ibn al-'Arābī . . . was not the passive monism that had been imagined, but a powerfully stimulating synthesis in which the human person, as microcosm in an infinitely meaningful cosmos was assigned vast potentialities in every phase of activity. (Hodgson, 1970)

It is true that the speculations of Ibn al-'Arābī did not provide a sufficient philosophical base to retrieve mechanistic Newtonianism for the *Nurcu* world picture. There were a number of difficulties of different orders that were concealed in the task Said had to accomplish in this respect. One was simply a matter of different emphasis. Even though traditional Islamic philosophy had developed a complex cosmology from the earliest time onward, the 19th century reformers of Islam had shown greater interest in faith, ritual, and conduct than in pictures of the cosmos.

Could Said Nursi introduce a new focus of religion that would prove as important? Another difficulty was that the centrality of the physical system of nature in human consensus—an aspect of the world-view derived from Newton—jarred with the direction of the mystic's thought. The latter leaned towards recapturing God's unity rather than studying the universe's diversity.

In other words, even though Sufi thinking was a sophisticated elaboration of ontology, since the direction of the mystic's speculations was away from phenomena and towards elucidating the mystery of Being in relation to the Creator, Said Nursi had to turn the Sufi point of view on its head. For this Sufi approach was an outlook which stressed that "entities do not 'borrow' existence from God. Nor do they share in Being, become 'connected' to it, nor act as 'receptables' for it. All of these expressions are only matters of speaking. They are images employed to explain a phenomenon whose reality is almost inexplicable . . . . " (Chittick, 1981, 181)

The strategic focus of the philosophical leap that Bediüzzaman had to undertake while maintaining his orthodox stand was the conception of the activity of God in nature. The orthodox *Ash'ārite* stand considered divine intervention into the movement of nature to be direct and continuous. Every movement of nature was an act of God. To elaborate a system where God was removed from the immediacy of His will, and where He worked through matter in movement, was not an easy task. Matter had to be accepted first as a basic element which either was pre-existent to God or was subject to laws which could be construed by literal interpreters of orthodox Islam as a limitation on the absolute power of God.

Some of the difficulties in reaching an accommodation with an idea of nature that bore the imprint of Newton's discoveries can be pinpointed by recollecting key aspects of the Enlightenment view of the universe and of the accommodation of deists to this new picture.

For the deists of the 18th century, man was part of a system of matter in movement, and his privilieged position in the center of the universe had already been withdrawn from him by the new scientific discourse. The sequence of the Great Chain of Being now went from God to the machinery of the universe, and from there to man. Many thinkers in Europe adduced the new discoveries and the system of Newton as evidences for faith and Said Nursi was to adopt the same position. However, the Enlightenment argument followed a path which differed considerably from that of his own. Thus in 1662, Simon Patrick, later Bishop of Ely, defended both latitudinarian religion and "the new and free philosophy" in the pages of a pamphlet (Gay, 1966, 315). This was possible because Patrick also took the movement of matter in the "theater of nature" to be an intermediate link between the Creator and Man. The regularities of nature, and its potential for generating effects did not need to be linked to the Creator's immediate intervention. By contrast, in the mystic's cosmology this intermediate was the "World of Archetypes," a realm which bore no resemblance to the enlightenment's nature. The mystic's "World of Archetypes" is clearly described by Chittick:

> The World of Spirits precedes the World of Corporeal Bodies *('ālam al-ajsām)* . . . both in being and in level. The Divine Succour which reaches the corporeal-bodies depends upon the intermediary of the Spirits between the corporeal-bodies and God. Moreover, the governing *(tadbīr)* of the corporeal-bodies is entrusted to the Spirits, but no inter-relationship can exist between the two sides, because of the intrinsic disparity between the composite and the noncomposite: All corporeal-bodies are composite, while the Spirits are noncomposite, so there is no affinity *(munāsaba)* between them, and thus no interrelationship. As long as there is no interrelationship there can be no actualization of the exercising and receiving of effects, . . . nor of the giving and receiving of succour . . . so God created the World of Image-exemplars as an Isthmus comprehending the World of the Spirits and the World of the Corporeal-Bodies, in order that each of the two worlds may establish a relationship with the other. (Chittick, 1982, 113–114 Quoting Sadrettin Konevi)

The names of Allah and his attributes set the archetypes that have the power to create the phenomenal world as perceived.

> The attribute of "sight" for example which on the one hand manifests itself in God's vision of Himself becomes manifested in all of the myriad possible forms it can assume as an independent—or rather semi-independent—reality. In the physical world it manifests itself in countless individuals as the sight of man and animals, the photo-sensitivity of plants, the vision of sages etc. Each mode of manifestation exists potentially within the reality of Sight within God's knowledge, but it exists in actuality only through separative existence in the manifested universe. (Chittick, 1979, 149)

Thus, for Said Nursi *"İsm-i Hakem* and *İsm-i Hakim"* (the name of Judge and Sovereign) *"İsm-i Adl ve Adil"* (the name of Justice and Just) together determine what we see as the regularity and balance of nature *(Lem'alar,* 228, cf. Fazlur Rahman, 1979, 92).

In terms of practical attitudes towards the study of nature, such a springboard would lead the innovator to concentrate on the mystery of the Names of God and His attributes in trying to derive new knowledge about the mystery of creation rather than on the regularities of nature. Said had to do both. We know that Bediüzzaman did effect the translation by giving considerable attention to the "theater of Nature" or, in his own words, "The Great Book of Nature."

In the Sufi's world, Adam, the archetype of the perfect man, is the specific intermediate between God and man, and he has a special relation to the physical world. "In the physical world all the celestial spheres, the elements, the animals, the vegetables and minerals are included within him" (Chittick, 1981), rather than as an autonomous realm outside him. "If it were not for the fact he acts as the isthmus unopposed to either of the two sides . . . the world would cease to exist" (Chittick, 1979, 153–154). Once more, what we see here is a reverse of the sequence of relations between the creator and nature which appears in the universe of 18th century deists.

One final difficulty which Said Nursi had to face was the attractiveness of the study of form as opposed to that of the discrete phenomena in the world of planets and atoms. "The *Sufis* understand 'form' *(surah)* to signify the means whereby unseen realities *(haqa'iq ghaybiyyah)*—which are disengaged *(mufarrad)* from and transcend physical reality—can be understood. In other words, the Form of a transcendent reality—perhaps symbol would be a better translation—in the means whereby that reality *(haqiqah)* or the meaning *(ma'na,* the term employed in contradistinction to *surah)* manifests itself in the physical world. The form is ontologically connected to its own meaning. Hence man as the form of Allah is ontologically the manifestation of Allah and the means whereby He is known in the physical world. Without man the Name "Allah" would have no single locus of manifestation" (Chittick, 1979, 145).

In the face of such a complex cosmology, one of Said Nursi's strategies seems to have been to advance the thesis (correctly in view of the preceding) that the world of archetypes *(âlem-i misal)* and the world of phenomena *(âlem-i şuhud)* are two different cognitive realms. The world of archetypes cannot be analyzed by means of concepts of the world of phenomena even though it is the source of that world of phenomena. Said Nursi attributes this idea to Ibn al-'Arabī and goes on from there to criticize crude populist ideas of religion which project the realm of phenomena onto the world of archetypes (*Muhakemat*, 1977, 56).

As to the world of phenomena itself and "nature" about which persons keep "blabbering" *(Muhakemat*, 1977, 112), it is nothing but the "corpse" *(ceset)* of creation. The most important characteristic of creation is that it is supported, or kept there so to speak, by an internal, Godly spring *(şeriat-ı fitriyye)*. Here Said Nursi seems to have been less willing than Ibn al-'Arābī to accord an autonomous unfolding to the externalization of God's attributes.

In another place in his writings Said Nursi explains his stand thus: there are three modern arguments concerning the dynamics of nature which have all distracted man: Causality, self-moving matter *(teşekkül-ü bi nefsihi)* and the "requisites of nature." All three are balderdash *(Lem'alar,* 167).

> "Let us think," argues Said, "of a clockmaker. Would it be easier for him to make the wheels of a clock and then set up the mechanism of the clock or to make a wondrous machine with these wheels and then give the manufacture of the clock to the machine? Or a secretary: he has brought ink, pen and paper. Is it easier for him to write the book himself or to make a more excellent, more difficult writing machine with the ink, pen and paper only for the composition of that particular machine devoid of consciousness *(şuursuz)* and say "Very well, write it now." *(Lem'alar,* 176)

Furthermore, God does not allow anything or anyone to share power with Him as would have been the case above *(Ibid.,* 177). And also, if the world of minerals, plants and animals has been created for man, how could one imagine that God would abandon these to an impersonal mechanism?

Said Nursi's explanation of the regularities to be found in nature was that (1) the regularities of lifeless matter can only be explained if the premise is accepted that an active intelligence set a pattern, a plan, for the regulations; (2) this pattern is written into the *lehv-i mahfuz* (the preserved tables) or the infinite set of regulatory devices which are contained in a "heavenly index" (Mürsel, 1976, 56 citing *Sözler,* 581–582).

Creation is of two kinds: an original act of creation of the varieties of inanimate nature and of the species, and an act of creation which is an art and which combines these primary elements. This process is characteristic of the regularities of organic nature. The innovation here is the idea of a *plan* which, in fact, goes beyond the cosmological mechanisms of Ibn al-'Arābī.

According to Said Nursi, there exists a homology—due to their common origin in a divine source—between the processes of nature and those that open up the perception and understanding of nature in man. This is the way in which a man grasps the processes of nature and has in him the ability to understand them.

Mektubat is one of his later works. In it Said unequivocally identifies nature as "a machine of the all-powerful" (1977, 212). Thus emerges what can only be described as a mechanistic view of nature. We can attribute this important shift of emphasis to the increasing importance—and prestige—that was given to science in the day-to-day life of the Turkish Republic, especially by secondary school teachers, who took the ideology of positive science into the provinces. This factor probably worked in tandem with another which appears quite early in the ideas of Said Nursi: namely, the admiration for the harnessing by man of the forces that lay dormant in nature and the power that it gave to nations. The easiest way to recapture this admiration is to follow the extent to which, from the beginning, Said Nursi's—and his followers'—vocabularies were infiltrated by conceptions taken from nineteenth century thermodynamics and electricity. Thus, one should "mount the train of religious law" (Bediüzzaman, 1976, 52); the world is a *fabrika-i kâinat* (factory of the universe) (*Lem'alar*, 287); life is a "machine of the future from the exalted benchwork of the universe" (*hayat kâinatın tezgah-i âzamında . . . bir istikbal makinesidir*) (*Lem'alar*, 371). Sabri, one of the first disciples of Bediüzzaman, speaks of "machines which produce the electricity of the *Nur* factory" when speaking of the work of disciples (Bediüzzaman, 1976, 173). Sabri himself is known as *Santral* (switchboard) Sabri. This interest in steam and electricity seems already to have marked "old" Said (*Lem'alar*, 166). Later the proof he adduces for the "centralized" command of God over the processes of nature is one where he uses as an analogy the rationality of giving the production of military equipment to "one factory and one ruler" (*Lem'alar*, 181).

While the speculations of the mystics brought up a fund of imagery which could trigger Said Nursi's accommodation with the Newtonian world view, there existed another popularized version of this type of thought, (see above pp., 196–197) which is best described by relating it to the Western idea of the Great Chain of Being, and this appears most clearly in his description of the biological world. One of the characteristics of Said Nursi's view of nature is the extent to which he subsumes it under biological processes. Thus birds and bees, flowers and trees, insects and gardens come immediately after the stars in his imagery of nature. Here again, one cannot but be reminded of the similar imagery of the mystics and particularly of the symbolism of plants that appears in Anatolian mysticism.

An example taken from his writings would be the following passage of which many variations can be found:

> And, for instance, just as a book may be found every line of which is itself a finely written book and every word of which is a *sura* of the *Qur'ān*, extremely meaningful, its propositions concerning each other and a wondrous compendium showing its scribe and author to be compassionate and powerful in the extreme, with no deviation, manifesting its scribe and producer's perfection and skill and thus the universe . . . which is only a single one of its

> pages—and in the spring—which is only one set of its pages—shows three hundred thousand different books as three hundred thousand botanical and zoological species, imbricated in one another, without error, without failure, without mixing things, without confusion, perfect and regular and revealing in a word that is a tree a qasīda, and in a point such as fruit's kernel a pen writing an entire index for a book which we can see writing without our own eyes in this infinitely significant cosmos and this majestic *qur'ānic* universe. . . . (*Şualar,* 174)

The symbolism of rebirth is also part of this imagery. Some of the deeper connotations of this imagery may be found in the insistence on the seed as an image. This, once again, points to elements which have to be studied in a psychoanalytic frame. For the moment these have to remain as cue for further explorations into Bediüzzaman's personality.

In the popular view of the Great Chain of Being Said Nursi had found a tradition which could make up for what late Islamic philosophy entailed as a "denial of trust in the natural properties and immanent processes of nature . . . " (Fazlur Rahman, 1979, 99). Already, in Suhrawardī, the illuminist who possibly may have influenced the young Bediüzzaman, there had been an infiltration of the "philosophical doctrine of the eternity of matter" (*Ibid.*). The popularized mystical tradition gave Said Nursi a means of using the Islamic version of Plotinus, i.e., the principle of the "grades of being" (*Ibid.,* 124).

The enduring quality of the mystic's imagery and symbolism was both a help and a hindrance to Said Nursi in trying to propagate a view of Islamic faith which had to address itself to a number of social classes and to persons with different educational achievements. Why, some of his followers asked him, did Ibn al-'Arabī state that the earth was made of seven different layers, a statement patently disproved by geography? Said Nursi answered that what Ibn al-'Arabī had seen was a vision. The statement was true only to the extent that the vision was true. But to draw conclusions concerning the phenomenal world from visions was wrong. It was wrong for two reasons: first, because the world of visions could not be assimilated to the world of phenomena, and second, because a vision could not be interpreted by the visionary himself (*Mektubat,* 74). Only those who, like the Brethren of Purity (*Asfiya*), were the touchstone of the true tradition of the Prophet could interpret these visions. What was meant by the Brethren of Purity was those who, in the tradition of Sirhindi, had not succumbed to a further corollary drawn from the theory that all was God: namely that all actions came from God and that therefore there was no clear line between good and evil or that God could be seen in the phenomena of nature themselves and did not have an existence outside them.

Bediüzzaman's stand in relation to this picture of nature thus straddles the mystical tradition: it is useful to paint a picture of nature more complex than that offered in the superficial interpretation of the *Qur'ān*, but dangerous if used by the masses to evade moral constraints.

Regardless of his view of nature as a machine, Said still considered the laws of nature to be appearances which heralded the presence of the real, i.e., the Godhead. Nature as a theophany of God and its study by science thus acquired a sacred quality. In the long run, this sacralization of science has resulted in a series of popularizations of science of a very high level published by the *nurcu* at their printing plant in Istanbul. The publications are devoid of propaganda and have such titles as "Cybernetics," "The Big Bang," "The Blood and Circulation," "Space and the World," "Energy and Life," "From the Cell to Man," or "The Air Around Us." The works are produced by reputable scientists, some with positions in the university, or by journalists who are careful to give a scientific account of the process they are studying. Only at the end is a theological point put forth: such extraordinarily involved but regular processes can only attest to the presence of a Maker, God.

Conclusion

IN THE MOST general sense my findings are concerned with human intelligence and with language and idiom as part of the adaptive instrumentalities of intelligence. But there are three general—and irreducible—qualitative aspects of the idiom I encountered. First, the idiom is concerned with "spiritual beings" and takes its force from a basic premise about the existence of God. Why a particular idiom would set out from this point is a question I do not investigage and for which I have no answer. But once this is accepted, I find that the idiom serves as an instrumentality for three things. First, for maintaining a sense of the mytho-poetic which works to produce a relation of enchantment or alternatively of daemonization with the ambient world. Power seems to me a force that originates in this locus. Again, I have no answer as to why the idiom I study should work through these channels. Second, the idiom to which I refer means that it can be used for what I can only describe as the expansion of one's personality or identity. Third, it serves to spin out a cognitive model of the universe and the world. None of these three dimensions prevail in their pure form. They have a mutual relation which is that of colors blending into one another, leaving some identifiable trails disappearing in the blend and reappearing at points as flakes or points.

Said Nursi's appeal to his followers—the problem that to me seemed most intriguing when I undertook the study—may be evaluated in the context of two main dimensions.

For one, the idiom that Said Nursi was reviving had also to be enriched. By enriched I mean enabled to confront the processes of a modern, more highly differentiated society. At this point we may refer to the ideas of Niklas Luhmann to bring out more clearly what this adaptation involved.

Luhmann is known for his work on the type of social communication that, in his view, has become characteristic of modern society. According to him, a difference exists between the sources which in "traditional" societies secrete the social cement productive of order as contrasted with those of modern societies. If *trust* in the way things will work themselves out in our lives—if, in other words, trust in society—is a basic component of this cement, then in traditional societies such trust depends on an emotional bonding with persons, or with myths or religion. But in modern times, members of society having been mobilized for wider participation, it is the workings of the system as a whole in which they have to place their trust. This requires a transition from reliance on a normative system to a system based on cognitive skills (Luhmann, 1979, 46). Ethical theory is, therefore, relegated to an auxilary role as legitimator. A typical example, relevant in the case of Said Nursi, would be *içtihad* elicited at weekly meetings of the brethren replacing the guidance of the *pir*.

The structural logic of Said Nursi's position was the need to achieve an accommodation with these specific external constraints that gave such a central role to flexible cognitive mechanisms. The problem which he encountered may thus be seen as a collapsing into a much shorter period of time of an extended Western experience in transiting from an earlier normative to a later cognitive phase. Today, when the young Turkish fundamentalists following in Said Nursi's path point out in the periodical *Girisim* (May, 1987) that what is needed for Islam is a 'paradigm' that will enable Muslims to draw meaning from the *Qur'ān* they are wending their way along a path opened up by said Nursi.

To complete this picture of transition to a new society we have to refer to still another dimension of Said Nursi's contribution. At this point he may be seen as having shaped the identity of a group among which the materials for identity had existed for a long time but which were brought to the fore by our sage. Remember that Said Nursi was seeking support among persons who had not climbed on the bandwagon of the modernist elite, i.e., among the underprivileged, who were still under the influence of their local culture. I would describe such persons as linked by a loose network and thus constituting a potential 'team' for concerted action in society. A characteristic of this "quasi-group" (Dahrendorf, 1958) was that it was made up of persons who, to a greater or lesser extent, took their value cues from and organized their daily life strategies around the so-called 'unbounded sea of the *şeriat*". This "virtual" group had a legitimation which was that of the just. Facing them was another team which took its values from sultanic practice—in the Weberian sense (or in more caricatural terms from "Oriental Despotism"). The boundaries of these two groups were the very product of Ottoman social organization, in the sense that the team of the just was also the group that paid taxes while the second group was that of persons exempted from taxes. We may therefore understand how the sultanic team, could be seen as the team of the unjust to which ordinary citizens gave habitual but no doubt often grudging obeisance. Cornell Fleischer has shown us how even one of the sons of an early Ottoman sultan rebelled against the practice of the unjust (unpublished speech, Istanbul, October, 1987).

Two characteristics of the team of the just need to be underlined. First, the elite of this team, the *'ulema* had often led the masses in movements that protested the practices of the unjust. Second, a more common form of protest against the unjust was the set of adversary, underground strategies directed to deflect and subvert the burdens generated by these policies. One of the more obvious of these tactics was gossip about the Great. Another, more clearly directed against the canon of the Great Tradition was the discourse of the central character in the Turkish shadow play, Karagöz. The *şeriat* played an important role in these strategies in the sense that it insured the protection of basic rights, including that of life and property, of the common citizen, in a way that was not true of the sultanic team. The *şeriat* therefore constituted a shield from behind which the popular *fronde* could be carried out.

These secret, and often semi-conscious and collective strategies have been studied by Michel de Certeau. He has highlighted the ways in which the totality of such stratagems subvert the canon of the discourse of the powerful, and has called this locus the "everyday" (*le quotidien*) (de Certeau, 1984). What Said Nursi was doing was fastening onto a fund of cultural resources—the religious idiom—which had an important place in the Ottoman everyday but also enriching it to fit the requirements of a modern society. Another, parallel, transformation was that by concentrating on the religious component of the everyday life of Ottomans and modern Turks he was able to bring it out with a new form, a collective identity which we could describe as populistic in mode.

Such an analysis of Said Nursi's ideas, however, only sets the broadest frame for their understanding. Other dimensions have to be evoked if we are to get a more precise understanding of *Nurculuk*. For one, Said Nursi's basic arsenal of a normative frame was not without its own philosophically compelling foundation. John Dunn, who takes up Locke's view of the subject, reminds us that "despite the indispensability of casual analysis of society . . . there is considerably more than we recognize today to be said from the pre-modern perspective on this question" (Dunn, 1934, 282). Locke's argument is that if *trust* is the prerequisite of any legitimation of a social order, this trust has to rest on ethical foundations rather than on cognitive technique.

Of related interest is the point which I have attempted to make a number of times, i.e., that the expanded external frame provided by the new world communications revolution also provides opportunities for expanding one's spiritual frame, which I define as one dimension of personality. The expansion of horizons which the modern state promotes through its educational policies brings not only the need for enhanced social status—an issue which has been studied many times—but also a need for spiritual plenitude. This does not mean that the process will work only in that direction. A cue that such a dimension of progress exists at all is provided more by the instances of its perversion in the modern world than by direct evidence. H. Rosenberg and his coterie of half-educated fascist intellectuals are not so far behind us that we may forget their own resolution of the issue in the form of the "Myth of the Twentieth Century": the vicious ideologies of totalitarianism may be interpreted as a need for spiritual plenitude which has gone awry. An apposite illustration may be given from the history of Muslim revivalism in Egypt.

In December 1981 in Cairo the manifesto appeared of an Islamic fundamentalist group entitled *The Forgotten Obligation* (Kepel, 1983). It was the work of a twenty-six year old Egyptian technician by the name of Abdessalam Faraj. In it Faraj gave his personal interpretation of some of the ideas of the great Islamic Medieval thinker Ibn Taimiyya (1263–1328). The brochure invited its audience to re-think the requirements of a truly Islamic society and reached the conclusion that Islamic political leaders who did not wholeheartedly work for the promotion of an Islamic society might as well be eliminated physically. The opuscule can be seen as the product and outcome of an enlarged educational system and the entry into the reading and writing public of a stratum of Egyptians mid-way between the rural masses and the learned *'ulema*. This new public did not rely any more on the authority of representatives of the "High" tradition to understand what their religion enjoined. The piece was consequently lambasted by the Azhar, the institutional representative of this culture in Egypt. But the most disturbing effect of the brochures was the impetus it provided to the assassination of A. Sadat.

The daemonic aspect of this particular development does not invalidate the need to consider spiritual dimensions on the reverse side of the coin. This is an item which is not adequately described when one mentions the need of modern men to have a picture of the cosmos or a map of social relations. It is related to a cognitive scheme, but it is also qualitatively different. In the case of Said Nursi, the Ottoman rural populations were not so far removed from the effects of modernization to fail to be aroused to a need for a new expansion of human horizons. This they could only express with the one language capable of carrying that weight, the language of religion. What I am arguing here is that students of social change who associate the growth of social communcation with an expanded vision of the world seem to forget that spiritual needs are also expanded as part of this change. This expansion comes at a time when a new populistic thrust is also emerging. Indeed, there is a democratized aspect in the very rise of *Nurculuk* since it provided an opportunity for persons with a lower class background to devise their own interpretation of the religious message.

This appears more clearly in Said's de-coupling of the linkage between esotericism and elitism in traditional Ottoman culture. Mysticism in one special form, i.e., the arcane knowledge of Islamic theosophy, the interpretation of the metaphorical content of the *Qur'ān* was considered to be the stuff that only persons with special intellectual and spiritual disposition could tackle, understand and control. In a sense, then, mysticism was the language of the elect, of a spiritual elite. This spiritual elite was not necessarily part of the ruling group of officials, but it had a special, preferred status which, through its cognitive selectivity, placed it in a position distinct from that of the mass of believers. Again, this does not mean the spiritual elect had no contact with the masses and did not serve their spiritual needs. The most intellectually aristocratic of the orders we know, that of *Melami,* who were bent on provoking outward blame only to contrast it with the immaculate nature of their internally held faith, were constantly in touch with the average believer. *İcaz,* the mystery, however, was a dimension of the *Qur'ān* into which they refused to bring this average believer.

By contrast, in the intellectual format of the ordinary believer there was a demand for ethical guidance, for spiritual support, for answers to problems posed by day-to-day life and for a sense of the enchantedness of the world rather than the search for the abstract, ineffable meaning of the *Qur'ān*. Modernization shattered this two-tiered religious stratification by propelling the ordinary citizen into an area which stood in between these two spheres.

Already in the nineteenth century there are indications that this cognitive boundary was softening. In modern times, a new, intermediate sphere, that of politics, arrived and drew philosophers, mystics and good burghers alike into participation; this also included what may be described as intellectual participation. During the three decades from 1930 to 1960, social mobilization, the penetration of the market nexus into the rural areas and the beginnings of political participation accelerated this tendency in Turkey. It could thus be predicted that to the existing material demands of the believers of rural areas would be added a demand for a picture of the world, for a cosmology (an ideology) more sophisticated than the one they had used in the past. This is one of the meanings of Said's emphasis on the proofs of Islam. But for Said, the time had also come when the middling religious man could and should be given a more extensive glimpse of the *icaz*. He still believed in the tiered nature of the religious message, but was ready to bring in an increasing number of believers and to show them the rich content, the layered nature, the multiplicity of explanations encapsulated in the message of the Prophet. It seems as if he thought that it is this richness rather than authoritative pronouncements which would draw his followers to the *Qur'ān*. Now the boundaries between the two tiers of religious knowledge had become more diffuse.

Underlying the new demand for a better understanding of religion we note the rise in effectiveness of what may be seen as a new "class," i.e., the middling level of the rural and small-town population in Turkey. This stratum is engaged in a diffuse and very tentative attempt to capture power for itself. Its main symbolic resource which it uses for this project is also the fund of religious symbolism. I have not had the opportunity to study this gradual, slow and diffuse process in detail or in depth. Nevertheless, once aware of such a development one realizes that the present revival of Islam in Turkey is better studied in this frame than from the vantage point of conspiracy theories of history. What seems involved here is a pre-political form of organization, itself influenced by the ambient politization of modern Turkey and held together by nothing more than a principle of hope, a principle which nevertheless has been taken seriously by at least one modern philosopher (Bloch, 1986).

In this class perspective Said Nursi may be considered to be an ideologue into whose preachings an infrastructural change, the "mobilization of the periphery," breathed new life. He was meeting a demand arising out of this mobilization. The idea that reformers such as Afgani "led" movements of Islamic reform could be reversed: It was the new social setting which propelled persons like Afgani into the role of reformers. Had this setting been missing they would not have been heard, just as the *müceddidî* failed to be heard by the men of the *Tanzimat*.

There are, however, specifically Muslim aspects which affected the unfolding of the *Nur* movement. Said Nursi's biography brings out a number of dimensions of the process of social change in an Islamic environment.

There is, first, the moral rearmament dimension of change, the emphasis on the revitalization of the ethical system. Studies of Muslim societies through the centuries show that this was a primary concern of Muslim religious thinkers. These studies also show that the concern acquired a sense of renewed urgency in India during the seventeenth century. Another, similar cluster of activity appears from the middle to the late eighteenth century and surfaces in Arabia, India and in the Maghrib. A third focus of ethical revivalism emerges in the more central regions of Islam during the nineteenth century. These three moments of Muslim ethical renewal may be unconnected, although in the case of India we can follow lines of continuity into the nineteenth century. Nevertheless, the three faces of Muslim revitalization have the same substratum, namely, the centrality of the ethically righteous community in Islam. What the Muslim reformers, who took the leadership of renovation, share, is a determination to create an Islamic activism based on faith as a guide for personal conduct. These views emphasize an outward, formalistic integument of practice which, they consider, will provide the primary channel into which faith will flow, but inner commitment is the goal they are after. This commitment also provides a new focus for Sufism: the externalities of "vitiated" mysticism are replaced by an inner search for God which pursues the same aim as the mystics but tames it with a constrictive morality. This new frame will also make good citizens of Muslims. In all three cases of Muslim revival, practices such as saint worship and the intercession of holy men are condemned, strict observance of ritual is enjoined, although the most difficult transition seems to be that which concerns the role of Holy men to which leaders themselves aspire and through which they receive a valuable formal legitimation. The reformist ethical thrust has also aspects which remind one of the history of Western European philosophy: Muslim scholars with an understanding of the Western intellectual tradition who have taken a retrospective look at the movement of religious revitalization see the ethical problem which confronted Muslim reformists as one of the "immanentization" of ethics. The issue is outlined by Fazlur Rahman:

> The question is not merely that of an antiquated cosmology in varying degrees, for this is relatively easy, but primarily that of "the other world" or the

> "hereafter," how to transfer their transcendence into some form of immanence. . . . Religion, in other words, must be secularized if the secular is to be made religious. But Islamic theology and dogma have not yet undergone this transformation to be acceptable to the modern mind. . . .

Here Said Nursi scores once more. To show his originality we may begin by setting the stage in the traditional Islamic sphere.

Let us take the great work of a Muslim theologian of the eleventh century, al-Ghazālī's *Iḥyā 'Ulūm ad-Dīn*. There are two main thrusts of his argument. First, a Muslim may capture the essence of his faith by the observance of ritual. His book, therefore, has a great deal to say about correct ritual (Ghazālī [Trs. 1975] I, 273–572). A second theme which he underlines is God as the source of all existence. God has no rival. Nothing such as the eternity of a *logos* which would have preceded His own active capacity should be placed on the same level with Him. By contrast Said Nursi's writings have relatively little to say about ritual. They are primarily concerned with the second theme, i.e., with affirming the unicity of God. The reason for this shift of emphasis is that Bediüzzaman is combatting the idea of an eternally existent nature, the theme propounded by his adversaries, the Ottoman materialists of his time. The primordial force of the universe that Said Nursi thus underlines is the very same force which sets the normative system of Islam. These normative obligations are not described by Bediüzzaman as *ritual* but instead as *moral* obligations. His own emphasis then is on the *meaningful* aspect of Islamic ethics rather than on its ritualistic aspect. His percipience thus appears in his understanding that *meaning* has become central in an age of intensified communication. This emphasis on *meaning* also allows him to draw a meaningful derivation from the idea of the unicity of God which is that of the wondrous world of nature created by Him. Through this type of argumentátion he can place himself in a different position than that of the naturists of the early nineteenth century such as Sayyid Ahmad Khan. In Bediüzzaman's thought, nature is *at one remove* from God and not on the same level as He. It also follows that none of the ethical obligations of a Muslim can be drawn *directly* from nature; a "higher" reference to the commands of God to Muslims is demanded. Thus ethics is saved for Muslims at the same time that the system of nature is legitimized; also the new stress on meaning "secularizes" religion.

The explanation is of considerable use in unravelling the otherwise obscure religious commentaries of Said Nursi. The same is true of the relevance of sociological concepts for the study of Muslim revitalization. In this sociological perspective, Muslim ethical revitalization movements may be studied as involving the transformation of symbolic systems, and the transformation of the symbolic system used as an approach to understanding the *Risale-i Nur* sheds light on aspects of Said Nursi's system of thought, which otherwise remains opaque.

The second major dimension of intellectual change in Islamic societies in the modern era arises somewhat later than the concern with ethical renewal. It consists of the felt necessity among nineteenth century Muslim thinkers to reach an accommodation with the world of Western science. This slant involves the building of a new cosmology which would bring Muslim thought, as it existed at that time, in harmony with the mechanistic views which underlay nineteenth century Western European science.

Finally, the psychological dissonance which caused Muslim thinkers to raise the issue in the first place and which gives these movements their peculiar force appears to have originated in a perception of a loss of power by Islamic societies. It is an outcome of the confrontation of Islamic societies with an alien cultural system infiltrating it. This perception is not limited to Muslim religious personnel but appears as a malaise affecting all strata of society. Once again, the peculiarities of Islamic society appear in the definition of the "other" as another religious system. Muslim publicists prefer to emphasize the Muslim drive towards ethical renewal in the process of social change. This approach is justified in the perspective which I have tried to underline, that of the centrality of religious organization for Muslim societies. Muslim societies are societies which—ideally—have to realize the kingdom of Heaven on earth. The stress of ethics which I find so central nevertheless beclouds the enormous importance of power in Muslim societies and the trauma caused by what is perceived as a loss of power. It therefore has to be counted together with other propellants of Islamic revitalization.

The involvement of Muslim society in power is transparent. Islam has been militant from the beginning, in a sense that Buddhism or Hinduism do not share. Because of the features of Middle Eastern society which I have already described, traditional Islam does not have an ecumenic tradition. It converts, conquers and relegates those who have not been taken into this net to the category of residuals. Second, Orthodox Muslims, and the traditional middle classes and lower classes which, in a sense, share the label of "People of the Hadith," carry the conviction of belonging to a community to which has been assigned the task of establishing a society framed and ruled by a religious message. They see Islam as having a destiny in this world which includes an international dimension. Two variants of this orthodox stand are those of Ottoman officialdom, which never concealed the primacy it gave to the state, and mysticism, which is the door through which a humanism, softening the stark fundamentalism of the "People of the Hadith," could enter Islam.

Bitlis, the area where Said Nursi spent his youth, was a region where opportunities for the seizure of power at the community level were highlighted by the history of the area. The entire setting of nineteenth century Bitlis highlighted power as an element of day-to-day life. It was ubiquitous in inter-tribal relations; it had been lost by the *mirs*, it was present in the form of the Ottoman administration, and it was a key element in the *müceddidî Nakşibendi* program of expansion. Islam's loss of power was symbolized by the presence of Protestant missionaries in Bitlis and by the educational and community achievements of the Armenians of eastern Turkey as well as by their revolutionary actions. This was the basic trauma which eventually propelled Said Nursi towards his version of pan-Islam. Even before this stage, however, Said was involved in seminary politics and in community power contests. It was because of the militancy of *müceddidî Nakşibendism* that his eyes were turned to the outer world. Again, it was because steam and the machines it propelled were metaphors of power that the terminology of thermodynamics and electricity occupied such a prominent place in Said's discourse. It was also its latent power-base that made modern science so attractive to him. All of this does not mean that power as a given of Islamic societies should be equated with brute force, but rather that it is associated with a tradition of seizing power at times when chaos threatens the Muslim community. Nevertheless, this fixation of Islam with power often results in Muslims bringing their own definition of society and its needs into contexts where their definitions do not apply. It is doubtful that without a number of innovations even the ayetullahs can equilibrate their regime with a definition of society as enduringly dependent on power relations as they have produced. Said Nursi was able to transcend this element through the humanitarian facet of his thought, which originated both in his personal character and in the mysticism from which he took his inspiration. This emphasis on the humanitarian bedrock of the *Qur'ān*, reminiscent of pietism in Europe, is one which has little relation to *Nakşibendi* puritanism. The latter, as we remember, also affected him in his views about inner discipline.

For the *'ulema* who represent the central traditions of Islam, the expansion of another creed at one's expense is a scandal. Sirhindi's movement in India and nineteenth century Muslim revitalization are clearly linked to reactions to an expanding rival creed. For Sirhindi, "the other" was Hinduism; for nineteenth century Muslims it was Western European culture. But Western European culture was identified with that of Christianity, an attitude which we can still locate in the ideas of Professor Erbakan, a contemporary Turkish Muslim ideologist and a leader of the now defunct National Salvation Party of Turkey. The eighteenth century setting is somewhat more difficult to analyze. But it is no coincidence that the Islamic proto-nationalism of the eighteenth century found such convenient moorings in religion. In the İsparta region, the lower class clerics (*lower* in the sense of modest, provincial origins) who gathered around Said Nursi brought one more element of power into the picture: they were set on saving the universe of discourse, which was the stuff of their influence and social position.

Power is also a central aspect of the life of an individual in Islamic societies. It is central for a paradoxical reason. Islamic socieities, with the possible exception of the Ottoman Empire, lack penetrative institutional structures in the traditional setting. They make up a social mosaic which I have attempted to describe on a number of occasions in this book. There is thus a recurring need for persons who can use power to seize it for the establishment of law and order at a number of levels of social organization.

The search for a charismatic leader which so often appears as one of the features of Islamic history and which is the central one in the case of Said Nursi is also an aspect of the search for order in times of disorder. Possibly this characteristic is a universalistic one: charismatic leaders are by definition persons who establish a new order in times of trouble. This feature acquires particular saliency in the case of Said Nursi: Bediüzzaman was offering a new Islamic solution to his followers, who had been deflected by the secularization of the Ottoman Empire and the Turkish Republic. The emphasis here is on the new as well as on the Islamic. Last, but not least, Bediüzzaman's new order was a paradigm for the solution of the every-day problems of life. The Turkish Republic was not interested in elaborating a map of every-day relations. In a society where persons defined their own stand in life and their power against the State through a religious idiom which served as such a map, this was a grave oversight. Said Nursi, by reviving the religious idiom, was revitalizing a total language for social life.

But "order" and "map" are still ambiguous constructions. In fact, Said Nursi set out to establish a new order at a number of levels. One of these was the revaluation of the family vis-a-vis the state. The core of personalism, an aspect of what I have named his discourse, is the familistic pattern. A second use of personalism was the re-setting of man's history in a context in which the cyclical time of history with its shattering turns (the time of Ottoman conquest, the time of Ottoman decline and the time of Republican success) was replaced by a more secure "time" with greater and more precise linearity. This was the time scale of Islamic destiny, one in which beginning and end were set. A third use of religious idiom and discourse was in providing an instrument for consensus. Now the Book, with a capital "B," the divine revelation in Arabic, was apprehended through the *book,* Said Nursi's *Risale.* The *Risale* became the means of forming Muslim opinion on a variety of items of every-day life. This is the function the book has kept today. It is through the dynamic of persons meeting every Saturday in a variety of houses throughout Turkey to discuss a passage of the *Risale* that the immanentization of ethics is taking place. A new form of *icma* consensus, through *içtihad* (exertion for interpretation), thus appears even though the gates of *individual* interpretation are still closed (see Peters, 1980). This transformation into a hermeneutic practice with a worldly base through an interpretation of the *Qur'ān*, which has its foundation in the speculations of a "reformed" mysticism, parallels what Voegelin tells us about a similar process in the West during the Renaissance, namely the overcoming of the uncertainty of faith "by receding from transcendence and endowing man and his intramundane range of actions with the meaning of eschatological fulfillment" (Voegelin, 1952, 129). Interestingly Voegelin ascribes this step to "gnostic speculation". First, *müceddidî Nakşibendism* had done away with semi-magical practices associated with mysticism. Nevertheless, the more humanistic background of mysticism had remained as a substratum in Said's thought.

I believe that Said Nursi did not fully realize that hermeneutics as applied to the *Risale-i Nur* would open up a new field of interpretation. He wanted to provide the widest access to the correct methodology of right religion. Nevertheless, the increasing range and variety of problems encountered in modern society have encouraged reinterpretations of his own *Qur'ānic* interpretations, which enable many practices of modern society to be legitimized as Muslim practices.

The immanentization achieved here concerns the interpretation of the *Qur'ān* as a guide to action in the every-day world. The substantive content of Islamic ethics among the *Nurcu*s has changed much less, and the literalness of the more precise injunctions of the *Qur'ān* is still evident in *Nurcu* approaches to ethics. This is a point of crucial importance in the study of Islamic modernization, for the same type of conservatism—an anti-hermeneutic attitude—is characteristic of a number of Muslim movements.

A tentative explanation of this characteristic would be that modern industrial society—and science in tandem—have forced modernizing Muslim societies to adopt the cosmology of Newton whether they like it or not. Faced by the Newtonian disenchantment of the cosmos, the dimensions of ethical systems—and of traditional mytho-poetic systems—enable individuals to preserve the basic fund of symbols which they have to use to come to terms with the world, and give a meaning to themselves as *persons* distinct from objects.

In the case of Said Nursi, the cosmology of Sufi theosophy was used to operate a smooth transition to an acceptance of the laws of nature as taught in the West. What remains for the *Nurcu*s to guide them through the process of self-formation—at whatever level and in whatever form this takes place—is ethical discourse, with its peculiar emphasis on the pitfalls of the animal self, the underlining of community life, the separate place of women, and uninterrupted communion with the Creator.

But in the final instance, the private mechanism of integration is probably overshadowed by the possibilities that inhere in the Islamic idiom for the creation of a private sphere which can then be defended against the incursions of the modern state. This is what makes the *political* revolutions of Islam revolutions which take their force from *religion*. That the Islamic revolution when carried out does not fulfill these hopes is beside the point: the Islamic idiom is a utopia and directs persons in the way other utopias have done. It is the *fund* of hope which the traditionalist *controls*, which he can manipulate because he knows how it works.

I have underlined an aspect of religion which we may label ideological but which itself consists of many layers. The outermost of these are the effects of privatization in the contemporary world. Atatürk wanted to make religion a private concern, but unanticipated social consequences soon caught up with him. As the boundaries of the private have become enlarged in Turkey an unforeseen development has occured. As private every-day life has increasingly been given a new richness and variety, religion has become a central focus of life and acquired a new power. Religion has received a new uplift from the privatizing wave; private religious instruction, Islamic fashion in clothes, manufacturing and music, Islamic learned journals, all of them aspects of *private* life, have made Islam pervasive in a modern sense in Turkish society, and have worked *against* religion becoming a private belief.

If there is a historical moral to the story I have been telling, it is that there are indeed watersheds in religious history, and that the history of Islam in Turkey is no exception. Turkish newspapers today write about the continuing influence of Turkish Sufi orders. The *Nakşibendi* order—the root organization from which *Nurculuk* emerged—is taken to task most frequently by them because of its pre-eminence in Turkish history. But if this is understood as the guidance of *şeyh*s, it is only completely true for regions of Turkey which had a special social tradition of Sufi influence. Here the *şeyh*s continue to fill a role as leaders of communities, as arbiters between disputes of tribal groups or of groups which take lineage as an anchor for group identity. Algar has claimed that, by contrast, in western Turkey the *Nakşibendi* order—as the source of spiritual learning of the highest order—has nowadays dwindled into insignificance. But this is because in a setting where universal education has been implemented with success, where industrial relations and mass communications are looming larger every day, Sufi orders are transformed into mass religious movements which show new distinctive characteristics. They may be described as faith movements. In these the charisma of the religious leader is rivalled by an increasing need to understand the message and to focus on the charisma of the text. The esoteric lore of the Sufi orders—its theosophy—has receded into the background and textual-Qur'ānic-interpretation plays a larger role than before in the life of the believer. The cosmology of the Sufi orders is replaced by a popularized Newtonian cosmology which has some overlap with what is taught in secular schools. Periodicals such as the *Nakşibendi İlim ve Sanat (Science and Art)* try to capture the discourse of secular intellectuals. Clients will join such a movement because it provides a bridge between the benefit of positive science and the internally consistent religious idiom of Islam. If such movements have an autonomous influence in the social sphere, it appears in the way in which the Islamic social idiom is still able to elicit social consequences. The very special social accommodation which Schiffauer's "Nurcu" woman achieves in West Berlin provides an example of such social consequences of an idiom and of the way it is used for self-placement. The deep primordially-anchored foundation for such an idiom, on the other hand was recently described by a Turkish psychiatrist writing in the daily *Cumhuriyet.* The theme he developed was that in his boyhood, spent in a Central Anatolian village, he had only known "ego ideals" derived from Islamic religious history, the sword of Ali "cutting fifty heads when it swung right, seventy heads when it swung left . . . the justice of the Caliph 'Umar. . . . "

At the national level the contemporary effects of the Islamic idiom appear primarily in the way in which social relations are conceptualized as family relations. The manner in which the present government of Turkey has been motivated to pass laws against the corruption of the young and the protection of the family (1985–1986) shows this influence. The Turkish cabinets may only have indirect connections with the *Nurcu,* but they harken to the same voice.

A word seems necessary, at this point, to assess the weight of Said Nursi's view of society; what I have, in the preceding pages, labelled "personalism." At a time when sociologists are rediscovering a conception of society as consisting of an interaction of individuals "embedded in a network of relationships and statuses—fathers, sons, masters, workers, burghers, peasants" (Plummer, 1983), this theory seems less unscientific than it would have been in the heyday of positivism. Its importance, however, lies in another aspect: it shows the element which most Muslims draw from their religious ideas for a construction of their own, private conceptualization of society. It is as if in the West, Lockean conceptions of the polity had been shared by his Christian audience in the construction of their own political views. Such a partial congruence no doubt existed, but seems stronger in the Muslim setting. Here, again, we achieve an understanding of the ubiquity of Muslim idiom.

What we have to offer for social theory at the end of this work is a mixed bag: a number of approaches to the study of religion are simultaneously vindicated. For one, there seems to be a sense in which methodological individualism allows us to penetrate into the religious universe of certain individuals whom I shall call "traditionals on the move." Said Nursi seems to have drawn his followers from this stratum. The label is quite different from that of "transitional"; it refers to a mix of traditionalism and modernity in which traditional values nevertheless keep their grip on the individual. What we have here are persons for whom the family as an institution, and way-stations in life—birth, adolescence, adulthood, marriage, old age, death—remain primordial social forces. Yet these persons are also moving into the more complex urban world of modernity. The traditional idiom serves both as a map of statuses and authority relations and at the same time defines a horizon of time-flow rates as well as life-expectations. The Islamic idiom which I postulated that Said Nursi recaptured and rejuvenated is what allows followers to conceptualize and reproduce these social relations.

Spirituality we find to be more complex than just a yearning for the absolute: in fact, as one transits from the old society to the new, the picture of a religious elite based on the distinction between the elect and the masses is transformed, and one observes the entry of the non-elect in a borderline area where spirituality and enlightenment comingle. But there still exists an irreducible aspect of spirituality and religiosity—the mysterium—which transcends both the use of religion as a map of social relations and its foundation for a theory of the elect, or, conversely, a means of social mobility. To me, after the research has ended, this still seems best explained by the way in which Islamic symbols were able to serve a person in building up an identity. Some of the idiosyncratic aspects of Islam, such as the absence of a society of blocks, and the necessity to uphold an identity at a personal and family level, underscore these processes.

At the end of my research I find that there still is much support for Durkheimian theories of "collective representations." When we look at our story as the unfolding of an historical process, we detect an aspect of Islam as communal cement and bond for solidarity, which easily belongs in that realm. With the special role that culture acquires in the modern nation state, the leaders of Islamic communities and states and persons who are propelled into new roles of leadership have used, manipulated and transformed these representations. If we are interested in studying these variables in detail, however, we shall have to use concepts such as authority relations, domination and legitimacy, and return to Weber at still another level.

It is by looking in at least the two aspects of methodological individualism and "collective representation" that we can make some sense of the process.

Bibliography

Abbott, Freeland (1962). "The Jihad of Sayyid Ahmad Shahid," *Muslim World* 52, 216–22.

——— (1902). "The Transformation of the Jihad Movement," *Muslim World 52, 288–295.*

Abdurraham, Şeref (1923, 1978). *Tarih Konusmaları.* Ed. by Eşref Eşrefoğlu, İstanbul, Kavram Yayınları. First published as *Tarih Musahabeleri.*

Abu Manneh, Butrus (1973). "Sultan Abdülhamid II and the Sharifs of Mecca (1880–1900)," *Asian and African Studies* 9, 1–21.

——— (1979). "Sultan Abdülhamid II and Shaikh Abulhuda al-Sayyadi," *Middle Eastern Studies* 15: 131-153.

——— (1980). "The Christians between Ottomanism and Syrian Nationalism: the Ideas of Butrus al-Bustani," *IJMES* 11:287–304.

——— (1982). "The Naqshbandiyya-Mujaddidiya in the Ottoman Lands in the Early 19th Century," *Die Welt des Islams*, 22: 1–36.

Adams, Charles J. (1983). "Mawdudi and the Islamic State," in *Voices of Resurgent Islam.* Ed by L. Esposito, New York, etc., Oxford University Press, p. 99–133.

Adıvar, Adnan (1944). *Tarih Boyunca İlim ve Din*, Istanbul, Remzi.

"Ahmad Djewdet Pasha," *E.I.*[2], I, 284–286.

"Ahmad Wafik Pasha" *E.I.*[2], I, 298.

Ahmed, Akbar S. (1976, 1980). *Millenium and Charisma among Pathans: A Critical Essay in Social Anthropology,* London, Routledge and Kegan, Paul.

Ahmet Haşim, (1969). *Bize Göre, Gurabahane-i Laklakan, Frankfurt Seyahatnamesi*, 2nd ed. Istanbul, Millî Eğitim Basımevi.

Ahmet Cevdet Paşa (1953–1967 ed.). *Tezâkir 1–12, 13–20, 21–29, 40 Tetimme;* Ed. by Cavid Baysun, Ankara, Türk Tarih Kurumu.

Ahmet Şerif (1909–1977). *Anadoluda Tanin*, Istanbul, Kavram Yayınları.

Al Faruqi, Isma'il (1967). "Science and Traditional Values in Islamic Society," *Zygon*, 2: No. 3.

Albayrak, Sadık (1973). *Son Devrin Islâm Akademisi*, Istanbul, Yeni Asya Yayınları.

Allen, W. E. D. & Muratoff, P. (1953). *Caucasian Battlefields*, Cambridge, Cambridge University Press.

Algar, Hamid (1976). "The Naqshbandi order: a preliminary survey of its history and significance," *Studia Islamica* 44: 123–152.

——— (1979). "Said Nursi and the *Risale-i Nur.* An aspect of Islam in contemporary Turkey," *Islamic perspectives—Studies in honor of Sayyid Abul Ala Mawdudi etc.*, Leicester, pp. 313–333.

——— (1985). "Der Nakshibendi-Orden in der republikanischen Turkei" in *Jahrbuch zur Geschichte und Gesellschaft des Forderen und Mittleren Orients 1984*, Berlin, Express.

Anchor, Robert (1967). *The Enlightenment Tradition*, Berkeley etc., The University of California Press.

Anonymous "*Içtihad* Meselesi," (April 1979), *Hareket* No. 2, pp. 84–86.

Armaner, Neda (1964). *Nurculuk. Islâm Dininden Ayrılan Cereyanlar*, Ankara, Millî Eğitim Basımevi.

Ayubi, Nazih N. M. (1981). "The Political Revival of Islam: the Case of Egypt," *IJMES*, 12: 481–499.

Albrow, Martin (1970). *Bureaucracy*, London, Pall Mall.

Aşçıdede Halil Ibrahim (1960 ed.). *Hatıralar* ed. Reşad Ekrem Koçu and M. Akbay, Istanbul. n.p.

Atay, Hüseyin (1981). "Medreselerin Islahatı" *Ankara Üniversitesi İlâhiyat Fakültesi Dergisi*, 25: 1–43.

Aydemir, Şevket Süreyya (1967). *Suyu Arayan Adam*, İstanbul, Remzi.

Aziz Ahmad (1964). *Studies in Islamic Culture in the Indian Environment*, Oxford, Clarendon Press.

Battal-Taymas, Abdullah (1958) *Musa Carullah Bigi*. Istanbul.

Barthold, V.V. (1958). *Four Studies on the History of Central Asia* Vol. II, Trs. R. V. Minorsky, Ulugh Beg. Leiden, E. J. Brill.

Bellah, Robert N. (1970). *Beyond Belief.* New York, Harper and Row.

——— (1975). *The Broken Covenant*, New York, Seabury Press.

Berger, Peter L. and Thomas Luckmann (1967). *The Social Construction of Reality.* Garden City, New York, Doubleday & Co., Anchor Books.

Berger, Peter L., Brigitte Berger and Hansfried Kellner (1973). *The Homeless Mind,* Harmondsworth, England, Penguin Books.

Benningsen, Alexandre and Chantal Lemercier–Quelquejay (1964). *La Presse et le Mouvement National chez les Musulmans de Russie avant 1920,* Paris, Mouton.

Berkes, Niyazi (1964). *The Development of Secularism in Turkey,* Montreal, McGill University Press.

——— (1978). *Türkiyede Cağdaşlaşma,* İstanbul, n. p.

Bernstein, Richard J. (1983, 1985). *Beyond Objectivism and Relativism*, Philadelphia, University of Pennsylvania Press.

Beşikçi, İsmail (1969). *Doğu Anadolunun Düzeni,* Ankara "E" Yayınları.

Binder, Henry (1887). *Au Kurdistan: En Mesopotamie et en Perse,* Paris, Maison Quantin.

Birken, Andreas (1976). *Die Provinzen des Osmanischen Reiches,* Wiesbaden, Dr. Ludwig Reichert Verlag.

Bishop, Isabella L. Bird (1891). *Journeys in Persia and Kurdistan,* 2 vols., London, J. Murray.

Bloch, Ernst (1986). *The Principle of Hope,* Trs. N. & S. Plaice and Paul Knight, Oxford, Basil Blackwell, 3 vols.

Bolay, Süleyman Hayrı (1967). *Türkiyede Ruhçu ve Maddeci Görüşün Mücadelesi,* İstanbul, Yağmur Yayınları.

Bouvat, L. (1921). "Le Code Familial Ottoman de 1917," *Revue du Monde Musulman* 43: 5–26.

Bremer, Marie Luise (1959). *Die Memoiren des Türkischen Derwichs Aşçi Dede Ibrahim* Bonn, n.p.

Brittain, Arthur (1977). *The Privatized World,* London, Routlege.

Brown, Leon Carl (1964). "The Islamic Reformist Movement in North Africa," *Journal of Modern African Studies,* II(1): 55–63.

Browne, Edward G. (1902). "Pan Islamism," In *Lectures on the History of the Nineteenth Century,* ed. F. Kirkpatrick, Cambridge, Cambridge University Press.

Burridge, K. O. L. (1967). *New Heaven, New Earth: a Study of Millenarian Activities,* Oxford, Basil Blackwell.

Burtt, E. A. (1924, 1980). *Metaphysical Foundations of Modern Science.* Rev. ed., London and Henley, Routledge and Kegan Paul.

The Cambridge History of Islam (1977). Volume 2B *Islamic Society and Civilization* Ed. by P. M. Holt, Ann K. S. Lambton, Bernard Lewis, Cambridge, etc., Cambridge University Press.

Carré, Olivier (1984). *Mystique et Politique.* Paris, Les Editions du Cerf.

de Certeau, Michel (1984). *The Practice of Everyday Life*, Berkeley etc., University of California Press.

Carstairs, G. Morris (1961). *The Twice-Born: a study of a Community of High Caste Hindus*, Bloomington, The University of Indiana Press.

Chadwick, Owen (1975, 1977). *The Secularization of the European Mind in the Nineteenth Century.* Cambridge, Cambridge University Press.

Charlton, D. G. (1963, 1970). *Secular Religion in France 1815–1870*, Oxford, Oxford University Press.

Chittick, William G. (1979). "The Perfect Man as the Prototype of the Self in the Sufism of Jami," *Studia Islamica* 49, 135–157.

——— (1981). "Sadr al-Din Qunawi on the Oneness of Being," *International Philosophical Quarterly* 21 (2): 171–184.

——— (1982). "The Five Divine Presences: From al-Qunawi to al-Qaysari," *The Muslim World.* 72, 107–128.

Chodkiewicz, Michel (1986). *Le Sceau des Saints*, Paris, Gallimard.

Cohen, Abner (1974). *Two-Dimensional Man: An Essay on the Anthropology of power and symbolism in Complex society*, London, Routledge and Kegan Paul.

Cuinet, Vidal (1895). *La Turquie d'Asie: Geographie Administrative, Statistique Descriptive et Raisionnée de Chaque Province de l'Asie Mineure*, 4 volumes, Vol II, 1891. Paris, Ernest Leroux.

Dahrendorf, R. (1959). *Class and Class Conflict in Industrial Society*, London.

Darkot, Besim and Mükrimin Halil Yinanç (1944). "Bitlis," *Islâm Ansiklopedisi* II: 657–66; 661–64.

Davison, Roderic H. (1963). *Reform in the Ottoman Empire 1856–1876*, Princeton, Princeton University Press.

Dekmejian, Hrair (1980). "The Anatomy of Islamic Revival and the Search for Islamic Alternatives," *MEJ*, 34: 1–12.

Dessouki, Ali E. Hillal (ed.) (1982). *Islamic Resurgence in the Arab World*, New York, Praeger.

Deutsch, Karl W. 2nd ed., (1966). *Nationalism and Social Communication: An Inquiry into the Foundation of Nationality*, Cambridge, MIT Press.

Devereux, Robert (1979). "The Feeling of Revolution," *Middle Eastern Studies*, 15:3–35.

Duguid, Stephen (1973). "The Politics of Unity: Hamidian Policy in Eastern Anatolia," *Middle Eastern Studies* 9: 139–156.

Dunn, John (1984). "The Concept of 'trust' in the Politics of John Locke" in *Philosophy in History* (Ed. Richard Rorty, J. B. Schneewind & Quentin Skinner), Cambridge, Cambridge University Press.

Durkheim, Emile (1893, 1947). *The Division of Labor in Society,* Glencoe, Free Press.

Edinger, Edward F. (1973). *Ego and Archetype,* Baltimore, Maryland, Penguin Books.

Eickelman, Dale F. (1976). *Moroccan Islam,* Austin, University of Texas Press.

——— (1978). "The Art of Memory: Islamic Education and its Social Reproduction." *Comparative Studies in Society and History.* 20: 485–516.

Eliade, Mircea (1960, 1976). *Myths, Dreams and Mysteries,* London, Harvill Press.

Eliot, Sir Charles (1908). *Turkey in Europe,* New Edition, London, Edward Arnold.

el-Zein, Abd el-Hamid (1977). "Beyond Ideology and Theology: the search for an anthropology of Islam." *Annual Review of Anthropology.* 6; 227–54.

——— (1974). *The Sacred Meadows,* Evanston, Northwestern University Press.

Enayat, Hamid (1982). *Modern Islamic Political Thought. The Response of Shii and Sunni Muslims to the Twentieth Century.* London and Basingstoke, the Macmillan Press.

Engelhardt, Edouard (1882–1884). *La Turquie et le Tanzimat,* 2 vols, Paris, Cotillon.

Ergin, Osman Nuri (1939–1943). *Türkiye Maarif Tarihi,* Istanbul, 5 vols.

Erişirgil, M. Emin (1956). *M. Akif-Islâmcı bir Şairin Romanı,* İstanbul, Inkilâp Yayınları.

Ertuğrul, İsmail Fennî (1979). *Hakikat Nurları,* İstanbul, Sebil Yayınları.

Esposito, John L. (ed.) (1980). *Islam and Development: Religion and sociopolitical Change,* Syracuse, Syracuse University Press.

Evans-Pritchard, E. E. (1949). *The Sanusi of Cyrenaica,* Oxford, Clarendon Press.

"Evkaf" *E.I.*[2], III, 1153. cf. "Vakīf" *İ. A.* Fasc. 137 (1982).

Farhi, David (1971). "The *Şeriat* as a political slogan—or the "Incident of the 31st Mart," *Middle Eastern Studies* 7: 275–300.

Farooqi, Naimur Rahman (1983). "Pan Islamism in the Nineteenth Century," *Islamic Culture,* 57:283–96.

Faroqhi, Suraiya (1981). *Der Bektaschi-Order in Anatolien* Vienna, Institut für Orientalistik.

Fazlur-Rahman (1955). "International Religious Development in the Present Century of Islam," *Cahiers d'Histoire Mondiale,* 2:868–79.

——— (1970). "Islamic Modernism: its Scope, Method and Alternatives,"

IJMES, I: 317–333.

——— (1977). "Revival and Reform in Islam," Ch. 7 in *The Cambridge History of Islam*. Vol. 2B, (Ed. by P. M. Holt, Ann K. S. Lambton, and Bernard Lewis), Cambridge University Press, pp. 632–656.

——— (1979). *Islam*, 2nd ed., Chicago and London, etc., University of Chicago Press.

——— (1982). *Islam and Modernity: Transformation of an Intellectual Tradition*. Chicago and London, The University of Chicago Press.

Felgenhauer, I. von (1887). "Die Militärbildungsanstalten in der Türkei und ihre Jüngsten Reformen," *Beiheft zum Militär-Wochenblatt*, Berlin.

[Fergan], Eşref Edip (1938). *M. Akif-Hayatı-Eserleri ve 10 Muharririn Yazıları*, İstanbul, Asâr-ı İlmiye Kütüphanesi.

——— (1965). *Risale-i Nur Muarızı Yazarların Isnatları Hakkında Ilmî bir Tahlil*, Istanbul, Sebilürreşad.

Foucault, Michel (1974, 1977). *The Archaeology of Knowledge*, Tr. A.M. Sheridan Smith, London, Tavistock Publications.

Frey-Rohn, Liliane (1974). *From Freud to Jung: A Comparative Study of the Psychology of the Unconscious*, Trs. from German by E. and K. Engreen, New York, Dell Publishing Co.

Friedmann, Johannan (1971). *Shaykh Ahmad Sirhindi*, Montreal and London. McGill-Queens University Press.

Gay, Peter (1966). *The Enlightenment: an Interpretation*, New York, Vintage Books.

Geertz, Clifford (1957). "Ethos, World-View and the Analysis of Sacred Symbols," *Antioch Review* 17: 421–37.

——— (1966). "Religion as a Cultural system," in *Anthropological Approaches to the Study of Religion*. Ed. M. Banton, London, Tavistock Publications.

——— (1968). *Islam Observed*. New Haven, Yale University Press.

Gellner, Ernest (1970). "Concepts and Society" in *Sociological Theory and Philosophical Analysis*. ed. and introd. Dorothy Emmet and Alasdair MacIntyre, New York, Macmillan.

——— (1972). "Doctor and Saint", in *Scholars, Saints and Sufis: Muslim Institutions in the Middle East since 1500* Ed. by Nikki R. Keddie. Berkeley etc., University of California Press, 307–326.

——— (1983). *Nations and Nationalism*, Ithaca and London, Cornell University Press.

Gerber, Haim (1976). "Guilds in Seventeenth Century Anatolian Bursa."

Asian and African Studies, 11(1): 59–86.

Ghazali, Abu Hamid al (1975 Trs.). *Ihyâu 'Ulumi'd-Din Tercümesi,* 4 vols, Istanbul, Bedir, Trs. Ahmet Serdaroğlu.

Gibb, H. A. R. (1947). *Modern Trends in Islam,* Chicago, The University of Chicago Press.

——— (1963). "The Comunity in Islamic History," *Proceedings of the American Philosophical Society* 107(2), 173–176.

Gibb, H. A. R. and Harold Bowen (1950, 1957). *Islamic Society and the West,* vol. 1, parts 1 and 2. Oxford, Oxford University Press.

Giddens, Anthony (1976). *New Rules of Sociological Method,* London, Hutchinson.

——— (1979). *Central Problems in Social Theory.* London, etc., The Macmillan Press.

——— (1984, 86). *The Constitution of Society,* Berkeley and Los Angeles, The University of California Press.

Gilsenan, Michael (1973). *Saint and Sufi in Modern Egypt: An Essay in the Sociology of Religion,* Oxford, Clarendon Press.

——— (1982). *Recognizing Islam,* Pantheon Books, New York.

Glock, Charles Y. and Robert N. Bellah (1976). *The New Religious Consciousness,* Berkeley, etc., The University of California Press.

Goody, J. and Watt, I. R. (1963). "The Consequences of Literacy," *Comparative Studies in Society and History* 5: 304–345.

Goody, Jack (ed.) (1968). *Literacy in Traditional Societies,* Cambridge, Cambridge University Press.

——— (1977). *The Domestication of the Savage Mind,* Cambridge, etc., Cambridge University Press.

Gökalp, Ziya (1959). *Turkish Nationalism and Western Civilization: Selected Essays of Ziya Gokalp.* Trs. and Ed. with an Introd. by Niyazi Berkes, London, George Allen and Unwin Ltd.

——— (1968). *The Principles of Turkism,* Trs. Ed. by Robert Devereux, Leiden, E. J. Brill.

Gökbilgin, M. Tayyib. "Hekīm Başhi," *E.I.*[2], III, 339–340.

——— (1971). "Kâtip Çelebi, interprète et rénovateur des traditions religeuses an XVII siecle," *Turcica,* 3:71–79.

Gölpınarlı, Abdulbaki (1931). *Melamilik ve Melamiler,* Istanbul, Devlet Matbaası.

Gouldner, Alvin W. (1976). *The Dialectic of Ideology and Technology: The Origins, Grammar and Future of Ideology,* London, etc., The Macmillan Press.

——— (1979). *The Future of Intellectuals and the Rise of the New Class,* London, etc., The Macmillan Press.

Gövsa, Ibrahim Alaettin (ed.) (1946). *Türk Meshurları Ansiklopedisi,* İstanbul, Yedigün Neşriyatı.

Gözütok, Ali (1971). *Müslümanlık ve Nurculuk,* Ankara, Altınok Matbaası.

Gran, Peter (1979). *Islamic Roots of Capitalism: Egypt, 1760–1840,* Austin and London, University of Texas Press.

Great Britain, Parliamentary Papers, Accounts and Papers, State Papers, Vol. 42, *Correspondence relating to the Asiatic Provinces of Turkey* (1890), 11 Feb., 1890–18 Aug., 1890. (1895).

Green, Arnold H. (1978). *The Tunisian Ulama, 1873–1915,* Leiden, Brill.

Griffiths, M. A. (1966). "The Reorganization of the Ottoman Army under Abdulhamid II, 1880–1897," Unpubl. Ph.D. Dissertation, UCLA.

Günay, Ünver (1974). "La Vie Religieuse a Küre." Unpubl. Ph.D. Dissertation, Sorbonne, VIe Section, Paris.

Gündüz, İrfan (1984). *Osmanlılarda Devlet-Tekke Münasebetleri,* Ankara, Seha Neşriyat.

——— (1984). *Gumüshanevî Ahmed Ziyauddin* (ks) Ankara, Seha Neşriyat.

Haddad, M. Robert (1970). *Syrian Christians in Muslim Society: an Interpretation,* Princeton, Princeton University Press.

Halbwachs, Maurice (1925–1975). *Les Cadres Sociaux de la Mémoire.* Paris, Mouton.

Halevy, Daniel (1948). *Essai Sur l'Accéleration de l'Histoire* Paris, 2nd ed.

Harik, Iliya (1968). *Politics and Change in a Traditional Society, Lebanon 1711–1845,* Princeton, Princeton University Press.

Heyd, Uriel (1973). *Studies in Old Ottoman Criminal Law,* Oxford, Clarendon Press.

Hillman, James (1974). "Archetypal Theory: C. G. Jung," in *Operational Theories of Personality,* ed. by Arthur Burton, New York, Brunner-Mazel, pp. 65–98.

Hirszowicz, L. (1972). "The Sultan and the Khedive 1892–1908," *Middle Eastern Studies,* 8: 287–31.

Historians of the Middle East (1962). Ed. by Bernard Lewis and P. M. Holt, London, etc., Oxford University Press.

Hodgson, Marshall G. S. (1970). "The Role of Islam in World History." *IJMES,* I:99–123.

——— (1974). *The Venture of Islam: Conscience and History in a World Civilization.* I: *The Classical Age of Islam,* Chicago, The University of Chicago Press.

Hourani, Albert (1962). *Arabic Thought in the Liberal Age,* London, etc., Oxford University Press.

——— (1972). "Shaikh Khalid and the Naqshbandi Order," *Islamic Philosophy and the Classical Tradition* ed. S. M. Stern, Albert Hourani and Vivian Brown, Columbia, South Carolina. University of South Carolina Press.

Huart, Clement. "Bibliographie Ottomane," *J. A.* Series 8, vol. 5, 232–VII; Vol. 16, p. 411; Vol. 19, p. 164, Series VIII, Vol. 5, pp. 229, 415; Vol. 9, p. 350; Vol. 13, p. 428; Vol. 17, p. 357.

Hudson, Michael C. (1980). "Islam and Political Development," in *Islam and Development: Religion and Sociopolitical Change,* ed. by John L. Esposito, Syracuse, Syracuse University Press.

Humphreys, R. S. (1979). "Islam and Political Violence in Saudi Arabia, Egypt and Syria," *MEJ,* 33:1–19.

Hurgronje, C. Snouck (1901). "Le Khalifat du Sultan de Constantinople," *Verspreide Geschriften,* Vol. III, pp. 363–375.

——— (1901). "Les confrèréries religieuses, la Mecque et le panislamisme," *Revue de l'Histoire des Religions* 44: 262–281.

Ibrahim, Saad Eddin (1980). "Anatomy of Egypt's Militant Islamic Groups: Methodological Notes and Preliminary Findings," *IJMES,* 12, No. 4.

Iğdemir, Uluğ (1937). *Kuleli Vak'ası Hakkında bir Araştırma,* Ankara, Türk Tarih Kurumu.

Imber, C. H. (1979). "The Persecution of the Ottoman Shiites according to the Muhimme Defterleri, 1565–1585," *Der Islam* 56 (2), 245–273.

Inalcık, Halil (1958). "Osmanlı Hukukuna Giriş: Örfi-Sultanî Hukuk ve Fatih Kanunlarī," *Siyasal Bilgiler Fakültesi Dergisi* 13: 102–126.

——— (1973). "Applications of the Tanzimat and its Social Effects,: *Archivum Ottomanicum,* V: 97–128.

"İsparta," *Yurt Ansiklopedisi,* Fascicule 63, 64, 65, pp. 3504–3615.

Issawi, Charles (ed.) (1966). *The Economic History of the Middle East 1800–1914: A book of Readings,* Chicago, The University of Chicago Press.

"Islah" *E. I.*[2], IV, 141–171.

Itzkowitz, N. and Shinder, J. (1972). "The Office of Şeyh ül-Islâm and the Tanzimat—A proposopographic Enquiry," *Middle Eastern Studies* 8: 93–101.

Jaffé, Aniela (1975). *The Myth of Meaning: Jung and the Expansion of Consciousness,* New York, Penguin Books.

Jameson, Frederic (1986). "On Magic Realism in Film," *Critical Inquiry,* 12 (2), 301–325.

Jansen, J. J. G. (1974). *The Interpretation of the Koran in Modern Egypt*, Leiden, E. J. Brill.

Jäschke, G. (1954). "Türkische Gesetzsammlungen," *Die Welt des Islams* N.S. III: 225–234.

——— (1951–1972). *Yeni Türkiyede Islâmlik*, Ankara, Bilgi Yayınevi. Translation of "Der Islam in der neuen Türkei," *Die Welt des Islams*,N.S. I (1951) 1–174; II (1953) 276–285 etc.

Jesperson, O. (n.d.) *Mankind, Nation and Individual from a Linguistic Point of View*, London, George Allen and Unwin.

Jung, Carl G., M. L. von Franz, Joseph L. Henderson, Yolanda Jacobi, Aniela Jaffé (1964). *Man and his Symbols*, Garden City, New York, Doubleday and Co.

Jung, C. G. (1938, 1976). *Psychology and Religion*, New Haven and London, Yale University Press.

"Ḳāḍī," *E.I.*[2], IV, 375; *I.A.* Fasc. 55 (1952), 42–46.

"Ḳānūn," *E.I.*[2], IV, 556–562.

"Ḳanūnnāme" *E.I.*[2], IV, 562–566.

Kaplan, Mehmet (1946). *Tevfik Fikret ve Şiiri*, Istanbul, Türkiye Yayinevi.

——— (1955). "Yunus Emre'de nebatlar," *Türkiyat Mecmuası*, 12: 45–56.

——— (1979). "Türk Edebiyatında Tipler: I. Oğuz Kağan Destanı," *Hareket*, 46–52.

Kara, Mustafa (1980). *Din, hayat, sanat açısından Tekkeler ve Zaviyeler*, 2nd ed. Istanbul, Dergân Yayınları.

Karakoç, Sezai (1968). *M. Akif-Hayatı, Aksiyonu ve Düşünceleri*, Istanbul, Yağmur Yayınları.

Karal, Enver Ziya (1954). *Osmanlı Tarihi VI: Islahat Fermanı Devri 1856–1861*, Ankara, Türk Tarih Kurumu Basımevi.

——— (1956). *Osmalı Tarihi VII: Islahat Fermanı Devri 1861–1876*, Ankara, Türk Tarih Kurumu Basımevi.

——— (1983). *Osmanlı Tarihi, VIII Birinci Meşrutiyet ve Istibdat Devirleri 1876–1907*, 2nd Printing, Ankara, Türk Tarih Kurumu Basımevi.

Karatay, Fethi Ethem (1956). *İstanbul Üniversitesi Kütüphanesi Türkçe Basmalar Alfabe Katalogu . . . 1729–1928.* Istanbul, Osman Yalçın.

Kâtip Çelebi ([1656], 1957). *The Balance of Truth*, Trs. G. L. Lewis. London, George Allen and Unwin.

Keddie, R. Nikki (1969). "Pam-Islam as Proto-Nationalism," *Journal of Modern History* 41: 17–28.

——— (1972). *Sayyid Jamal ad-Din "al-Afghani" A Political Biography*, Berkeley, etc., University of California Press.

——— (ed.) (1972). *Scholars, Saints and Sufis: Muslim Religious Institutions in the Middle East Since 1500*, Berkeley, etc., University of California Press.

Kepel, Gilles (1984). *Le Prophète et Pharaon*, Paris, Maspero.

——— (1984b). "L'Egypte Aujourd'hui: Mouvement Islamiste et Tradition Savante," *Annales*, 667–680.

Kerr, Malcolm H. (1966), *Islamic Reform: The Political and Legal Theories of Muhammad Abduh and Rashid Rida*, Berkeley, etc., University of California Press.

Keskiöglu, Osman (1962). "Cemaleddin Efgani," *Ilâhiyat Fakültesi Dergisi*, 10: 91–102.

——— (1964). "Musa Carullah," *Ilâhiyat Fakültesi Dergisi*, 12: 63–74.

——— (1970). "Muhammed Abduh," *Ilâhiyat Fakültesi Dergisi*, 18: 109–136.

Kissling, Hans Joachim (1954). "The Sociological and Educational Role of the Dervish Orders in the Ottoman Empire," in *Studies in Islamic Cultural History*, ed. G. von Grunebaum, *American Anthropologist Memoir* No. 76.

Kodaman, Bayram (1979). "Hamidiye Hafif Suvari Alayları," *Istanbul Üniversitesi* Edebiyat Fakültesi Tarih Dergisi 32: 427–480.

——— (1980). *Abdülhamid devri Eğitim Sistemi*, Istanbul, Ötüken.

Kolakowski, Leszek. *The Alienation of Reason:* Trs Norbert Guterman, Garden City, N. Y., Doubleday.

Köprülü, Fuad (1976). *Türk Edebiyatında ilk Mutasavvıflar*, 3rd. ed. ed. Orhan Köprülü, Ankara, Diyanet Işleri Başkanlığı.

Kuntay, Mithat Cemal (1939). *Mehmet Akif Hayatı-Seciyesi-Sanatı-Eserleri*, Istanbul, Semih Lûtfi Kitabevi.

——— (1949). *Namık Kemal Devrinin Insanları ve Olayları Arasında*, Vol. 2 (1), İstanbul, Millî Eğitim Basımevi.

Kuran, A. Bedevi (1954). *Osmanlı Imparatorluğunda Inkilâp Hareketleri ve Millî Mücadele*, Istanbul, Baha Matbaası.

"Kurds" *E.I.*[1], IV, 1132–1155; *E.I.*[2], V, 462.

Kushner, David (1977). *The Rise of Turkish Nationalism 1876–1908*, London, Frank Cass.

Kutay, Cemal (1966–1967). "Nurculuğun Kurucusu Bediüzzaman . . ." (Series with varying titles.), *Tarih Sohbetleri* I: (1966) 201–212; II; 193–222; III; 261–311; IV (1967): 207–225; V (1967): 192–209.

Kutluay, Yaşar (1959–1960). "Mezhepler Tarihi Yönünden Said Nursi ve Nurculuk." *Islâm Tetkikleri Enstitüsü Dergisi* III: 211–225.

"Ibn 'Abd al-Wahhāb," *E. I.*,[2] III, 677–679.

Lasswell, Harold (1980). "The Future of World Communication and Propaganda," in Lasswell, Lerner and Speier, Vol. III, p. 516f.

Landau, Jacob M. (1971). *The Hejaz Railway and the Muslim Pilgrimage: A Case of Ottoman Political Propaganda,* Detroit, Wayne State University Press.

Lawson, Fred H. (1981). "Rural Revolt and Provincial Society in Egypt," *IJMES*, 13 (2): 131–153.

Le Chatelier, A. (1910). "Politique Musulmane," *Revue du Monde Musulman*, 12:1–157.

Lee, Dwight E. (1941). "The Origins of Pan-Islamism," *American Historical Review*, 47: 278–287.

Levy, Avigdor (1971). "The Ottoman Ulema and the Military Reforms of Sultan Mahmud II," in *The Ulama' in Modern History* Ed. by Gabriel Baer, *Asian and African Studies*, Vol. 7, 1971, Jerusalem, The Israel Oriental Society.

Lewis, Bernard (1968). *The Emergence of Modern Turkey,* 2nd ed., London, etc., Oxford University Press.

——— (1980). "The Ottoman Empire and its Aftermath," *Journal of Contemporary History*, 15:27–36.

Lewis, Joan (ed.) (1977). *Symbols and Sentiments*, London, etc., Academic Press.

Lewis, Norman N. (1955). "The Frontier of Settlement in Syria 1800–1950." *International Affairs*. 31:48–60 in Issawi, 1966, 259–268.

Lovejoy, Arthur O. (1936, 1960). *The Great Chain of Being: A Study of the History of an Idea*, New York, Harper Torchbooks.

Luhman, Niklas (1979). *Trust and Power*, ed. T. Burns and G. Puggi, Chichester, and New York, John Wiley.

Lyman, Stanford M. (1978). "The acceptance, rejection and reconstruction of histories: on some controversies in the study of social and cultural change," in *Structure, Consciousness and History*, ed. by Richard Harvey Brown and Stanford M. Lyman, Cambridge, etc., Cambridge University Press, pp. 53–105.

Makeen, Abdul Majid Mohammed (1980). Unpublished Paper.

Ma'oz Moshe (1971). "The 'Ulamā' and the process of Modernization in Syria during the mid-Nineteenth Century," *Asian and African Studies*, Vol. 7. "The 'Ulama' in Modern History," Ed. by Gabriel Baer, The Israel Oriental Society, Jerusalem, 1971, pp. 77–88.

Mardin, Ebul'ula (1946). *Medenî Hukuk Cephesinden Ahmet Cevdet Paşa (1822–1895).* Ölümünün 50nci yıldönümü vesilesiyle. Istanbul, Cumhuriyet Matbaası.

Mardin, Şerif (1972). "Center Periphery relation a key to Turkish politics?" *Daedalus.* Winter.

——— (1979). "The Modernization of Social Communication," in *Propaganda and Communications in World History,* ed. Lerner, Speier and Laswell, p. 381–443.

Martin, David (1978). *A General Theory of Secularization,* Oxford, Basil Blackwell.

Meeker, Michael (1976). "Meaning and Society in the Near East: Examples from the Black Sea Turks and the Levantine Arabs," *IJMES* 7:243–270, 383–422.

Mehmed Ziya. (n.d.) *Yenikapı Mevlevihanesi,* Ed. Yavuz Senemoğlu, İstanbul, Tercüman 1000 Temel Eser.

"Mekteb" *İ. A.,* VII, 652–659.

Melikoff, Irène (1973). "Yunus Emre ile Hacı Bektaş," *Istanbul Edebiyat Fakültesi Türk Dili ve Edebiyatı Dergisi* 20: 26–47.

——— (1975). "Le Problème Ḳïzïlbaş," *Turcica,* 6: 49–67

——— (1982). "L'Islam Hétérodoxe en Anatolie," *Turcica,* 14: 142–154.

Merad, Ali (1967). *Le reformisme musulman en Algerie de 1925a 1940: Essai d'histoire Religieuse et Sociale,* Paris and The Hague, Mouton.

Meriç, Cemil (1976). *Bu Ülke,* Istanbul, Ötüken.

Metcalf, Barbara Daly (1982). *Islamic Revival in British India: Deoband 1860–1900,* Princeton, Princeton University Press.

——— (ed.) (1984). *Moral Conduct and Authority,* Berkeley, The University of California Press.

Minnes, Mattison (1975). "Islamisation and Muslim Ethnicity in South India," *Man,* 70:404–419.

Ministère des Affaires Etrangères: *Documents Diplomatiques: Affaires Arméniennes. Projet de Reformes dans l'Empire Ottoman 1893–1897,* Paris, Imprimerie Nationale.

Mitchell, R. P. (1969). *The Society of Muslim Brothers,* London, Oxford University Press.

Mohammed Ayoob (ed.) (1981). *The Politics of Islamic Reassertion,* London, Croom Helm.

Mottahedeh, Roy P. (1980). *Loyalty and Leadership in an Early Islamic Society,* Princeton, Princeton University Press.

Muhammad 'Abduh (1966). *The Theology of Unity,* London, George Allen and Unwin.
"Mudir". *İ. A.,* VIII, 784–786.
Mürsel, Safa (1976). *Bediüzzaman Said Nursi ve Devlet Felsefesi,* İstanbul, Yeni Asya, Yayınları.
Mustafa Sabri (Şeyhulislâm) (1341 A. H.–1969 A. D.) *Dinî Mücedditler,* İstanbul, Sebil Yayınevı.
Myths, Rites, Symbols: A Mircea Eliade Reader, (1975). ed. Wendell C. Beame and William G. Doty. New York, etc., Harper and Row, 2 vols.
"Naip", *İ. A.,* IX: 50–52.
Nalbandian, Louise (1963). *The Armenian Revolutionary Movement: The Development of Armenian Political Parties through the Nineteenth Century,* Berkeley and Los Angeles, University of California Press.
Nasr, Sayyid Husayn (1961). "Religion and Secularism, their meaning and manifestation in Islamic history," *The Islamic Quarterly Review, the Islamic Quarterly V–VI,* 118–126.
——— (1978). *An Introduction to Islamic Cosmological Doctrines,* Rev. ed., Boulder, Shambala.
Neumann, Erich (1969). *The Origin and History of Consciousness,* Princeton, Princeton University Press.
Nicholson, R. N. (1921, 1980). *Studies in Islamic Mysticism,* Cambridge, etc., Cambridge University Press.
van Nienwenhuijze, C. A. O. (1969). "The Ummah—An Analytic Approach," *Studia Islamica,* 10: 5–22.
Nisbet, Robert (1969). *Social Change and History,* New York, Oxford University Press.
Nurculuk (1968). Ankara. Çicek Yayınevi.
Okay, M. Orhan (n. d.). *İlk Türk Pozitivist ve Natüralisti Beşir Fuad,* Istanbul, Dergâh Yayınları.
Ong, Walter (1982). *Orality and Literacy* London, Methuen.
Orhonlu, Cengiz I. (1968). "Türkçe Yayınlanan İlk Gazete, Takvim-i Vekayi," *Belgelerle Türk Tarihi Dergisi,* 35–39.
Otto, Rudolf (1929). *The Idea of the Holy,* Trs. John W. Harvey, London, etc., Oxford University Press.
Özön, M. Nihat (1938). *Namık kemal ve İbret Gazetesi* Istanbul, Remzi.
Pakalın, M. Zeki (1971–1972). *Osmanlı Tarih Deyimleri ve Terimleri Sözlüğü,* 3 vols, 2nd printing, Istanbul, Millî Eğitim Basımevi.
Palmer, Richard E. (1969). *Hermeneutics,* Evanston, Northwestern University Press.

Parkin, David (1982). "Introduction" in *Semantic Anthropology,* ASA Monograph 22, London, etc., Academic Press.

Peters, Rudolf (1980). "Idjtihad and Taqlid in 18th and 19th Century Islam," *Die Welt des Islams,* NS 20 (3–4), 131–145.

Pinson, Mark (1979). "Demographic Warfare: An aspect of Ottoman and Russian Policy," Unpubl. Ph.D. Dissertation, Harvard University.

Plummer, Ken (1983). *Documents of Life,* London, George Allen & Unwin.

Popper, Karl R. (1968). *Conjectures and Refutations: the Growth of Scientific Knowledge,* New York and Evanston, Harper and Row.

Propaganda and Communication in World History (1980), Vol. III, ed. by Harold D. Lasswell, Daniel Lerner and Hans Speier, Honolulu, The University Press of Hawaii.

Quelquejay, Chantal (1959). "Le 'vaisisme' a Kazan: Contribution a l'étude des confréries musulmanes chez les Tartares de la Volga," *Die Welt des Islams,* N. S. 16: 91–112.

Ramsay, William M. (1896). *Impression of Turkey during Twelve Years Wanderings,* London, Hodder.

——— (1915–1916). "The Intermixture of Races in Asia Minor . . ." *Proceedings of the British Academy.*

Reed, H. A. (1957). The Religious Life of modern Turkish Muslims," in R. N. Frye (ed.) *Islam and the West,* The Hague, Mouton, 108–148.

Repp, Richard (1972). "Some Observations on the Development of the Ottoman Learned Hierarchy," pp. 7–32 in *Scholars, Saints and Sufis: Muslim Institutions in the Middle East since 1500.* Ed. by Nikki R. Keddie, Berkeley, etc., University of California Press, 17–32.

Repp, R. C. (1977). "The Altered Nature and Role of the Ulema," in *Studies in Eighteenth Century Islamic History,* Ed. by Thomas Naff and Roger Owen, Carbondale and Edwardsville, Southern Illinois University Press, 277–287.

Safa, Peyami (1938, n.d. 2nd. ed.). *Türk Inkilâbına Bakışlar,* 2nd ed., Istanbul, Inkilâp Kitabevi.

——— (1978). *Din, Inkilâp, Irtica,* Ed. by Ergun Göze and Nevzat Kösoğlu, Istanbul, Ötüken.

Safrastian, Arshak (1948). *Kurds and Kurdistan,* London, The Harvill Press.

Şahiner, Necmeddin, (ed.) (1977). *Said Nursi ve Nurculuk Hakkında Aydınlar Konusuyor,* İstanbul, Yeni Asya.

——— (1976–1986) (ed.) *Son Şahitler,* Istanbul, Yeni Asya, 3 Vols.

——— (1979). *Bilinmeyen Taraflarıyla Bediüzzaman Said Nursi,* Istanbul, Yeni Asya.

Schiffauer, Werner (1984). "Religion und Identität," *Revue Suisse de Sociologie* 2: 485–516.

Schimmel, Annemarie (1975, 1978). *Mystical Dimensions of Islam,* Chapel Hill, The University of North Carolina Press.

——— (1985). *And Muhammad is his Messenger,* Chapel Hill, The University of North Carolina Press.

Scholem, Gershom London (1969). *On the Kabbalah and its Symbolism.* Trs. Ralph Mannheim, New York, Schocken Books.

Scott, R. B. (1965). "Turkish village attitudes towards religious educa tion," *The Muslim World* 55 (3): 22–229.

Sennett, Richard (1973). *The Uses of Disorder,* Pelican Books.

Shahrani, M. Nazif (1985). "Popular knowledge of Islam and Social Discourse in Afghanistan and Turkistan in the Modern Period," unpublished paper.

Shaw, Stanford (1970). "The Central Legislative Councils in the Nineteenth Century Ottoman Reform Movement before 1876," *IJMES.* I: 51–84.

Shaw, Stanford J. and Ezel Kuran Shaw (1977). *History of the Ottoman Empire and Modern Turkey.* Vol II: *Reform, Revolution and Republic: the Rise of Modern Turkey, 1808–1915.* Cambridge, London, etc., Cambridge University Press.

Shippee, Arthur W. (1974) "Mircea Eliade's Concept of Myth . . . " Unpublished Doctoral Dissertation, The Hartford Seminary.

Siegel, James (1969). *The Rope of God,* Berkeley and Los Angeles, The University of California Press.

Smith, Wilfred Cantwell (1962). "The Historical Development in Islam of the Concept of Islam as an Historical Development" in Bernard Lewis and P. M. Holt eds., *Historians of the Middle East,* London, Oxford University Press, 484–562.

Sotiriu, Dido (1980). *Benden Selam Söyle Anadoluya,* Trs. Atilla Tokatlı, Istanbul, Sander.

Spuler, C. (1973). "Nurculuk," *Bonner Orientalische Studien* 27: 100–182.

——— (1977). "Nurculuk-Eine moderne islamische bewegung," *XIX Deutscher Orientalistentag* (ed. Voigt), Wiesbaden.

Steiner, Franz (1981). "Zur Organisationsstruktur der Nurculuk Bewegung," *Studien zur Geschichte und Kultur des Vorderen Orients. Festschrift fur Bertold Spuler zum siebzigsten Geburstag* (Ed. H. R. Roemer and A. Noth), Leiden, E. J. Brill, pp. 423–442.

Stone, Frank Andrew (1984). *Academies For Anatolia,* New York & London, Lanham.

Studies in Eighteenth Century Islamic History (1977). Ed. by Thomas Naff and Roger Owen, Southern Illinois University Press, Carbondale, Ill.

"Tahsin," *Aylık Ansiklopedi*, V., 1485–1486.

Tahsin Paşa (1931), *Abdulhamit ve Yıldız Hatıraları, Istanbul, Ahmet Halit.*

Tansel, Fevziye Abdullah (1946–1951). "Ahmet Hikmet Müftüoğlu-Hayatı ve Sanatı," *Türkiyat Mecmuası*, 9: 1–34.

——— (1962). "Muallim Naci'nin Dini Eserleri," *Diyanet Işleri Baskanlığı Dergisi*, Vol. I, 161–177.

Tanzimat: Yüzüncü Yīldönümü Münasebetiyle (1940). Istanbul, Maarif Matbaasf.

Tekin, Latife and Savaşır, İskender (1987). "Yazı ve Yoksulluk," *Defter* I, Oct.–Nov., 133–147.

Temo, İbrahim (1939). *İttihat ve Terakki Cemiyetinin Teşekkülü*, Mecidiye, Romania.

Ter Minassian, Anaide (1984). *Nationalism and Socialism in the Armenian Revolutionary Movement*, Cambridge, Mass., The Zorian Institute.

Tokgöz, Ahmet İhsan (1930). *Matbuat Hatıralarım I, (1888–1903)*, Istanbul, Ahmet İhsan.

Toprak, Binnaz (1981). *Islam and Political Development in Turkey*, Leiden, E. J. Brill.

Trimingham, J. Spencer (1971, 1973). *The Sufi Orders in Islam*, London, Oxford, etc., Oxford University Press.

Troll, Christian W. (1978). *Sayyid Ahmad Khan: a Reinterpretation of Muslim Theology*, New Delhi, etc., Vikas Publishing House.

Tunaya, Tarık Z. (1962). *Islamcılık Cerayanı: Meşrutiyetin Siyasî Hayatı Boyunca Gelişmesi ve bugüne bıraktığı meseleler*, Istanbul, Baha Matbaası.

——— (1984–1986). *Tükiyede Siyasal Partiler*, Vols. I, II., Istanbul, Hürriyet Vakfı.

Türk Meşhurları n.d. (1946). Ed. by Ibrahim Alaettin Gövsa, Istanbul, Yedigün Yayīnlarī.

Turner, Bryan S. (1974, 1978). *Weber and Islam: A Critical Study.* Henley and Boston, Routledge and Kegan Paul.

Turner, Victor (1967, 1970). *The Forest of Symbols: Aspects of Ndembu Ritual*, Ithaca and London, Cornell University Press.

——— (1969). *The Ritual Process*, Chicago, Aldine.

——— (1974). *Dramas, Fields and Metaphors*, Ithaca, Cornell University Press.

"The 'Ulamā' in Modern History," Studies in Memory of Professor Uriel Heyd (1971). *Asian and African Studies*, Vol. 7, Jerusalem. The Israel Oriental Society.

Ülken, Hilmi Ziya (1966). *Turkiyede Cağdaş Düşünce Tarihi*, 2 vols. Konya, Selçuk.

——— (1969). "L'Ecole Vudjudite et son influence dans la pensée turque." *Wiener Zeitschrift fur die kunde des Morgenlandes*, 62: 193–208.

Unat, Faik Reşit (1964). *Türkiye Eğitim Sisteminin Gelişmesine Tarihî bir Bakış*, Ankara, Millî Eğitim Başımevi.

Us, Hakkı Tarık (1940–1954). *Meclis-i Meb'usan 1293–1877: Zabıt Ceridesi*, 2 vols., Istanbul, Vakit.

Uşaklıgil, Halit Ziya (1969). *Kırk Yıl*, İstanbul, Inkilâp ve Aka.

Uzuncarşılı, Ismail Hakkı (1965). *Osmanlı Devletinin İlmiye Teskilâtı*, Ankara, Türk Tarih Kurumu.

Vambery, A. (1898). *La Turquie d'Aujourd'hui et d'Avant Quarante Ans*, Paris, P. V. Stock.

Van Bruinessen, M. M. (1978). *Agha, Shaikh and State: On the social and political Organization of Kurdistan*, Rijswik, Europrint.

———(1985). "Von Osmanismus zu Separatismus: Religiose und ethnische Hintergrunde der Rebellion der Scheich Said," in *Jahrbuch zur Geschichte und Gesellschaft des Vorderen und Mittleren Orients 1984*, Berlin, Express Edition.

Voegelin, Eric (1952). *The New Science of Politics: An Introduction*, Chicago, The University of Chicago Press.

Van Ess-Bremer "Fehmi" *E.I.²*, II, 878f.

Wallace, Anthony F. C. (1956). "Revitalization Movements" *American Anthropologist* 58: 264–281.

Wallis, Roy (ed.) (1975). *Sectarianism*, London, Peter Owen.

——— (1978). *The Rebirth of the Gods: On the New Religions of the West*. Belfast.

Watt, W. Montgomery (1960). "The Charismatic Community in Islam," *Numen* 7: 77–90.

Weber, Max (1946). *From Max Weber* (ed. Trs. Hans Gerth and C. W. Mills), New York, Oxford University Press.

Wilson, B. R. (1970). *Religious Sects*, London, Weidenfeld and Nicholson.

[Yalman], Ahmet Emin (1930). *Turkey in the World War*, New Haven, Yale University Press.

Yaşar, Muammer (1971). *Anadolu'da ilk Türk Gazetesi: Envar-ı Şarkiyye*, Ankara, Türk Tarih Kurumu Basınevi.

Yıldırım, Dursun (1972). "Dede Korkut ve Yunus Emre'de Hayat, Tabiat, Tanrı ve Ölüm," *Istanbul Üniversitesi Edebiyat Fakültesi: Türk Dili ve Edebiyatı Dergisi*, 20: 37–47.

Yörükkan, Yusuf Ziya (1953). "Vahhabilik," *İlâhiyat Fakültesi Dergisi* I: 51–68.

Young, George (1905–1906). *Corps de Droit Ottoman*, 7 Vols., Oxford, The Clarendon Press.

Zaehner, R. C. (1961). *Mysticism: Sacred and Profane: An Inquiry into Some Varieties of Preternatural Experience*, New York, Oxford University Press.

Books by "Bediuzzaman" Said Nursi

(1960) *Şualar*, Istanbul.

(1960) *Risale-i Nur Kulliyatindan Barla Lahikası*, Sinan Matbaasi, Istanbul.

(1913) *Munazarat*, Istanbul, Matbaa-i Ebuzziya.

(1959) *Risale-i Nur Kulliyatindan Emirdag Lahikasi*, Istanbul, Sinan Matbaasi.

(1975) *Fruits of the Tree of Light*, Trs. Hamid Algar (Author: Bediuzzaman Said Nursi.) The Risale-i Nur Institute of America, Albany, Calif.

(1976) *Belief or Unbelief: The Results of a Choice*, Trs. Ümit Şimsek, The Risale-i Nur Institute of America, Albany, Calif.

(1976) (BSN) *Risale-i Nur Külliyatı Muellifi Bediuzzaman Said Nursi Hayatı-Mesleki-Tercume-i Hali*, Istanbul, Sözler Yayınevi.

(1976) *Sincerity and Brotherhood*, Albany, Calif.

(1976) *Risale-i Nur Kulliyatindan Asa-yi Musa*, Istanbul, Sözler Yayınevi.

(1976) *Risale-i Nur Kulliyatindan Lem'alar*, Istanbul, Sözler Yayınevi.

(1977) Bediuzzaman Said Nursi, *Risale-i Nur Kulliyatindan Mesnevi Nuriye.*

(1977) *Risale-i Nur Kulliyatindan Mektubat*, Istanbul, Sözler Yayınevi.

(1977) *Muhakemat*, Istanbul, Sözler Yayınevi.

(1980) *Resurrection and the Hereafter: A Decisive Proof of their Reality*, Berkeley, Calif.

(1326) *Nutuk*, Istanbul, Kütüphane-i Içtihad.

(1960) *Risale-i Nur Külliyatindan Sikke-i Tasdik-i Gaybî* Istanbul, Sinan Matbaası.

Appendix

Inclosure 3 in No. 4.

Extract from the "Bitlis Gazette" of October 17, 1889.

(Translation.)

ARREST AND PUNISHMENT OF BRIGANDS IN SASSOUN.—When Sassoun Caza is spoken of, most of our readers would doubtless think of a well-ordered place where the inhabitants are blessed with the advantages of civilization.

In respect of this caza, though it is hoped that under the Sultan's auspices the order, tranquillity, and civilization imagined by our readers, who are ignorant of local conditions, will be established—yet its present condition is entirely wanting in such order and civilization.

This district comprises over a hundred villages, and depends for its civil administration on Moush, and for its judicial on Sert; it is about fourteen or fifteen hours distant from the former, and ten or eleven from the latter town.

Besides the importance of this caza, and the wild and nomad character of the inhabitants—so to speak, just as in the Cazas of Modiki and Carzan, the fact of its being surrounded by these cazas and Khyan and Pernashin and such-like "nahiyyes," and that it should be limitroph with such difficult of access, but important spots, clearly gives special reasons for its local importance being greatly augmented.

In view of the wildness of the inhabitants, local conditions having prevented any census* being taken so far, the exact number of inhabitants is unknown, but, males and females together, it may be approximately taken as exceeding 6,000, of whom four-fifths are Kurds, and the rest Armenians.

If, on account of its mountainous situation and remoteness, Sassoun has remained quite obscured from the rays of careful attention, inspection,

*Colonel Everett estimated in 1884: Armenians, 5,957; Kurds, 3,043.

and reform, no less has that which depends on the light of prosperity—education—entirely failed to penetrate.

Inasmuch as they had none among them capable of explaining the true creed, or of appreciating law and morality, the inhabitants, both Moslem and non-Moslem, have remained in gross ignorance and abjectness of understanding, and, whilst knowing nothing of religious duties or institutions, have even forgotten their language.

The language they at present generally use, which resembles a species of Arabic without any system, is in suitable relation to the strange barbarism which has produced it from the blending and mixing up of the Kurdish, Zaza, and Armenian languages.

Kurds and Armenians converse in this tongue, and the individuals of both nations in the exercise of brute violence are as wild beasts, and in their actions and habits perseveringly give free licence to villany and aggression.

That the Government functionaries of this caza, which from time to time has had to be administered by military force, have been compelled to accommodate their ideas and action to the requirements of local conditions, and that often enough in respect of necessary local business inaction has been incumbent, is no secret.

For the purpose of establishing and rendering firm the necessary security under His Majesty the Sultan as against this peace-breaking condition, which occasions local perturbation, and for the seizing of the murderers of a certain Stepan who was killed by robbers in his house at night, a recent effect of this savageness, two detachments of troops were lately dispatched to the caza by Imperial command.

When news was received that this force was unequal to cope with the situation and to re-establish order effectively, two battalions of infantry summoned from Moush and neighboring posts and placed under the command of Mehmed Bey, a Lieutenant-Colonel of the regulars from Van, together with two mountain guns, were further sent, so that the chastising force thus attained a sufficient degree of efficiency.

When for some days nothing was heard of the operations of this force, upon repeated communications to the proper quarter whereby the necessity and importance of taking measures and action was pointed out by the Vali's representative *pro tem.*, the Defterdar, for this most urgent pursuit—to sum up the official information handed in, the prescribed measures followed out by Mehmed Bey in accordance with the communications and desires of the central authorities resulted in complete success.

The military force returned safely to Khato, the caza town of Sassoun, having seized under the Sultan's authority the four wicked robbers, the sons of Bedr Khan, suspected of having ventured on the odious deed of murder, and renowned in crime, with their abettors they were found in the village Morshen of Garzan, where they had taken refuge but were unable to escape the military power. The inhabitants of Sassoun, practised and accomplished in wickedness, were reduced to complete submission by the troops, who were successful in this manner.

That so great a solicitude which must be reviewed in relation to the difficulty and predisposition of the situation, taken together with the wild and wandering habits of the inhabitants, should have been done away with by the above described gentle and safety-giving methods, through the wonderful effects produced by the Sultan, whose study is the causes of prosperity, devoting his special quality of majesty and his private talents of grace to removing every difficulty and obstacle to make way for facility and ease, which is all in accord with his dignity, therefore do we offer special prayers on behalf of His Majesty in pure devotion of spirit, and record gratefully the serious efforts, zeal, and measures which have happily resulted in these high fortunate events as desired by the Vali and the troops, and in particular their commander, and by the local authorities.

Index